Themes in Comparative History

Editorial Consultants: Alan Milward
Harold Perkin
Gwyn Williams

This series of books provides concise studies on some of the major themes currently arousing academic controversy in the fields of economic and social history. Each author explores a given theme in a comparative context, drawing on material from western societies as well as those in the wider world. The books are introductory and explanatory and are designed for all those following thematic courses in history, cultural European or social studies.

Themes in Comparative History

General Editor: CLIVE EMSLEY

PUBLISHED TITLES

Clive Emsley
POLICING AND ITS CONTEXT 1750-1870
Raymond Pearson
NATIONAL MINORITIES IN EASTERN EUROPE 1848-1944
Colin Russell
SCIENCE AND SOCIAL CHANGE 1700-1900

FORTHCOMING

David Englander and Tony Mason
WAR AND POLITICS: THE EXPERIENCE OF THE
SERVICEMAN IN TWO WORLD WARS
John Stevenson
POPULAR PROTEST IN THE MODERN WORLD c.1750-1970
R.F.Holland
DECOLONISATION 1918-1980
Jane Rendall
THE CAUSE OF WOMEN: NINETEENTH-CENTURY
FEMINISM IN BRITAIN, FRANCE AND AMERICA
Joe Lee
PEASANT EUROPE IN THE 18th and 19th CENTURIES

NATIONAL MINORITIES IN EASTERN EUROPE

1848–1945

Raymond Pearson

M

First published 1983 by
THE MACMILLAN PRESS LTD
London and Basingstoke
Companies and representatives
throughout the world

ISBN 0 333 28888 2 (hc)
ISBN 0 333 28889 0 (pbk)

Typeset by Memo Typography Limited,
Nicosia, Cyprus

Printed in Hong Kong

Contents

Illustrations

Acknowledgements

Maps 2, 3 and 6 are taken from Martin Gilberts' *Recent History Atlas* and are reproduced by permission of Weidenfeld and Nicholson Ltd. Map 5 is taken from *Europe, 1880-1945* by J. M. Roberts and is reproduced by permission of the Longman Group Ltd.

General Editor's Preface

SINCE the Second World War there has been a massive expansion in the study of economic and social history generating, and fuelled by, new journals, new academic series and societies. The expansion of research has given rise to new debates and ferocious controversies. This series proposes to take up some of the current issues in historical debate and explore them in a comparative framework.

Historians, of course, are principally concerned with unique events, and they can be inclined to wrap themselves in the isolating greatcoats of their 'country' and their 'period.' It is at least arguable, however, that a comparison of events, or a comparison of the way in which different societies coped with a similar problem – war, industrialisation, population growth and so forth – can reveal new perspectives and new questions. The authors of the volumes in this series have each taken an issue to explore in such a comparative framework. The books are not designed to be path-breaking monographs, though most will contain a degree of new research. The intention is, by exploring problems across national boundaries, to encourage students in tertiary education, in sixth-forms, and hopefully also the more general reader, to think critically about aspects of past developments. No author can maintain strict objectivity; nor can he or she provide definitive answers to all the questions which they explore. If the authors generate discussion and increase perception, then their task is well done.

Clive Emsley

Preface

SINCE the sheer variety of human settlement, social development and political experience in eastern Europe renders any definitive coverage of national minorities within a single volume a patent impossibility, self-interest rather than conventional modesty dictates that the introductory nature of this study be emphasised from the outset. The universally acknowledged complexity of eastern Europe has had two unfortunate effects academically : the intimidation and alienation of a more general readership; and the defensive concentration by professional historians on narrow lines ·of enquiry, most commonly the career of a particular nation. The latter phenomenon often exacerbates the former: historiographical coverage of eastern Europe reflects its national fragmentation, promoting an unhealthy academic 'tunnel vision' in which wider horizons are reduced to a vaguely perceived peripheral blur. In large measure, it is this feature that serves as the justification for the present study: despite the obvious pitfalls, an attempt at a general overview of national minorities in eastern Europe seems timely. The sanguine objective of the following necessarily idiosyncratic treatment covering the century following 1848 is to interest a broader educated readership without outraging the specialist.

I would like to thank my colleagues in the History Department of the New University of Ulster, most particularly Tom Fraser, Alan Sharp, Dennis Smith and Ken Ward, for broadening my own academic horizons by many impromptu discussions on the worldwide incidence of national minorities. More generally, I must offer belated thanks to a decade of second-year university students who participated in my Area Study of Nineteenth- and Twentieth-Century Eastern Europe, to whose successors this introductory study is largely addressed.

It has been estimated that during the First World War as many as ten civilians were needed to maintain one soldier at the Russian front. I must express full, even fulsome, gratitude to my wife Margaret for doing the work of ten during the preparation and especially the writing of this book. Naturally the errors of commission and omission on the academic front remain my own exclusive responsibility.

R.P.

OCTOBER 1981

1. The Demographic Inheritance

A 'mosaic of shifting stones', a 'patchwork quilt' and a 'living kaleidoscope' are just a sample of the metaphors resorted to by specialists finding their descriptive powers taxed to the limit by contemplation of the ethnic variety of eastern Europe. The complexity of the national pattern in eastern Europe is attributable to the combination of two principal features. Considering that the area of eastern Europe is comparable to that of western Europe, the number of resident nationalities in the east is almost three times that in the west, effecting an intimidatingly lengthy *dramatis personae*. The second feature is the diffused nature of ethnic distribution: although the conventional taxonomy of population distribution is into 'compact', 'mixed' and 'diaspora' settlement, a single glance at the ethnic map of eastern Europe (Map 1) reveals how practical reality can mock the artifice of the social scientist. S ome ethnic groups may legitimately be classified as 'compact' in settlement: the Czechs and Albanians, for example, are basically concentrated in a single consolidated mass, with a relatively negligible proportion resident outside the ethnic heartland. At the other extreme, the Jews and Gypsies represent 'diaspora' settlement, the human detritus of an outward flow of population which left them scattered haphazardly over a wide geographical area, without either their original homeland or a convincing claim to territorial status. The great majority of ethnic groups, however, fall into the intermediate category of 'mixed' settlement: the Magyars and Serbs, for instance, possess defined

MAP 1 Ethnic Distribution in Inter-War Eastern Europe

East Slavs:	West Slavs:	South Slavs:		Non-Slav people:			
A - White Russians	D - Czechs	G - Serbs	J - Macedonians	M - Estonians	P - Lithuanians	T - Rumanians	W - Turks
B - Ukrainians	E - Poles	H - Croats	K - Bulgarians	N - Germans	R - Italians	U - Greeks	X - Danes
C - Russians	F - Slovaks	I - Slovenes	L - Bosniaks	O - Latvians	S - Hungarians	V - Albanians	

Source: two-page map in A. Polonsky, *The Little Dictators* (London: Routledge and Kegan Paul, 1975) pp. 12–13.

ethnic heartlands but feature a relatively high proportion of their populations in separate enclaves in close proximity to other groups. The overall result has been a 'shot-silk' ethnic pattern, a bewildering demographic inheritance which nationalism was to convert into a political challenge to the east European establishment.

The primary explanation for the ethnic pattern of Europe lies in its progressive colonisation from the east over approximately the first millennium AD. The present population of eastern Europe may be divided, theoretically at least, into the descendants of the original autochthonous residents and of the immigrant tribal settlers from Asia. Although the origins of races lie in the shadowy disputed period where history, archaeology and anthropology meet, 'Europeans' have been identified as the peoples whose ethnogenesis dates from the late Bronze Age 'Urnfield Complex' of central Europe, who around 800 BC were separating into three distinct groups: the proto-Celts to the west, the proto-Illyrians in the eastern Carpatho-Danubian area, and the proto-Slavs in the north-east Lusation region. The spontaneous dispersal of these groups was hastened and complicated by the mass immigration of a succession of Asiatic tribes, a process deplored by the European residents as the 'Invasion of the Barbarians' and excused by the Asiatic newcomers as a *Völkerwanderung*, a natural and entirely justifiable shift of population into Europe.

Why such diverse Asiatic tribes, ranging from the Huns and Goths of the fifth and sixth centuries through the Avars and Magyars of the ninth century to the Mongols of the thirteenth century, should decamp to Europe is still a matter of guesswork rather than definitive judgement. A beguiling explanation is founded upon the observation that migratory movements are overwhelmingly westerly rather than easterly; in following the setting sun in search of a land where there was no night, the primitive migrants hoped to steal a march on time, with the goal of a longer life and ultimately even immortality. Modern scholarship, more inclined to emphasise materialistic motivation, has tended to presume that population pressure in Asia, with primitive societies outrunning their meagre material resources, was the more likely and principal determinant. Although the 'Barbarian Onslaught' has often been portrayed as a succession of 'waves', a physical metaphor suggesting tidal inevitability, the biological metaphor of the 'swarm' is probably more apt: separate tribes independently reached the economic or psychological trigger-point when mass exodus towards a West affording better prospects became irresistible, penetrating Europe neither as a steady migrant trickle nor as a cataclysmic flood but in a succession of sudden movements over relatively short distances by the entire tribe.

Whatever the mysteries of motivation, the impact of the Asian influx upon Europe was profound. The effect of the invasion of Germanic tribes over the fifth and sixth centuries AD was to scatter the Slavs to the four winds, forcing them north to the Baltic, west into Bohemia and Slovenia, north-east into Russia and south into Macedonia and Bulgaria. Although comparative population figures for the 'residents' and 'immigrants' can only be speculative, it may well be that the original 'Europeans' were forcibly converted into ethnic minorities by this process of *Überfremdung*, or demographic overwhelming of the original inhabitants by massive alien immigration. The distribution pattern of the 'Europeans' altered radically as they fled before the invaders, transforming their status from unchallenged territorial monopolists to pressured minorities in both the numerical and political senses. Although the ultimate disaster of genocide was generally avoided by flight, notably to the mountains and marshes, the inhospitable terrain in which the 'Europeans' had now to survive produced an impoverishment of their civilisation which often came close to ethnocide. Apologists for the smaller autochthonous groups, like the Albanians, have stressed the legitimate claims of the 'Europeans' against what amounted to a flood of illegal Asian immigrants. Forced outwards to the continental periphery by an immigrant pressure which threatened to sweep many of them into the sea, 'Europeans' dreamed of the day when they might recover some semblance of their former territory and status.

The process of forcible colonisation from the east was not unnaturally resisted, initially by the 'Europeans' alone, later by the early immigrants who resented the competition of Asiatic groups following in their tracks. The resident population understandably played up the threat posed by the incoming tribes, scenting pillage, murder and ethnic atrocity. In many cases, the ferocious behaviour of the 'invaders' matched up to, or even exceeded, expectations: the Magyars, for example, invading the middle Danube in the late ninth century, became a by-word throughout Europe for unbridled rapacity. Even so, the conventional scenario of honest worthy peasants gratuitously slaughtered by bloodthirsty Asiatic marauders probably requires some qualification. Although their claim is hotly contested by the Rumanians, the Magyars insist that their tribes peacefully occupied an under-populated, essentially empty 'Hungary' and the element of violence and duress involved was therefore minimal. It may well be that most immigrant tribes prevailed less through terror and atrocity than by a combination of intimidating military superiority and weight of numbers. In an eastern Europe underpopulated relative to its resources, there was for a considerable time room for all, with incoming tribes overwhelming the resident population not through pitched battles but by demographically swamping the locality.

Competition for territory increased as the queue of Asiatic claimants showed no signs of ending and each group acquired property which it self-interestedly denied to all others. Squabbles over territorial 'ownership' became sharper and more frequent as the 'land pool' diminished and the variable value of the land became known. Rival tribes and races came into conflict. Perhaps the most successful were the Finno-Ugrian tribes. Finnic groups like the Estonians, Livonians, Lapps, Karelians and Finns took early possession of the eastern littoral of the Baltic while the Cheremiss, Mordvin, Udmurt and Samoyed tribes retained the interior of northern European Russia. In the south, the Magyars burst upon a surprised central Europe to conquer or occupy (depending upon whom you believe) the area of Hungary and defended this valuable piece of real estate with a tenacity which has never failed to exasperate their neighbours. Perhaps the least successful at either (quite literally) making inroads on rivals' territory or even retaining their own were the Slavs. Although 'genuine Europeans', the Slavs were displaced by their later rivals and compelled to rest content with spare, often agriculturally inferior land while the most valuable property was seized by more aggressive, recent interlopers from Asia.

The atmosphere of tribal competition over territory has never disappeared from eastern Europe. Although much of the explanation for the resilience of the tradition of tribal warfare (especially in the Balkans) has been attributed to 'national character', the time-scale factor plays at least as large a role. As the earliest immigrant swarms occupied central Europe, the later swarms (with notable exceptions like the Magyars) piled back on one another towards the departure point of their migrations in the east in a crude process of filling up Europe from west to east. The societies of the west were therefore always more sedentary, stable and advanced than those of the more recent immigrants in eastern Europe. To the West, the East was primitive and barbaric, or – more charitably – represented an evolutionary phase through which it had long passed. To eastern Europe, the West represented the goal which it expected to reach in the fullness of time. To travel latitudinally across Europe from, say, Paris to Moscow constituted a journey in both space and time: to move from west to east was to visit the past; to move from east to west was to be granted a vision of the future. Leaving aside the dubious concept of a 'natural' hierarchy of national character, the ethnic groups of eastern Europe comprised a society up to almost a millennium younger than the West and predictably displayed features which were quite literally more 'primitive'. The demography of Europe incorporates an historical time-lag on a graduated scale broadly from west to east.

The natural hierarchy of social and political development resulting from progressive settlement of Europe from west to east was accentuated by a final onslaught from Asia. In the mid-thirteenth century, the Mongols (or Tartars) invaded the West, the last in a long line of Asian-born threats to the European status quo. The long-term effect of their incursions was not radically to affect western or central Europe but to overlay the society of much of eastern Europe. Towards central Europe, groups like the Poles, Czechs and Magyars either developed their own distinctive civilisations or were drawn along by the development of the West in a cultural 'tow effect'. The east Slavs however found themselves arbitrarily cut off from the progressive West. Shortly after the promising but possibly premature experiment of an early Russian state based on Kiev in the tenth and eleventh centuries, almost the entire territory of the east Slavs – broadly occupied by the Russians, Ukrainians and Belorussians – was forcibly incorporated into the Mongol Empire. Almost overnight, 'Russia' was converted from the most easterly province of Europe into the most westerly province of Asia. Controversy still rages about the relative stagnancy and cultural poverty of the Mongol Empire but it seems undeniable that the east Slavs received less benefit from their enforced cohabitation with the Mongols than they would have enjoyed from voluntary intercourse with the West.[1]

For three full centuries, the east Slavs languished under Mongol rule while resources needed to promote the development of society and state were instead siphoned off by order of the khans. Most disastrous of all, the east Slavs were forcibly quarantined from Europe at its most critical and progressive phase. In the early modern period, when the foundations of what was to emerge as the modern world were being laid in the West – the concept of the state, the rule of law, the ideal of the university, the tradition of a civil service and the value of science and technology – the east Slavs were not permitted to participate. The natural 'backwardness' of the most eastern areas of Europe was compounded by centuries of the 'Mongol Captivity'.

The combined effect of the accidents of European geography and history was to accentuate the qualitative variety of the ethnic entities of eastern Europe. The quantitative advantage of the east Slavs was offset by their qualitative inferiority: the Russians and Ukrainians were the largest groups numerically but were unable to match the technical standard or collective self-consciousness of smaller groups to the west like the Czechs and Magyars. As a result, the competition between rival ethnic groups was broadly equalised: with no natural hegemony by a single dominant people, the scene was set for a long-standing and probably internecine struggle for power.

With the passage of time, the number of identifiable ethnic groups remained quite stable. Factors promoting the reduction of groups – ethnic extinction, eclipse and amalgamation – all proved historically low-key. Instances of ethnic extinction, whether by natural internal degeneration or calculated genocide, were relatively rare. The autochthonous Dalmatian people gradually succumbed to immigrant Slav pressure – an example of one 'European' group destroying another – yet lingered on the Adriatic island of Krk until the nineteenth century. The Polabs, an isolated Slav tribe living east of the Elbe, disappeared in the eighteenth century under sustained German attack. The Pruz, a Baltic Slav tribe, suffered what came very close to a deliberate programme of genocide at the hands of the Teutonic Knights but still counted some survivors until the sixteenth century. The lingering death agony of these groups should not be allowed to obscure the point that only the smallest and unluckiest peoples suffered ethnic extinction and even these few took a very long time to die.[2] The historical experience of eastern Europe would suggest that even Mohicans last an unconscionably extended period before expiring.

By contrast, there are many examples of ethnic eclipse, where a self-conscious group was temporarily overwhelmed by a stronger neighbour but re-emerged safely at a later date. The Czechs were forcibly 'eclipsed' by the Habsburgs after the Battle of the White Mountain in 1620, a benighted condition which continued for almost two centuries. The Magyars suffered a similar fate at the hands of the Turks at the Battle of Mohács in 1526 and did not surface again for 150 years. The Bulgars after 1388, the Greeks after 1453 and the Serbs after the Battle of Kosovo in 1389 furnish further instances of ethnic entities overlaid by more powerful neighbours but who still found the resilience to present strong claims for nationhood by the nineteenth century. If an ethnic group possessed a clear identity and self-consciousness, the enforced disappearance of its political expression – the national state – certainly did not consign it automatically to extinction. In some cases, as for example in nineteenth-century Poland, the suppression of the state actually strengthened the self-consciousness and commitment of the group.

The incidence of ethnic amalgamation, separate groups voluntarily surrendering their identities to form a new composite nation, was significant (though not always genuine). The examples of the Szeklers, Montenegrins and Ruthenes acceding respectively to the Magyars, Serbs and Ukrainians demonstrate that clearly differentiated ethnic groups could and did voluntarily abandon their exclusivity in the interests of physical survival. Most other 'amalgamations' prove on closer inspection to be nearer to forcible takeovers by a dominant 'partner': two cases in point would be Lithuania's incorporation by Poland in 1569 and, more controversially, the Czech absorption of Slovakia in 1919.

Proving less common or less dangerous than might have been expected, the factors of ethnic extinction, eclipse and amalgamation were balanced by the phenomenon of a growth of 'nations' through progressive fissiparous reproduction. Non-Slav groups like the Magyars and Rumanians, well aware of their numerical disadvantage, followed an instinctive policy of 'solidarity for survival' which could, as we have seen, countenance ethnic amalgamation. But the Slavs' natural numerical hegemony seemed to render an obsession with ethnic unity unnecessary. As time brought different experiences and diverse fortunes to the far-flung members of the 'Slav diaspora', the dispersed tribes quite spontaneously placed greater emphasis on local allegiances, implicitly downgrading the sense of membership of the wider Slav community. Unheard-of Slav 'nations' emerged (like the Ruthenes). Old Slav nations re-emerged after periods of involuntary eclipse (like the Czechs, Serbs and even the Russians). Slav nations like the Ukrainians and Belorussians recovered from what have been termed 'ethnic comas'. The territorial and ethnic fragmentation of the Slav camp undermined its natural numerical ascendancy and once again tended to equalise the competition between the steadily more self-aware nations of eastern Europe.

The final factor in determining the range and distribution of ethnic groups was state (especially imperial) policy. By the early modern period, the 'natural' legacy of past colonisation was being significantly adjusted (though rarely transformed) by the self-interest of the dominant political authorities. As the size and power of empires increased, so did the ambition of imperial government to alter the inherited distribution of ethnic groups in the interests of security, stability or prosperity. Although the governments concerned did not necessarily articulate their demographic strategy in such terms, they effectively had seven options from which to choose: acquiescence, genocide, ethnocide, attraction, expulsion, dispersal and concentration.

'Acquiescence', accepting the ethnic status quo in the sense of precluding direct and positive action, was always common (if only as an excuse for lazy or timid government). At its more constructive, this attitude conceded the primacy of natural and spontaneous population trends, an elemental and continuous process which it was the business of government to reflect rather than to attempt to determine.

'Genocide' was rarely either a desirable or practical official policy: if an ethnic minority was important enough to be politically intolerable, it was usually too populous for physical liquidation: if a minority was tiny enough for genocide to be a practical proposition, it was invariably insufficiently important to warrant the effort, expense and bad publicity. Genocide had no real place until racial fanaticism and the technology of mass murder coincided in the twentieth century.

'Ethnocide' however was not beyond the ambition of imperial governments (though it usually proved to be beyond their grasp). The suppression of an ethnic culture was considered less reprehensible and considerably more feasible than the attempted annihilation of an entire people and was generally adopted. A number of examples have already been cited under the heading of 'ethnic eclipse': many more could be added. The Habsburg and Ottoman Empires in the eighteenth century and the Romanov Empire in the nineteenth century provide a variety of instances of what may be described as attempted ethnocide.

In the seventeenth and eighteenth centuries, the east European empires toyed with the policy of selective 'attraction'. Occasionally the line sprang from conscious humanitarianism and even philanthropy. The kings of Poland offered refuge to the persecuted Jews of the continent who, taking up the invitation with grateful alacrity, flooded into the Polish territories on a scale which was soon embarrassing their royal benefactors. An increasingly favoured policy was to attract foreign ethnic or religious groups of a higher economic or social standard for the purpose of both raising the national average and undermining the position of truculent resident groups. Perhaps the best-known example was Catherine the Great's patronage of German immigrants. By offering harassed German Stundists assisted passage, subsidised land and guaranteed privileges within the Romanov Empire, Catherine hoped to utilise the superior quality of the group for the betterment of Russian agriculture. The substantial colonies which developed on the Volga and Black Sea, largely offsetting the volatile local Tartar communities, represented an example of deliberate, state-sponsored induction of an ethnic minority for the furtherance of imperial authority.

If empires were inclined to favour superior-calibre ethnic minorities from outside their borders, they also considered expelling resident troublesome or inferior-calibre groups. The policy of raising standards by exporting one's problems possessed the obvious relish of killling two birds with one stone but, in general, both the will and the means were commonly lacking. When mass emigration did occur in the later nineteenth century, with ethnic minorities indeed playing a role disproportionate to their numbers, state attitudes towards population release still tended to be grudging rather than enthusiastic. Only in the isolated case of tsarist treatment of the Jews was the state line towards the departing minority so aggressive as to approach a policy of enforced expulsion.

A tactic much favoured by the Habsburgs was 'ethnic dispersal', the redistribution of resident minorities to lend the government maximum advantage. A compact settlement of an ethnic minority might well foster a sense of solidarity (and later nationalism) which could prove inconvenient or even dangerous to the imperial establishment. Perhaps the best illustration of the Habsburg technique came when the Turks were expelled from Hungary in the late seventeenth century. After the depopulating effect of the 'Ottoman Captivity', Hungary constituted a demographic vacuum which promoted a spontaneous infilling from neighbouring areas over the course of the eighteenth century. But having reclaimed territory lost for 150 years, the Habsburgs recolonised the area not only with long-dispossessed local Magyars but with a variety of favoured minorities from elsewhere in the empire. To the understandable disgust and fury of the Magyars, their claims had to compete with those of German ('Swabian' and 'Saxon'), Serb and Slovak groups artfully favoured by the Habsburgs in a spirit of divide and rule. The Habsburg 'plantations' of lesser minorities to inhibit and contain the more dangerous Magyars left a permanent mark on the ethnic map of Hungary.

The last option regarding the geographical location of ethnic minorities available to the dynastic empires was 'concentration'. Drawing opposite conclusions on the optimum distribution of minorities from the 'dispersalists', the 'concentrationists' believed that respectable society must be protected by the rigorous quarantine of potentially disruptive groups. Like the American government in its Red Indian policy, proponents of 'concentration' held that an ethnic minority could best be controlled and rendered harmless by confinement to a clearly defined 'reservation'. Tsarist treatment of the Jews fell increasingly into this category. The Jews were forcibly confined to that area of Poland which they had settled before the disappearance of the Polish state by imperial partition. The portion of Poland appropriated by the tsars after 1795 became the basis for an official 'Pale of Settlement' for all Jews. Even within the Pale, ghettos and *shtetls* further segregated the Jews from more-favoured subjects of the tsars, perversely combining the functions of prison and refuge. Converted from Polish to Russian subjects without moving a step, the resident Jews fell victim to the movement of the frontiers, first exchanged through the exigencies of international diplomacy, then confined and concentrated by tsarist domestic policy.

Without pushing too far the distinction between 'natural' and 'artificial' factors, the geographical distribution of ethnic groups in eastern Europe may be seen as a combination of the spontaneous pattern of original colonisation and the contrived objectives of subsequent political agencies. Given the limited logistical and managerial resources available to governments before the nineteenth century, however, their contribution could essentially be only to modify the demographic matrix established by the *Völkerwanderung* of the first millennium AD.

The Austrian Chancellor Metternich has been credited with the dismissive remark that 'Italy is a geographical expression', an opinion often smugly repeated to demonstrate the political myopia of the Habsburg establishment and therefore the inevitability of its demise. In reality, the bewildering heterogeneity of eastern Europe had little more than academic significance before the early nineteenth century: the welter of ethnic exhibits lent eastern Europe all the curiosity value of a permanent exhibition of the biological sciences. In so far as this ethnic overabundance impinged upon politics at all, it featured principally as an administrative inconvenience in the conduct of imperial government. The ethnic mosaic had few political implications until the nineteenth-century emergence of the concept of the 'nation'. No minorities problem beyond that of practical nuisance existed until the hitherto politically inert ethnic, demographic and linguistic inheritance of eastern Europe was transmuted by the advent of the revolutionary new force of nationalism.

2. Minority Nationalism

NATIONALISM has fascinated and frustrated historians for almost two centuries. The fascination has stemmed from the exotic variety, arcane dynamism and almost supernatural resilience of nationalism, the frustration from the paradoxes of a phenomenon at once universal and quintessentially particular, simultaneously demanding comprehension through historical context yet so often defying rational analysis. More recently, political scientists and sociologists have joined the historians in attempting to identify the 'leaven of nationalism', the doctrine, class, circumstance or combination of elements which invariably transforms often the most inert and unpromising social material into a dynamic, frequently irresistible nationalist movement. Although significant progress has been recorded, it is probably fair to suggest that the sheer range of nationalist experience has prevented any 'magic ingredient' of nationalism from yet being identified. With the historian's instinctive aversion to mono-causal explanation, it may be more instructive to pursue a less sensational line of enquiry by considering minority nationalism under three complementary headings: the traditional factors considered indispensable to the emergence of modern nationalism; the new external stimuli which prompted the dramatic take-off of nationalism in the nineteenth century; and the internal components which lent nationalism so much appeal and force.

TRADITIONAL FACTORS

The tribal pattern of human settlement inherited from the past made some racial constituent in the character of nationalism in eastern

Europe inevitable. The practice of exogamy (or marriage outside the tribe) was comparatively rare : local social taboos and an almost instinctive reluctance to cross the tribal divide were compounded in the nineteenth century by a growing fear for the disappearance of the race as a recognisable entity in a half-breed, hybrid population. Although the social dislocations of war and migration could on occasion foster an exogamous phase in tribal society, it was historically untypical. Endogamy (or marriage within the tribe) was the general rule, and the prospect of extensive miscegenation, interbreeding between races, was tacitly or openly condemned in favour of maintaining the racial or tribal identity. As a general observation, it may be true that more developed, sedentary and secure societies tend to be tolerant of exogamy while more primitive, nomadic and threatened societies are most insistent about endogamy. The prevalent endogamous tradition ensured that the fundamental racial pattern of eastern Europe was only blurred and never transformed by the marriage choices of successive historical generations.

This is not to state that race as either an anthropological fact or a subjective perception necessarily dominated the nationalism of eastern Europe. Over the nineteenth century, race played only a minor role in the nationalism of the Slavs. As in the remote colonising past, the Slavs relied upon numerical size and weight of bodies to win undramatic but decisive victories: the demographic hegemony of the Slavs bred the quiet, almost unstated conviction that they must ultimately prevail. Despite lip-service to the idea of Pan-Slavism, Russian, Ukrainian and even Polish nationalism featured only a low-key racial component. Only when an isolated Slav group was menaced by neighbours of another race did a defensive sense of racial community surface: for example, the Bulgar campaign against the Turkish, Rumanian and Greek threat in the late nineteenth century promoted a more explicitly racial response from Slavs elsewhere in eastern Europe. Otherwise, Pan-Slavism and its early twentieth-century updating of Neo-Slavism were overwhelmingly cultural and even sentimental in flavour, invariably demonstrating chronic Slav disunity whenever more ambitious schemes for racial solidarity were entertained.

Race figured much more in the nationalism of the non-Slavs. Individually and collectively in the minority, the non-Slavs readily appreciated the inherent demographic weakness of their position. Positive action had to be organised to prevent the natural erosion of their beleaguered 'ethnic islands' by a sea of Slavs. Those races in a particularly exposed position – like the Magyars and Rumanians – were most vigorous, even savage, in their defensive campaigns for what they regarded as ethnic survival. The ubiquitous spectre of the last of the Mohicans was repeatedly invoked, with alarmist prophecies of ethnic extinction at the hands of the culturally impoverished but numerically overpowering Slavs whipping the Magyars in particular into an almost fanatical over-reaction. Other isolated non-Slav groups like the Finns, Albanians and even Bohemian Germans adopted an identical siege-mentality, ever suspicious of Slav intentions and intransigent in their determination to preserve or augment any ethnic privileges. In a nineteenth-century world becoming increasingly aware of names like Darwin and Spencer, and concepts like 'the survival of the fittest', the lessons for mankind from the biological sciences seemed ominous: confronted by the 'scientific' possibility of irreversible extinction, the minority races of eastern Europe were galvanised into campaigns of militant defensive nationalism to secure their ethnic futures.

Overall, the racial factor in east European nationalism, although pandemic, was only selectively critical, notably amongst vulnerable minority nationalities. The Nazi racialism of the twentieth century marked a substantial departure from the defensive nationalism of even the late-nineteenth-century Magyars, whose policy of 'Magyarisation' (however reprehensible to the liberal mind) never included such principles as the physical liquidation of minorities or even the immutability of racial identity. Although the various pan-racial movements which appeared threatened, albeit rather ineffectually, to introduce a hitherto-underplayed racial dimension into international politics, it was not until the era of Nazi Europe that the factor of race played a leading role in the fates of the east European minorities.

The philosophy of racialism, with its fanatic insistence on the impermeability of the racial divide, was a relatively late, even a twentieth-century phenomenon. Racialists like Hitler and Alfred Rosenberg asserted that the race of an individual was a blessing or a curse from birth, an immutable genetic fact which predetermined his future, with no concessions to such compromise social devices as 'assimilation' and 'conversion'. But the Nazi assertion was that the racial factor had been scandalously neglected in the past. Accepting reluctantly and regretfully that the German nation had already compromised itself genetically by intermarriage with racial inferiors, the Nazi mission was to purge away the biological taints of the past. The logical impossibility of the task – once lost, racial purity (like virginity) can never be reclaimed – did not inhibit the campaign. The liquidation of racial half-breeds, the prohibition of marriages of mixed race and the promotion of extensive Aryan breeding were all related fronts in the eugenics war waged by the Nazis to 'save' the German race. Yet it was only towards the middle of the twentieth century that the agents and instruments of mass social control were available to make feasible a political philosophy based so uncompromisingly on the principle of race.

Territory, the concept of 'patriotism of place', has always been regarded as fundamental to nationalism. Although political, social and economic explanations for the drive for territorial possession have never been lacking, expositions from the anthropological and even psychological disciplines have recently been advanced to augment or upset more traditional arguments. In *The Territorial Imperative*, Robert Ardrey advances a series of claims about national behaviour on the premise that man can only be understood as a human animal. 'Man is a territorial species . . . [with] an inherent drive to gain and defend an exclusive property'. Moreover, 'the territorial nature of man is genetic and ineradicable', rendering all other explanations for land acquisition as at most subsidiary. A territory becomes a 'power-kingdom' which satisfies three needs obsessive in human nature: 'Motivation for territory is psychological, not physiological . . . it arises from twin needs in the animal for security and stimulation, and that is satisfied by the territorial heartland and the territorial periphery . . . [while] identity is another animal need which territory satisfies'. Although the persuasiveness, even the validity, of Ardrey's argument has been questioned, its effect has been to re-open and enrich the conventional debate on the role of territory in nationalism.[1]

Aside from blatant military conquest, the two means of claiming territory are fundamentally the 'historic' and the 'demographic', the former insisting that past ownership constitutes legitimisation of the current claim, the latter stipulating majority settlement as the ultimate criterion for ownership. In many instances, of course, the historical and demographic claims coincide, constituting a universally recognised right of ownership. But in eastern Europe the two approaches have frequently clashed. Transylvania, for example, was until the twentieth century ruled by the Magyars but probably featured a Rumanian majority from the eighteenth century. To whom did Transylvania morally belong? The Magyars predictably presented an 'historic' argument, the Rumanians a 'demographic' (albeit buttressed by their self-serving Daco-Roman interpretation of local history). Both arguments exhibit many flaws. What does the 'historic' claim mean? The *longest* chronological span of ownership? The *earliest* significant period of ownership? The *latest* or the most *beneficial* period of ownership? In practice, claimants select the criteria favouring their own case, transforming past history into present politics in the process. Since almost every territory has come under the rule of another at some point in the tangled history of eastern Europe, the question of 'ownership' often rests on the choice of historical date. Polish expansionists chose 1611 as their optimum date, the year when the Polish Commonwealth included Muscovy in domains which swept majestically from the Baltic to the Black Seas. Russians could of course retaliate by selecting any date between 1846 and 1914, when no Polish state of any kind existed and most of Poland was under tsarist sway.[2]

The 'demographic' argument, though ostensibly more straightforward and judicious, also has hidden snags. Statistics, elections and plebiscites can be – and in eastern Europe often were – rigged. Almost all the official censuses of the pre-1914 empires and post-1919 states exaggerated the demographic dominance of the establishment and minimised the representation of national minorities. The elusiveness of reliable statistics, especially over contested territory, made a just decision difficult and tended to inflame rather than settle local grievances. Moreover, if it were to be generally conceded that the 'demographic' claim took automatic precedence over the 'historic', a breeding-war might well result, with rival ethnic groups seeking the demographic edge by prodigious and selfless feats of reproduction.

Some ethnic groups lost out completely on both historic and demographic grounds, a predicament leading directly to the question of whether a minority without territory can qualify as a 'nation'. Some specialists have argued that 'national aspirations without a strong historical connexion with a territory do not constitute a nation'. In a subsequently celebrated check-list of features which entitled a 'nationality' to recognition as a 'nation', Stalin in 1913 insisted upon territorial possession as an indispensable condition: 'A nation is . . . an historically developed, stable community of people, arising on the basis of language, territory, economic life and psychological pattern,

manifested in a community of culture'.[3] The landless ethnic minorities which provided the test-case in eastern Europe were the two
diaspora groups, the Jews and Gypsies.

Although the Jews had been settled in Poland and Russia for
centuries, there was never any question of advancing an 'historic'
claim to ownership: and although they constituted a substantial
proportion of the local population, their position as a numerical
minority undercut any 'demographic' argument. The landlessness of
the Jews was always regarded as sinister, casting them in the
perennial role of (quite literally) outlandish outsiders in the folk
culture of their host societies. The Jews have been identified – almost
simultaneously – as the prime operatives of capitalism at its most
unacceptable and communism at its most diabolical. Testifying to the
intimate inter-relation between territory and identity, Ardrey goes so
far as to argue that 'the "Jewish personality" is nothing but a bundle
of mannerisms preserving the identity of a de-territorialised man'.[4]
Without that 'legal' territory which satisfied the basic needs of
security, stimulation and identity, the Jews have long suffered a
crippling handicap which might well have condemned them to early
extinction but for three countervailing factors. The diaspora itself offered
some advantages, lending Jewish minorities the hope of organising
international protection in the face of local persecution. Religion became a
substitute for territory in preserving the self-consciousness of the Jews.
Finally, the very concentration of the Jewish population in Poland and
Russia, partly natural settlement, partly tsarist confinement, offered a
self-sustaining surrogate territory which greatly boosted Jewish nationalism. To quote Anthony Smith:

> The effective support for Zionism came from the rapidly-
> expanding Jewish population of the Russian Pale, which consti-
> tuted an enforced territory for Russian Jewry, in which they
> formed dense, compact communities, resembling an autonomous
> 'state within a state' hemmed in by tsarist restrictions. Without
> that geopolitical framework, it is doubtful if Jewish nationalism
> would have achieved a powerful following.[5]

The concentration policy of the tsars unwittingly provided the
Russian Jews with a substitute for the one major component their
nationalism so conspicuously lacked, contributing powerfully to its
maturation.

The Gypsies, by contrast, were unable to employ a distinctive religion as a territory-substitute and, without the sustaining literary tradition of the Jews, their decline has been predictable and possibly irretrievable. Arriving in Europe from the Indian sub-continent as a belated post-script to the *Völkerwanderung* in the fourteenth century, the Gypsies were compelled by the unavailability of spare land to continue their migrations on a permanent nomadic basis. Too late, too few and too backward, the last of the Asiatic tribes to enter Europe could make no impression on the entrenched social and territorial establishment and was forced to attempt a livelihood on the fringes of legality. Without any territory except their tents and caravans, the Gypsies could only retain their identity by rigorous self-segregation, a recourse which only further antagonised *gadjo* (non-Gypsy) society and increased their vulnerability as a minority. Whether Romani is a genuine language or a thieves'argot, it failed to provide as effective a substitute for territory as religion had for the Jews. As a result, the Gypsies were all too often caught between physical decline (with death from disease, accident and violence all well above average), deliberate genocide (most horrifically at the hands of the Nazis in the Second World War) and well-meaning but misguided efforts to sedentarise and integrate the disruptive 'vagrants' which amounted to ethnocide.

Ethnic groups without established territorial claims were at very least dangerously disadvantaged and probably on the 'extinction list' in an eastern Europe where pressure on land was always on the increase. Many Russian Jews in the early twentieth century followed the 'territorialist heresy' that any territory was better than none: Palestine was of course the ideal, but if it proved unavailable, the Jews had no alternative but to accept offers like Uganda or even Madagascar. With the survival of the Jewish people contingent on the acquisition of a homeland, it would be a tragic and irrevocable mistake to hold out for the most desirable piece of national real estate.

Even so, the possession of territory was far from being a guarantee of ethnic survival: all three east European nationalities known to have become extinct (the Dalmatians, Polabs and Pruz) found native territory no protection against their fate. In a climate of mounting competition for land, the occupation of a valuable tract of territory often attracted envious eyes and increased the chances of forcible dispossession by a stronger neighbour.

The intensity of nationalist feeling varied appreciably according to territorial size and location. It is well known that extreme nationalists tend to come from the borderlands, the friction zones of their nation. 'Border dwellers' are more sensitive about national identity and loyalty through day-to-day proximity to the state frontier, develop firmer commitments through awareness of the alternatives and are most subject to neuroses about territorial adjustment and therefore national security. The capital city, where the government's eagerness to parade its responsible conduct of the nation's business combines with remoteness from the danger zone and the more cosmopolitan climate of city life, is typically less nationalist. Least nationalist of all is likely to be the population of the rural heartland of a territory, where the demands of economic self-interest and the absence of contact with aliens lull the 'core dwellers' into a comfortable, even complacent sense of well-being. Ardrey dubs this phenomenon the 'castle and border' view of territory, with the castle providing the security and the border the stimulation necessary to successful nationalism.[6]

Many nations in eastern Europe had territories on their peripheries which provided the regular nationalist stimulation required by the state. Examples include Karelia for the Finns and Russians, Bessarabia for the Russians and Rumanians, the southern Dobrudja for the Bulgars and Rumanians, Transylvania for the Magyars and Rumanians and – most spectacular of all – Macedonia for the Serbs, Bulgars, Greeks and Albanians. Constantly changing ownership provided an almost perpetual stimulus to extreme nationalism, repeatedly re-firing flagging national antagonisms and reviving national pride. Invested with enormous nationalist commitment (and often with mystical, talismanic significance), these contentious border territories became so emotionally charged as to pass beyond the scope of rational argument or solution.

The relationship between nationalism and territory was frequently convoluted, far from the natural, organic coincidence of 'nation' and 'state' so painstakingly portrayed in nationalist propaganda. A power-territory might have its justification entirely in the ability of its rulers to fend off competitors but the prevailing trend was to promote a variety of complementary, mutually reinforcing allegiances. As traditional commitments like dynastic loyalty and religious creed steadily lost influence, nationalism in its manifestation of patriotism of place provided the new legitimisation. A state territory might be a paragon of ethnic self-determination but was more than likely to be a haphazarad agglomeration of different properties, the product of historical chance and accident. The neutral expanse of landscape which comprised territory was now required to inspire (or be invested with) a sense of patriotism, an emotional commitment by the population at large. Starting with the new Balkan states in the nineteenth century and spreading to all the 'Successor States' in the early twentieth century, a pattern of artificial 'nationism' (as distinct from spontaneous nationalism) emerged. Provincialism, regionalism and particularism within the power-territory were suppressed in the interests of the solidarity of the whole. The superiority of the fatherland or motherland was insistently proclaimed, the inferiority and artificiality of neighbouring 'nations' taken for granted. National territory was perceived as a living, organic entity which could not be partitioned without endangering the entire body politic.

To possess territory in eastern Europe was always dangerous; but to possess none was even more dangerous. The deafening message of the rising force of nationalism from the mid-nineteenth century was the stark necessity of territory for either recognition as a nation or biological survival. The 'territorial imperative' of nationalism was paramount: landless national minorities could expect no mercy from the political law of the jungle; territory was an irreplacable asset in the struggle of nations for the 'survival of the fittest'.

Religion played its most significant role in the early phases of nationalism. The fragmentation of the medieval unity of Christendom undoubtedly set in train developments which were to favour the emergence of nationalism in the early modern period. The frequent power struggles between church and monarch often led to both sides seeking reinforcement against rival authority but, while the Papacy in particular was not averse to raising proto-nationalism as a tactical ploy in the contest with temporal authority, no church intended to sponsor the nationalism that actually resulted. In general, the attitude of the various churches was to favour nationalism in its initial phase out of self-interest but to become increasingly antagonistic as nationalism developed into first a rival and then a threat to traditional faiths and hierarchies.

In a world where religious values still predominated, what was later revealed as embryonic secular nationalism naturally found expression in religious form. A blurring of religious and nationalist motivation was often characteristic: were the Hussites of the fifteenth century, for example, predominantly Protestant or Czech? In the modern period, religion and emerging nationalism became mutually reinforcing interests, with religion gradually losing its status as senior partner to nationalism. Examples of the coincidence of religion and nationalism in eastern Europe are legion. The Lutheranism of the Finns doubly differentiated them from the Orthodox Russians. The Calvinism of many Magyar nationalists added an extra dimension to their quarrel with the Catholic Austrians. The Orthodoxy of the Serbs and Catholicism of the Croats represented a fundamental divide against which a common language and race proved helpless. The later emergence of a Bosnian identity based on Muslim religious adherence rather than ethnic unity further complicated the career of Yugoslavia. Similarly, the religious differences between the Hussite Czechs, Catholic Slovaks and Uniate Ruthenes encouraged distinctive styles of nationalism which proved most troublesome to Czechoslovakia.

The greatest service that the church provided for nationalism was as a last bastion of national identity. Ikons, relics and shrines which comprised an ultimate repository for religious identity became national symbols too. The Black Madonna of Czestochowa for the Poles and the Virgin of Vladimir for the Russians assumed immense national importance as mystical rallying-points in time of emergency. The church appeared historically as the custodian of the cultural identity of the nation, playing the most invaluable role if secular authority collapsed. When Muscovy succumbed to Polish invasion during the Time of Troubles in the early seventeenth century, it was the Orthodox hierarchy which orchestrated the national revival and the Patriarch Filaret who organised the accession of the Romanov dynasty to rally the Russian people. It was the hierarchy of the Uniate Church, employing Orthodox liturgy under papal licence, which agitated in the mid-eighteenth century for Habsburg recognition of the Vlach-Rumanian people as a political 'nation' in Transylvania. When the Polish state was partitioned between Orthodox Russia, Catholic Austria and Protestant Prussia, it was the local Catholic hierarchy which seized the opportunity both to preserve the self-consciousness of the Polish nation and to extend its own authority over Poles to the point of religious monopoly. By the mid-nineteenth century, it was virtually unthinkable to be a Pole without being a Catholic, a tribute to the success of the church's self-portrayal as the guardian of the Polish national identity.

The common factor was the eagerness of the church hierarchy to assume a national role when that nation was overlaid by a conqueror of a different religious persuasion, especially one committed to the intolerant concept of *cuius regio, eius religio*. The combination of a religious and national threat was guaranteed to galvanise all levels of the local church into leading the resistance movement in alliance with the burgeoning forces of nationalism. Not only the church hierarchies but the local parish priests could be relied upon to assume a militant religious-cum-national stance. Partly because of the churches' early monopoly over popular education and literacy, partly through an instinct to proselytise, local priests (frequently of a 'populist' variety) were exceptionally active as self-proclaimed defenders of nations under threat. In Transylvania in the late eighteenth century, Uniate priests nursed Vlach cultural self-consciousness into the beginnings of Rumanian nationalism. At the turn of the nineteenth century, the nascent nationalism of Belorussia was fostered by the local Catholic priests. In Croatia and Slovenia, Catholic priests always bulked large in the anti-Serb, anti-Orthodox agitation which bedevilled the unification of the South Slavs. Finally, it was no coincidence that, well into the twentieth century, Catholic priests like Hlinka and Tiso should lead the Slovak resistance against the real or imagined onslaught of the Czechs.

If religious persecution was almost invariably a nationalist stimulant, religious tolerance on the part of authority proved little more effective against the march of nationalism. The Ottoman Empire, for example, was a territorial entity based upon neither dynasty nor nationality but the faith of Islam. Under Islamic law, the Ottoman state could neither compel unbelievers to conform to the Muslim faith nor direct their lives. The practical result was the social quarantine of non-Muslims in religious communities called 'millets', a policy which at first acquaintance suggests a commendable spirit of tolerance but was in reality closer to a gesture of contempt. Reasonably autonomous so long as regular tribute was paid, the Christian millets became almost states within the state and gradually developed political ambitions. As the millets improved their status, the declining Ottomans complaisantly permitted them to acquire disproportionate economic importance, with the Greek minority becoming the most prosperous community. It comes as no surprise therefore that it was the Greeks who first successfully employed their millet as a nationalist springboard for political independence. The Bulgar nation too was preserved through its darkest ethnic 'eclipse' by a combination of the dedication of scholar-clerics like Father Paisii of Athos and judicious exploitation of the Ottoman millet system. Incapable of either performing the function of a nationalist safety-valve or adapting into a modern national federation, the millet system provided the catalyst for converting the religious communities of the Ottoman Empire into nations and eventually into states.

But however significant the role of religion and the church in the early phase of nationalism, the new movement rapidly acquired an independent momentum which soon left them far behind. The role of the church in time of emergency was soon forgotten, sometimes even resented, in peace time. The priests who led the popular defence of faith and nation were overtaken by more ambitious and modern leaders, most frequently from the new class of the intelligentsia. Religion became relegated to the position of a reinforcing or (occasionally) a surrogate factor: the Jews in particular sought to compensate for their lack of territory by extra emphasis on their religious identity. The slow but steady decline of religion and the church, under fire from the Enlightenment in the eighteenth century and from materialism and science in the nineteenth century, ensured that the nationalism to which the church contributed when expedient would inevitably shrug off its early influence and develop an independent dynamism.

Language was the final traditional factor which influenced nationalism most profoundly. Until the modern period, two varieties of language were current ; the parochial, low-status and lower-class vernaculars and the cosmopolitan, cultivated and upper-class *lingua franca*. The abandonment of Latin as the international written language came all the quicker in eastern Europe where remoteness from the Roman tradition had already prevented Latin from acquiring a wide currency. Imperial attempts to replace Latin as an international means of communication, notably by French and German, had little success. The plan of the Habsburg 'Enlightened Despot' Josef II to impose the German language on all his subjects in the late eighteenth century actually provoked his Magyar (and to some extent Czech) educated classes into rebellion and a determination to develop their own vernacular languages. However the Magyars' subsequent campaign to promote their own language in no way inhibited them from imposing it upon other linguistic minorities when the opportunity arose. Once the genuine international medium of Latin was tacitly abandoned, no successor which commanded any

comparable allegiance could be discovered and it became apparent
that there existed a linguistic fragmentation of eastern Europe to
match its ethnic heterogeneity. With no generally acceptable *lingua
franca*, the result could only be a linguistic free-for-all.

The awareness of linguistic diversity had few political implications
before the nineteenth century. If any explanation of linguistic
heterogeneity were required, it could be found in Holy Writ: the
Tower of Babel had earned God's punishment on erring mankind for
its sins of pride and ambition. The bewildering linguistic map must be
viewed as a divine reprimand, before which the wise and devout
would bow in submission. Only with the linked decline of conventional religion and the rise of nationalism did new generations draw a very
different lesson from the Babel of languages than that of the necessity
of meek acceptance of God's will.

The great advantage of language as a criterion of nationalism was
its provision of a line of clear-cut differentiation between 'natives' and
'aliens'. One could dissemble over race and religion but not over
language: instant and accurate identification of a linguistic group
made language the closest to a foolproof test of nationality. Language
was a very personal possession which simultaneously provided the
public service of indisputable identification. As a direct result, early
nationalism developed the criterion of language for nationality
membership further than any other. The 'shibboleth concept' was
introduced, the proposition that language marked man out for fortune
or death, the essence of his identity and therefore his fate.[7] At very
least, language could provide a nation with a spurious sense of
superiority: the inability of foreigners to articulate Greek had led to
their being dismissively labelled 'barbarians' (stammerers); the
uncomprehending silence of Germans in the presence of Russians
earned them the contemptuous label of *nemtsy* (dumb). Although the
Gypsies had no territory and no formal religion, the exclusive
language of Romani offered some compensation and proved a prime
sustainer of their identity. With no convincing grounds for elevating
one vernacular language above another, minorities deficient in every
other respect seized upon language as the criterion which granted
their nationalism equal status with any other.

There was no lack of linguistic complications to torture the
relationship between language and nation. Sometimes an otherwise
identical language was divided by the convention of script: the
Serbo-Croat language is almost perversely split by the practice of

Serb being written in Cyrillic script and Croat in the Western alphabet. Occasionally, a nationality employed two distinct languages, one literary-religious, the other oral-popular, which invariably led to heated arguments over the necessity (and choice) of a single national language. The Jews, for example, employed Hebrew together with a variety of vernaculars appropriate to their physical location (with the strange hybrid of Yiddish enjoying the widest currency).

Many of the languages which nationalists wished to elevate to high status were peasant vernaculars of limited expression, vocabulary and flexibility. To answer the needs of the modern world, the unsophisticated tongues of backward nationalities had to be systematised and – most controversially – augmented. There were only two methods of 'lexical coinage', of acquiring the necessary modern and technical vocabulary: to borrow foreign words brazenly (which was regarded as patriotically demeaning and unacceptable) or to invent words from the existing semantic raw material (which seemed ludicrously pedantic and contrived). The incidence of foreign loanwords soon became a reliable indicator of the intensity of local nationalism. Most commonly, a three-phase sequence occurred: initially foreign words for which no equivalent existed were simply abstracted as 'calques'; at the height of nationalist xenophobia, linguistic purism forced the semantic concoction of new-but-old words; and finally, common sense prevailed with an attempt at a judicious selection of native and foreign, often with greater concessions to the latter. The truly cyclical career of the Russian word for 'bicycle' is a banal example: starting as a *velosiped* (velocipede). it served an uncomfortable term as a *samokat* (self-driver) before being allowed to revert to its French-derived label.

The promotion of language as the touchstone of nationalism prompted some (admittedly feeble) attempts at counter-attack. Pan-Slavism, never a doctrine famed for the precision of its programme, considered adding a linguistic dimension to augment its limited political appeal. It was proposed to abstract a common Slav language from the existing variants to serve as a new Slav *lingua franca*, which in turn would foster the cultural and political solidarity of the race. The ambitious scheme foundered on the practical difficulties of concocting an artificial *lingua slavonica* from many variants which was still recognisable enough by all participants to command a common and equal allegiance. A desperate attempt to salvage something from the doomed enterprise could only come up with the tactless proposition that all Slav minorities abandon their own languages in favour of the Slav tongue spoken by the largest proportion, in other words Russian. Predictably, this ingenuous suggestion was immediately condemned as 'linguistic imperialism', confirming the non-Russians in their instinctive suspicion that Pan-Slavism was no more than a cover for tsarist expansionism. The proposed international Slav language was unmasked as an imperialist ploy and instantly discredited.

Following the line of Johann Herder that language enshrines a nation's essence and supreme individuality, nineteenth-century nationalism elevated language to the status of a sacred heritage. 'If territory is the body of the nation, language is its soul' ran the nationalist credo.[8] The hyper-sensitivity of nationalists over language was institutionalised by almost every emergent nation of eastern Europe. The *Académie Francaise*, standing guard over the purity of the French language, an exclusive and sometimes inflexible institution contrasting sharply with the linguistic *laissez-faire* attitude of the English-speaking world, was copied throughout eastern Europe over the nineteenth and early twentieth centuries. Fervent nationalists objected not only to foreign semantic intrusions but even to well-intentioned foreigners manfully attempting to speak their language, an effort interpreted not as a gesture of respect but as an attempted infringement of the nation's monopoly of access to its sacred inheritance. The Greek constitution of 1911 made corruption of the national language a punishable offence, in effect banning the use of the language by any but Greeks! Thus the obvious pragmatic advantages of language to nationalism – like promoting a monolithic linguistic solidarity within the national territory and asserting the separate identity and high status of the nation before an international audience – were soon overlaid by a mystical, semi-religious aura. With communion reserved for the chosen people and deliberately withheld from outsiders, language became the sacrament of nationalism.

EXTERNAL STIMULI

Of all the new influences of the nineteenth and early twentieth centuries, overpopulation probably had the most profound repercussions on east European society. The tabulated statistics for population growth over the century after 1800 present convincing evidence of a population explosion of unprecedented proportions (see Table I). The explanation for the sudden meteoric rise in population continues to tax demographers. The most plausible cause was a sudden fall in the average death rate: with the rapid advance of medical science and welfare provision, famine and disease claimed fewer victims than ever before and the average life expectancy was dramatically extended. The puzzle is that despite being notoriously insulated from the benefits of modern science, eastern Europe had a higher population growth rate than the continental average of 80 per cent. The growth rate of the Finns and Russian Poles was *three* times the European average and by the later nineteenth century the Russians, Rumanians and Bulgars were increasing at the phenomenal annual rate of over 40 per 1000 of their populations, triumphantly heading the continental league table. Confronted with statistics which are frequently confused and incomplete, historical demographers of eastern Europe have been left to surmise that the population explosion resulted less from a falling death rate, the prevailing factor in western European society, than from a still-unexplained but patently decisive rising birth rate.

Although the population density of eastern Europe was appreciably lower than that of western Europe in 1800, the effect of the differential growth rate was to bring significant proportions of the East up to the continental average by 1900. Indeed by 1914 Hungary, 'Poland' and 'Czechoslovakia' had population densities above the European average of 86 inhabitants per square kilometre. It is no coincidence that it was the populations of these same regions which campaigned most vigorously for nationalist expression and political independence. The low-density settlement of eastern Europe had hitherto defused many a squabble over territory but by the later nineteenth century social and political sensitivity to territory reflected the unprecedented demographic pressure on land. Rocketing demand set an increasingly high value on the land a nation possessed or claimed. Morever the growing tendency for the smaller, underdeveloped nationalities to feature a higher growth rate than the larger, established nations augured even stiffer competition for territory in the future. The 'minorities' were serving demographic notice on the 'majorities', the nationalities were serving political notice on the nations. The Poles, Magyars and especially the Czechs felt the demographic pressure to claim territory and independence from their imperial masters before they were overhauled in the competition for people and power by minority nationalities whom they were now

TABLE I ESTIMATED POPULATION INCREASE IN EASTERN EUROPE
1800–1900 IN MILLIONS[9]

State	1800	1900	% increase
'Poland'	4.0	14.0	250
Finland	0.83	2.65	220
European Russia	38.0	103.3	170
Hungary	3.25	7.0	115
Rumania	5.5	11.0	100
Bulgaria	2.0	4.0	100
Greece	2.25	4.5	100
'Yugoslavia'	4.75	9.5	100
'Albania'	0.4	0.8	100
'Czechoslovakia'	6.75	12.25	80
Europe overall	200	390	95

Notes. 1. None of the states cited maintained a continuous stable
territorial identity throughout the period 1800 to 1900. Poland,
Yugoslavia, Albania and Czechoslovakia did not exist at all during
the nineteenth century and the remainder all experienced substantial boundary changes. The figures can therefore only be composite
estimates of 'geographical expressions'.
 2. Mass emigration profoundly affected all the states listed,
masking an even higher population increase than suggested by these
estimates.

compelled to treat as rivals. At the opposite end of the hierarchy of
nationality, those ethnic groups which had failed to lay successful
claim to territory in the relatively relaxed past, like the Jews and
Gypsies, now had no chance whatsoever of gaining access to the
commodity which might ensure their survival in eastern Europe.

As population size outstripped the available traditional sources of
sustenance, a classic definition of overpopulation, four possible
solutions presented themselves, two stressing a reduction in demand,

two a growth in supply. The easiest and most universally acceptable recourse was mass emigration to destinations of ample resources but low population density. The second presupposed natural or man-made disaster on a massive scale to reduce the current population level. Man had fallen into his customary trap of solving one problem by posing another: medical science had exacerbated the population crisis in the name of humanity by increasing the odds against a recurrence of the Black Death. Moreover the nineteenth century proved lamentably parsimonious in its indulgence in major wars, leaving to the twentieth century the experiment of attempting to solve overpopulation by mass destruction. In the meantime, the Four Horsemen of the Apocalypse could no longer be relied upon.

Attempts were made to improve both the quantity and quality of land available to the peasantry, the social class comprising the overwhelming majority of the population. More land became available through modern technology, with deserts irrigated and swamps drained and reclaimed. In some areas, the peasantry acquired the chance of a higher proportion of the land through the generosity or (more often) the economic decline of the traditional landowners: in European Russia, for example, the nobility's share of the total land fell from around 70 per cent in 1850 to about 25 per cent in 1914, with the emancipated peasantry receiving the largest proportion of the property released. Modern agricultural techniques like mechanisation and artificial fertilisers could greatly improve the productivity of the available land, although their application in eastern Europe was generally slow and selective. Yet without underestimating the advances made in agriculture and agrarian society, there can be no doubt that these relatively modest improvements fell very short of providing an answer to the chronic question of overpopulation.

The healthiest and most progressive prospect was that the changing economic pattern of society would make available new or transformed resources which could sustain a continuously mounting population. As the Industrial Revolution spread eastwards across Europe in the nineteenth century, the new industrial, commercial, entrepreneurial and service enterprises which developed with such speed promised to absorb the excess labour force which a sated agriculture could no longer employ. Even if the strengthening industrial economy proved unable completely to answer the challenge of overpopulation, the hope remained that it might prevent a dangerous social phenomenon from becoming politically explosive.

Urbanisation, the leading demographic by-product of industrialisation, favoured the development of minority nationalism. As towns and cities began to spring up in eastern Europe, the fortunes of individual nationalities became largely contingent upon the possession of an urban base. The countryside, with its high birth rate, provided the demographic weight, the raw material that might be fashioned into the troops of nationalism. Towns supplied educated nationalist cadres and the organisation necessary to mount sustained campaigns for national objectives. But only a city could constitute that mass concentration of forces that enemies found impossible to ignore and practically indestructible. Commanding demographically and politically, the city served as the bastion of the nation, a refuge in times of oppression and a headquarters at moments of national opportunity.

As serf emancipation passed across eastern Europe, transforming the Habsburg Empire after 1848 and the Romanov Empire after 1861, the resulting legal mobility of labour encouraged a large proportion of excess peasantry to migrate to the towns and cities. In minority areas, the trend amounted to a nationalist time-bomb. Cities had previously been political and demographic citadels of the imperial nationality: in the pre-1848 Habsburg Empire, Budapest and Prague were German cities in (respectively) Hungarian and Bohemian locations. After emancipation and the provision of sufficient industry to provide continuous mass urban employment, the provincial centres of the Empire were converted demographically into the would-be capital cities of emergent nations. Budapest, a city which was 75 per cent German-speaking in 1848, experienced an influx of population from the surrounding countryside to become 80 per cent Magyar-speaking by 1900.[10] The imperial majority was converted into a minority; the local nationality took possession of a ready-made city, an enormous boost to nationalist ambition.

Demographic takeover did not necessarily mean a political revolution, only an irreversible shift in that direction. In Prague, the Germans may have been reduced to a 14 per cent minority in an overwhelmingly Czech city by 1880 but they kept a disproportionately high number of powerful and remunerative positions. Similarly, in Helsingfors the Swedish minority retained an economic and social stranglehold on the city which almost defied the Finnish demographic revolution. In general, while the provincial cities were stormed demographically by the local nationality, the imperial minorities conducted an effective rearguard action to preserve much of their political, social and economic preponderance.

It is probably judicious to suggest that those nationalities without a city always experienced difficulty developing their nationalism beyond the cultural stage, had to rest content with a longer time-scale of national development and in the meantime were painfully vulnerable to imperial repression. The majority of nationalities which failed to gain wider acceptance as a nation or state were those without a city, for example the Macedonians, Ruthenes and Belorussians. The Jews provide an interesting instance of a nationality which lacked territory but could claim more than one city, notably Vilna and Kishinev but to a lesser extent Warsaw, Lvov and Odessa, thereby offsetting their most conspicuous disadvantage. A nationality without a city rarely achieved sovereignty and independence; a nation acquiring a city could rarely be denied.

As economic revolution spawned social revolution, class complicated the development of nationalism. Though class self-interest always fuelled east European nationalism, the dominant class was not always the same. When nationalism first penetrated to eastern Europe from Germany, it was perceived as a reinforcement of traditional arguments in favour of the established order, most particularly to bolster the conservative stand of the provincial nobility against imperial plans for reform. Where the Magyars, Poles and Croats were dominant, the nobility reserved for themselves alone the rights, responsibilities and privileges of the 'political nation', usually in defiance of imperial authority. 'Magyar', 'Pole' and 'Croat' were initially at least as much labels denoting class privilege as ethnic affiliation. It was said that a Croat aristocrat would sooner admit his horse to membership of the Croat 'nation' than a peasant. The nobility demanded a monopoly of political power within their own territory and perverted the new concept of the nation to their own interests, advancing 'nationalism' as justification for class-serving social and political conservatism.

By the definition of Marx, eastern Europe in the early nineteenth century was polarised between 'Historic' and 'Un-Historic' entities, with the distinction broadly between the rulers and the ruled in the past, or between what may be termed 'nations' and 'nationalities'. The Historic nations based their aristocratic nationalism on the legitimacy accorded by history. To the historical concepts of traditional territory and 'constitutions' agreed between the nobility and imperial authority was added a mystical appeal centred on the legendary crown. The crown was viewed as the symbol of ultimate historic and divine legitimacy by all Historic nations, provoking an atmosphere of intense co mpetition between rival 'crownlands': the Poles venerated the Crown of Poland, the Magyars the Crown of St Stephen, the Croats the Crown of Zvonimir and the Czechs (on the occasions they were accorded Historic status) the Crown of St Wenceslas. The initial effect of nationalism was therefore to establish a hierarchy of nations and nationalities based ostensibly on historical precedent but fundamentally on the class dominance of the nobility.[11]

The economic revolution of the nineteenth century tended to undermine the hegemony of the nobility and promote a broad middle class encompassing commercial, industrial and professional compo-nents, which entertained ambitions for converting its formidable economic influence into political power. Nationalism was again the obvious (though not the only) vehicle for class ambition and, by the mid-nineteenth century, 'aristocratic nationalism' was having its monopoly challenged by 'bourgeois nationalism'. The overall effect was both to strengthen nationalism by extending its allegiance beyond a single class and to provoke a power struggle between the classes for exclusive possession of what each termed 'true national-ism'.

Two factors however restricted the role of the middle class in east European nationalism. The first was the relative smallness of the bourgeoisie because of the slow progress of industrialisation: of all the various movements, probably only the Czech and Finnish featured a bourgeois leadership. Even in Bohemia, an early compact between aristocratic and middle-class nationalist camps only gradually evolved into the principally bourgeois Czech nationalism of the late nineteenth century. Moreover, despite the weakness of the local aristocracy and relative strength of the middle class, the Czech nationalist campaign was deliberately based upon the traditional crownland rather than the increasingly authoritative (but territorial-ly disadvantageous) argument of ethnic self-determination.

The second bar to the primacy of bourgeois nationalism was the fact that, for much of eastern Europe, the bourgeoisie was not of the same nationality as the majority of the population. Among the Historic nations, the aristocracy shunned trade, commerce and industry as socially demeaning, with the result that what middle.class emerged in Poland and Hungary was by default almost entirely

German and Jewish. Similarly in the Ottoman Empire, the Turkish distaste for economic enterprise let the initiative slip to the Armenians and especially the Greeks, who soon almost monopolised the small but prosperous local bourgeoisie. In these circumstances, Magyar or Polish bourgeois nationalism, for example, was a social and political impossibility. In the early twentieth century, the economic influence and social privilege of such 'bourgeois minorities' as the Germans, Greeks and especially the Jews were to prove a great embarrassment to the new nation states of eastern Europe

Popular nationalism, expressing the aspirations of the lower classes of society, was the last variety of nationalism to evolve and has attracted the most criticism. International socialists have claimed that nationalism represents at very least a 'false consciousness', which diverts the masses from the true path and positively retards the advent of socialism. More specifically, nationalism has been attacked as a cynical device by which the upper classes retain power: so-called 'popular nationalism' was less the spontaneous (if mistaken) expression of the masses than the contrived and artificial concoction of an aristocracy or bourgeoisie anxious to project an image of what might be called 'national nationalism'. The object of raising pseudo-nationalism in the nineteenth century was of course to intimidate the imperial power into concessions which were promptly monopolised by the upper classes. The classic example in eastern Europe was Magyar nationalism. By raising the spectre of popular nationalism, the Magyar gentry managed to browbeat the Habsburg establishment into the *Ausgleich*, which offered them a virtually free hand in Hungary. After 1867, the new Magyar establishment repressed and exploited both the non-Magyar minorities and the Magyar lower classes but took care to establish a two-tier system of differential discrimination by which an appeal to nationalism united all Magyars against non-Magyars.

It would be quite unhistorical to suggest, however, either that working-class nationalists did not exist in eastern Europe or that they were all pathetic dupes of the bourgeoisie. The weakness or absence of both a local aristocracy and middle class clearly contributed to the success of essentially peasant Serb and Bulgar nationalism. The peasants who invaded the cities to become the proletariat of the future very often found nationalism more attractive than socialism: 'growing cities were a fertile breeding-ground for national feeling; this, with religion declining, was the readiest emotional compensation for the strangeness of urban and industrial life ·to the first generation of incomers from the countryside'.[12] Although it may well be true that nationalism was never the mass movement its champions have claimed, the role of the lower classes was rarely negligible, often significant and occasionally crucial.

The relationship between nationalism and class was invariably controversial and often convoluted. As a general rule, the leadership and social emphasis of nationalism (as with most movements) tended to permeate down the social pyramid from its apex. Aristocratic nationalism declined overall, albeit proving remarkably resilient in Poland and Hungary. Bourgeois nationalism appeared but the economic backwardness of eastern Europe prevented it ever playing a major role except in Bohemia. Popular nationalism featured more prominently towards the twentieth century although, perversely, Serb nationalism was among the very earliest successes. Competition between classes for the 'right to nationalism' became obsessive even as the adherents of liberalism and socialism condemned all varieties of nationalism as socially reactionary or diversionary. Whether genuine or bogus, nationalism was employed as a weapon to threaten imperial masters and as a device for social control over volatile populaces. The overall social trend was that nationalism became less likely to be the property of a single class, more inclined to evolve a cross-class appeal (however superficial) which made the movement increasingly formidable.

Mass education was a final new development in society which had enormous implications for nationalism. As one would expect, eastern Europe was less literate than western Europe, with the population of the Ottoman Empire most unlettered but the Habsburg Empire approaching a Western level of popular education. As late as 1897 the Romanov Empire had an illiteracy rate within European Russia of 81 per cent. By comparison, in 1890 the Habsburg Empire featured an illiteracy rate of only 23 per cent. Predictably, female illiteracy was universally significantly higher than male. At the same time, progress towards the reduction of illiteracy was steady: over the period 1874 to 1894, the illiteracy rate of conscripts to the Habsburg army fell from 41 per cent to 22 per cent and that of conscripts to the Romanov army from 79 per cent to 62 per cent. In the capital cities in particular, a striking improvement was being registered: in 1897 the illiteracy rate in St Petersburg was only 31 per cent; in 1900 the rate in Vienna was down to 3 per cent, 1 per çent lower than Paris.[13] High urban literacy underlined the role of the city in the development of nationalism.

With literacy transforming social expectations and the prospect of an 'Age of the Masses' boosting the demand for education, nationalist movements became outstandingly successful in recruiting the newly literate, freshly aware social classes. The critical social group which developed nationalism from an elitist and abstruse ideology into a movement of cultural respectability, broad appeal and political authority was the 'intelligentsia'. Relatively over-educated in societies still struggling to overcome mass illiteracy, the intelligentsia still had to suffer the frustration of exclusion from the social and political establishment. Culturally misplaced and underemployed, the intelligentsia – especially the academics, lawyers and journalists – were the natural 'social bearers' of nationalism. Under the general heading of popular education, the intelligentsia set itself the task of converting geographical expressions first into cultural entities, then into social nations and finally into political sovereign states.

The critical initial phase of the nationalist education programme was the creation of a 'culture-community', a consciousness-raising exercise by the intelligentsia to invest territory which was otherwise ethnically deficient or inert with an identity which the populace would embrace. Linguists like Kopitar in Slovenia, Gaj in Croatia and Dobrovsky in Bohemia toiled to produce grammars and dictionaries as the linguistic basis for future cultural development. Folklorists like the Miladinov brothers in Bulgaria, Karadzić in Serbia and Lönnrot in Finland scoured the countryside in search of the ancient folk-culture of the nation, as manifested in custom, song, costume and dance.

Historians, with the Czech Palacký as the most successful, played an indispensable role, labouring to provide nations with a sense of historical identity, contemporary respectability and future legitimacy. Often the historicist exigencies of nationalism carried academics far beyond the traditional confines of their disciplines. No nationality would admit to newness; all solemnly subscribed to the concept of national 'revival'. The assertion that one cannot revive what has never existed and many nationalisms were historically and politically untenable fabrications – as frequently advanced by propagandists of empire – urged on nationalist historians to fresh excesses of wish-fulfilment. Literally every self-respecting nationality laid claim to a glorious past: the Rumanians looked back to Stephen the Great in the fifteenth century; the Albanians to the heroic Skanderbeg also in the fifteenth century; the Serbs to Dushan in the fourteenth century; the Ruthenes to the thirteenth-century principality of Halich; the Slovenes unearthed the tenth-century Freising Manuscripts; the Ukrainians expressed touching nostalgia for the 'Golden Age of Kiev' in the tenth century; the Slovaks claimed the ninth-century Moravian Empire as the first state in central Europe; and the Bulgars revealed that they had been the cradle of Slavic civilisation. Factual accuracy was an early casualty in the competition for long historical pedigrees. With 'the Dark Ages being lit by the garish beams of chauvinistic scholarship', historians were soon reduced to operatives in nationalist myth-making factories. It became easy to identify with Renan's jaundiced judgement that 'to forget and – I will venture to say – to get one's history wrong are essential factors in the making of a nation'.[14] The ultimate shame and degradation came in the 1880s with the forging of manuscripts by Hanka, the director of the library of the Czech Museum, to 'improve' the longevity of the pedigree of Czech civilisation.

At a less exalted level, the nationalist mythopeic obsession became ever more ludicrous. Preposterous claims, often on the sales principle 'the poorer the product, the harder the pitch', became the rule. A favourite self-indulgence was out-bidding one's rivals with famous national sons: the Bulgars claimed Napoleon had Bulgar blood; the Croats discovered America (or alternatively, two of Columbus's sailors were Croat, presumably recruited to show him the way); Alexander the Great was revealed as a Gypsy; Jesus Christ was a Serb; the Magyars claimed Adam; everybody claimed God.

Infinitely more dignified and productive was the promotion of 'national music'. To cater for public participation in music-making, choral societies became a major nationalist vehicle. Following the German model, the Czech *Hlahol* adopted the motto, 'Through song to the heart, Through the heart to the homeland'. In societies where illiteracy was often the rule rather than the exception, music played an indispensable role in promoting a sense of cultural identity and pride. Morever, by employing the truly international language of music, the so-called national composers like Chopin, Sibelius, Kodaly, Janaček, Smetana and Dvořak became the most effective publicists for national identity and the best ambassadors for east European nationalism to the wider world.

In the final analysis, all publicity was good publicity since it raised the level of the population's national consciousness. Once the masses had learnt to recognise and appreciate their cultural identity, even if it was little more than a confidence-trick pulled on a trusting populace, the educational drive became more overtly political. Once the intelligentsia had performed its historic role as the midwife of nationalism, the newly aware population could be drawn into full membership of the nation and mobilised in its campaign for national sovereignty.

INTERNAL COMPONENTS

A new sense of legitimacy was the earliest of the more intangible internal components to galvanise nationalism. A feeling of grievance was not an inevitable response to bad treatment or wretched conditions, which were regularly borne with only statutory complaint. A more complex conjunction of popular perceptions was necessary to found a new legitimacy. When a plague epidemic, brutal treatment by the local landowner or even higher taxes were viewed as divine punishments, the vanity of railing against God's will (and inviting further retribution) bred an attitude of reluctant fatalism. But with the fragmentation and then decline of the universal church, a growing tendency towards individualism also bred the hope that human action might secure a better deal in this world, rather than trusting to divine compensation in the next. A sense of legitimate grievance also presupposed that the offending circumstance was perceived less as a sentence of divine justice than the product of a very different, inferior 'morality'. The value-system on which society based its code of morality and justice naturally varied widely according to time, place and social class. For the privileged upper classes the law was paramount, but even an unlettered peasant soon appreciated that secular law was class-based, often serving as little more than an aristocratic machinery to preserve sectional vested interests. As God's justice – revealed somewhat cryptically in Holy Writ and administered rather high-handedly by the church – lost universal allegiance, and the laws of man proved blatantly discriminatory and self-serving, a moral crisis of confidence manifested itself.

The vacuum in traditional consensus morality favoured the development of liberalism, nationalism and socialism as variants of a new concept of 'natural justice'. The new movements all emphasised that the ultimate morality was not divinely imposed but a natural, organic outgrowth of the maturation of society. Heaven could wait; modern man should not and would not wait. As nationalism asserted a novel morality based upon the principles of the sovereignty of the people and the right of the nation to pursue its chosen fate, all other systems were explicitly or tacitly condemned as false, artificial and therefore 'unjust'. The appeal of conventional religion and the authority of the church had been irretrievably undermined by their prolonged cohabitation with the 'illegal' social and political establishment. Nationalism reached its 'take-off ' point to become a major political force once its adherents passed the psychological barrier of acting as rebels against the established moral system to believing themselves to be executors of the incoming morality against an illegitimate establishment. The conviction of nationalist legitimacy had been born and proved unshakable: once Right was on your side, Might would sooner or later follow!

The concept of responsible activism was a logical corollary. The character of nationalist leadership was necessarily moulded by its perception of the dynamic of nationalism. The nation was a natural 'organism', a biological necessity, immutable and irresistible in its logic, morality and ability to survive. It was emphatically not an artificial 'apparatus', an accidental and contrived agglomeration of random components like the current dynastic empires. The inner logic of nationalism made its eventual triumph inevitable, offering its adherents the comforts of 'historical legitimacy' and the assurance that they had joined the winning side.

At the same time, the role of leadership was at least by implication downgraded: if the triumph of nationalism was certain, was not the nationalist leadership historically superfluous? The conventional wisdom of nationalism countered that while victory was pre-ordained, its timing was negotiable. Whilst nationalists could not force the pace of nationalism, they bore the social responsibility of ensuring that victory occurred at the earliest point sanctioned by History. Abandoning the fatalistic passivity of past generations, the activist had the moral duty to foster the fastest natural rate of nationalist development and to prevent the temporary arrest or retardation of nationalist progress by defending empires or rival movements. Nationalism thereby plausibly blended the ingredients of moral legitimacy in an imperfect world with responsible activism within the context of inevitable victory.

As a crusade for youth, nationalism fulfilled a deeply felt nineteenth-century need. A cause which combined a moral challenge to the jaded political establishment and a 'legitimate' channel of expression for youthful high spirits exercised an ineradicable fascination. Elie Kedourie has pointed out the degree to which early nationalist movements were almost children's crusades, deliberately sporting such labels as 'Young Italy' and 'Young Poland'.[15] Setting aside for one moment the phenomenon of aristocratic nationalism, the vanguard of bourgeois and popular nationalism was almost invariably from well-educated youth, particularly university students destined to become the new intelligentsia. It is likely that a component in youth's virtual monopoly of nationalism in its early phase sprang from a sense of disappointment: too young to participate in the excitement of the Revolutionary and Napoleonic eras, irrepressible youth was provoked by the banality of the post-1815 world into a self-conscious Romanticism. Reinforcing the familiar generation gap, the post-Revolutionary generation demanded a sense of purpose in a humdrum, reactionary period. If necessary, rebels without a cause would invent one rather than abandon their oppositional stance. If the cause of Revolution was dead, a glamorous substitute must be found: Lord Byron showed the way by espousing, publicising and then dying for the independence of Greece, 'for Freedom's Battle'.

Youth's commitment to nationalism was manifested in a variety of forms. The *Burschenschaft*, a society of radical students founded in 1815 at the University of Jena to promote German unity, established many of the character traits of later conspiratorial nationalism. Asserting the principle that the righteous man recognises no external law, the *Burschenschaft* took as their ideal Jesus Christ, whom they hailed as the definitive model of the uncompromising zealot. The premise that 'morality proceeds from self-legislation' led directly to the belief that the 'nationalist is a law unto himself ' and on to the terroristic conclusion that 'the end justifies the means'.[16]

The 'Gymnastic Movement' was another variant form. In 1811 Friedrich Jahn established a student gymnastic fraternity, the *Turnverein*, as a front organisation behind which to raise a 'regenerative elite' for the German nation. Committing their bodies and souls, the 'gymnasts' were to serve as a 'catalyst of national regeneration', transcending the regionalism and (to some extent) the class structure of Germany. The expanded *Turnerbund* played a leading part in what has been termed 'nationalisation', the propagation of nationalism among the mass of the population, and incidentally became the international matrix for nationalist youth organisations. Parading as innocuous sporting associations, the Czech *Sokol* clubs in particular were amongst the most influential promoters of popular nationalism in nineteenth-century eastern Europe.

The gymnastic tradition paid an unexpected bonus when the revival of the Olympic Games at the turn of the nineteenth century presented nationalities with a world stage for asserting their identities. In a world almost uncannily free from major conflict, it was natural that the Olympics were from the very start a war substitute, what George Orwell later called 'wars without the shooting'. The Olympics were also exploited for sectional political purposes: the Czechs, thanks to the strength of their *Sokol* organisation, secured recognition for a Bohemian team in the Olympics decades before Czechoslovakia existed as a state, thereby accustoming world opinion to the reality of the Czech identity which must eventually be accorded political status.

Another youth-monopolised aspect of nationalism was the 'Apostles of Freedom' movement. Most influential in Rumanian and Bulgar nationalism, this missionary concept of spreading the gospel of liberty to benighted nations was a development of the revolutionary examples of Mazzini and Garibaldi. Always idealistic and often insufferably self-indulgent, the heroic 'Apostles' made a strong contrast with the disciplined 'Gymnasts' within the overall nationalist youth tradition. But whether expressing itself through the more controlled, evolutionary nationalism of central Europe or the more flamboyant, revolutionary nationalism of the Balkans, the role of temperamental youth in the movement as a whole cannot be exaggerated.

It was as a surrogate religion that nationalism made its widest appeal of all. The rational aspects of nationalism were throughout its career challenged by an almost irresistible emotional fervour. Renan claimed that 'a nation is a great solidarity founded on the consciousness of sacrifices made in the past and the willingness to make further sacrifices in the future'.[17] The mysticism implicit in this definition becomes more explicit in the concept of the nation as 'a community of fate': individuals are predestined to membership of a nation, a personal fate which can never be denied; the role of free will is reduced to the quality of service that the individual can bring to the cause of the nation. As the bandwagon of nationalist activism gathered momentum, rationality was regularly sacrificed on the altar of nationalism: intoxicated by the grandeur of their cause, nationalists became victims of their own propaganda and abandoned themselves to transports of self-deception.

As nationalism approached the peak of its self-assurance (and before the nationalist movements were sobered by the practical experience of independence), the resemblance to a secular religion became uncanny but unmistakable. Most of the social and psychological behaviour-patterns conventionally associated with traditional religion, and particularly with persecuted messianic sects, were on public show. The phenomenon was comprehensible enough: with even human nature abhorring a vacuum, the decline of traditional religion had to be accompanied by the rise of a substitute 'faith'. Whilst consciously rejecting the comforts of religion together with the self-serving conservatism of the church, the new anti-clerical and atheistic generations were unable to make a clean break with the past and subconsciously elaborated a substitute ideology with most of the features they had earlier despised. Starting life as an ideological response to a moral crisis, nationalism intentionally or involuntarily evolved into a secular faith.

The tag *vox populi, vox dei* took on a new meaning. In opposition to the reactionary establishment, a political equivalent of 'catacombs Christianity' emerged. The doctrine of 'ethnocentrism' replaced Christian ethics as the basis for moral superiority. Nationalism provided a liturgy which codified the duties and responsibilities of the individual in a comforting, sustaining corpus of ritual. A therapeutic 'blanket response to emotional strain and social deprivation', the nationalist creed proved self-justifying, morale-boosting and emotionally cathartic.[18] A strong revivalist element suffused popular nationalism, in the senses both of an uplifting emotional crusade in a morally grubby world and a return to a frequently mythical but hallowed set of 'original' values. Nations achieving independence gave thanks to their national god, a curiously biddable Being who had yet apparently emerged the victor in some celestial 'Battle of the Nations'. Nations failing to secure independence were far from discouraged, revelling in their martyrdom and claiming self-sacrifice as the ultimate demonstration of a nation's validity and self-esteem. Suffering for the cause became almost welcome: the Poles for example claimed the coveted role of 'Christ of Nations' for Poland, tormented unremittingly throughout the nineteenth century for the real or imagined sins of other nationalities.

All too soon faith passed beyond the orbit of rationality altogether. Debatable doctrine became inflexible dogma. Nationalist emotion grew into quasi-religious hysteria. Starting as a gospel of emancipation for all, the creed of nationalism continued the analogy of Christianity by developing all the unsavoury features of the Inquisition and the Wars of Religion. The nationalist campaign recalled the crusade's blend of ideological sanctimoniousness and sordid self-interest. The excommunication of apostates and heretics was updated in a new conformist tyranny which swept all emergent nations. The sectarian abomination of other faiths was translated into xenophobic chauvinism, with aliens (and national minorities) reduced to mendacious stereotypes as a deliberate de-humanising exercise to justify discrimination. The original idealistic dream turned into a nightmare, and most especially for the minorities. The devaluation of all other 'nationalities' and the fanatical exaltation of one's own 'nation' as the 'chosen people' perversely set European nationalism on the road to Auschwitz.

The traditional factors of race, religion, territory and language jointly (and often separately) fostered senses of distinctive national identity and unity against outside threat. The external stimuli of the nineteenth century, most notably overpopulation, urbanisation, class consciousness and mass education, provided a cumulatively massive boost to the development of nationalism. Internal components like a new perception of political legitimacy, the concept of responsible activism, the attractions of a youth crusade and a religion for a secular age endowed nationalism with an appeal – even a charisma – which guaranteed mass recruitment and determined commitment. The end-product was a dynamic political and social movement whose challenge to the imperial establishment of nineteenth-century eastern Europe seemed formidable to the point of being totally irresistible.

3. The Imperial Perspective

THE reputation of 1848 as the 'Springtime of Nations' seems at first sight grossly inflated. All the nationalist fervour generated at the time and all the retrospective evaluations of 'the watershed of nineteenth-century Europe' cannot disguise the glaring limitations of the 1848 exercise in revolution. Although many nationalist movements either stirred for the first time or had their most successful showings to date, not a single permanent or substantial victory was scored by nationalism: the imperial structure of eastern Europe survived the nationalist onslaught of 1848 without a casualty. And yet if the concrete achievements of the 'Year of Revolutions' were so meagre, with the challenged Habsburg and Romanov Empires surviving territorially almost intact into the twentieth century, why have contemporary nationalists and subsequent historians accorded 1848 so much respect? The present chapter sets out to compare the Habsburg and Romanov Empires over the period 1815 to 1914 in order to assess the long-term significance of 1848, the viability of the defending imperial establishments and the historical progress of their national minorities.

THE HABSBURG EMPIRE

The Habsburg experience of '1848' was traumatic, a stream of profoundly shocking developments which reverberated throughout the Empire for the remainder of its career. Although the new phenomenon of socialism (which played so dominant a role in France) made a variety of cameo appearances, 1848 to the Habsburg

Empire meant overwhelmingly a full-scale nationalist challenge to the imperial establishment. Almost by dint of sheer longevity, the Habsburg dynasty had acquired over the centuries an astonishingly varied territorial legacy, part through military conquest, much through expedient marriage. The bewildering range of ethnic material gathered arbitrarily (and on occasion almost absent-mindedly) by the Habsburgs in the years before nationalism became a threat represented an historical inheritance which was converted almost overnight by 1848 from an administratively inconvenient mishmash into a political nightmare. Table II demonstrates the problem posed the Habsburg Empire by the advent of nationalism. If the neutral or inert ethnic pattern were invested with political dynamism, converting the Empire from a poly-ethnic to a multi-national entity, the prospects for the Habsburgs were grim. The wide variety of nationalities, a major problem in itself, was compounded by the relative population distribution. No nationality commanded even one-quarter of the total population of the state: there was no national majority in the Empire, only a spectrum of national minorities of variable size and quality. The pertinent political distinction cannot therefore be between 'majority' and 'minorities' but only between 'dominant' and 'subordinate' minorities. The demographic size of the various minorities provided a crude hierarchy of population which was to provide the basis for the political pecking-order of nationalities: once the Magyars, the second largest minority, were promoted by the Germans to the rank of 'junior dominant minority' in 1867, the Czechs, the third largest minority, automatically became head of the nationalist queue for admission from subordinate to dominant status.

The most dangerous of the nationalist challenges of 1848 predictably came from the Magyars. As already remarked, Magyar nationalism was notable for its taxocentric, aristocratic nature. Although the nobility comprised only some 5 per cent of the total population of 'Hungary' (in 1840), its 80 per cent Magyar dominance ensured that the development of Hungarian nationalism was always closely tied to the aristocratic or gentry classes. After the late eighteenth century, when nationalism was employed as a reinforcing argument for the maintenance of noble privilege and the feudal class-nation against the Germanisation plans of Emperor Josef II, the concept of nationalism became extended. The gloomy prediction from Herder that the Magyars stood no chance of surviving intact as an ethnic entity and would soon be absorbed by the surrounding Germans and Slavs

TABLE II Composition of Austria–Hungary in 1910
(rounded in millions)[1]

(a) *Ethnic Distribution*

Nationality	Population	% of total
Germans	12.0	23.9
Magyars	10.0	20.2
Czechs	6.5	12.6
Poles	5.0	10.0
Ruthenes	4.0	7.9
Rumanians	3.25	6.4
Croats	2.5	5.3
Slovaks	2.0	3.8
Serbs	2.0	3.8
Slovenes	1.25	2.6
Others	2.9	3.5
Total	51.4	100.0

(b) *Religious Affiliation*

Religion	Population	% of total
Roman Catholic (incl. Uniate)	39.0	77.2
Protestant	4.5	8.9
Orthodox	4.5	8.9
Jewish	2.1	3.9
Muslim	0.5	1.1
Total	50.6	99.8

galvanised the Magyar upper classes into a broader nationalist
campaign. From the 1820s, a Romantic revival was staged to

strengthen the Magyar sense of cultural identity and to expand the social appeal of nationalism in Hungary. For many Magyar nobles, this course was a regrettable but necessary infringement of their political monopoly for the sake of survival, although more liberal nationalists like Count Istvan Széchenyi preferred to welcome what he envisaged as the ennoblement of the nation.

Magyar nationalism was being driven on by two new social forces by the 1840s. A small but articulate Magyar intelligentsia, just beginning to emerge after decades of being overshadowed by the local German and Jewish minority communities, was epitomised by the Byronic Sandor Petöfi. An increasingly radical nationalism, fuelled by the frustrations of the impoverished gentry class, was headed by the charismatic Lajos Kossuth, who was, to quote C. A. Macartney, 'a member of that dangerous class which possesses birth and brains but no means'.[2] Both Petöfi and Kossuth represented emerging or newly motivated social classes which, in the absence of a strong native Magyar middle class, played the crucial roles in the nationalist campaign of 1848–9. It was Kossuth who, in March 1848, led the delegation of the Hungarian Diet that wrung from an unnerved imperial government concessions amounting to full autonomy for the Magyars. A new government representing a fair spectrum of Magyar opinion was created, encompassing the moderate Széchenyi, the liberal Ferenc Deák and the radical Kossuth.

The crisis came when the imperial government in Vienna began its counter-revolution, summarily cancelling the 'March Revolution' on the pretext of Magyar duress in September 1848. Under siege from the Habsburgs, Magyar nationalism entered its heroic phase. Kossuth led Magyar opinion in refusing to countenance an arbitrary imperial cancellation of the 'lawful revolution' and opting to fight for Hungary. A Hungarian army (the *Honvéd*) was raised, a 'sacred union' of all Magyars proclaimed and a 'holy war' for the physical survival of the Magyar people fanatically preached. The confrontation between Magyars and Habsburgs assumed social and political dimensions unprecedented in eastern Europe.

The Hungarian cause was probably ultimately doomed for reasons outside the control of the Magyar nationalists but they did make one substantive contribution to their fate over 1848–9. The Magyar attitude to the non-Magyar nationalities within the territory of Hungary had always been, to say the least, ungenerous. The Magyar self-perception was of an heroic people decimated fighting against the

Turks, a selfless martyrdom which had been shamelessly exploited by non-Magyar groups to encroach upon Magyar land in their time of weakness. In the emotionally charged atmosphere of 1848–9, all gestures towards toleration were forgotten. Petöfi, perhaps because of his mixed Serb-Slovak parentage, kept his head better than most, combining burning Magyar patriotism with a politick regard for non-Magyar sensibilities. Kossuth however seemed to go out of his way to alienate the minorities, declaring that Croatia was not worth a breakfast and claiming to be unable to locate Slovakia on any map. Kossuth's increasingly rabid public pronouncements could only antagonise the non-Magyars. Caught between the Habsburgs and the Magyars, the minorities had little hesitation in preferring the former and passively or actively favouring counter-revolution. The most overt demonstration came with the military intervention against Hungary of the formidable Croats, headed by Josip Jellačić a leader more fanatically anti-Magyar than any Habsburg. Realising the enormity of the blunder, the Hungarian Parliament played a last desperate card in July 1849 by granting equality to all non-Magyars; but the timing was too crude and the motive too transparent to dent the unanimous hostility of the minority nationalities.

Without more general support outside and inside Hungary, the Magyars were isolated and vulnerable. The Habsburg establishment was increasing in self-confidence by late 1848. The military chastisement of the Italians and Czechs was complete. The shedding of the incompetent Emperor Ferdinand in favour of the personable Franz Josef in December 1848 offered the Empire the dynastic pretext to renege on its earlier concessions and launch the military counter-revolution against Hungary. Given the probable eventual subjugation of the Magyars by Habsburg power alone, the intervention of Tsar Nicholas I in mid-1849 served not to determine the outcome but to hasten it. In an atmosphere of acrimonious in-fighting, the Magyar revolution turned on its chief architect and rejected Kossuth as the national leader in favour of General Görgey in August 1849, but nothing could prevent the victory that Russian arms handed to the Habsburgs. The Magyars had insufficient of the classic ingredients of the nationalist success formula to win in 1848–9: the imperial power was too strong, Great Power patronage was conspicuously absent and the nationalists made a significant (though probably not decisive) contribution to their own defeat by their intolerance towards their minorities.

Even so, the defeat of 1849 was to be only temporary, only a postponement of the achievement of Magyar self-determination. Once the broader Magyar commitment had been forged, it could not be dissolved. The Habsburgs unwisely played into the hands of the Magyars by a vindictive campaign of reprisals. The punitive action associated with General Haynau, who promised the Emperor 'no more revolution in Hungary for a hundred years', culminated in the public hanging of thirteen Magyar generals in October 1849. Far from aiding the Habsburg cause, the savage repression supplied the Magyars with the martyrs that every nationalist movement needs to buttress its sense of moral outrage. The repartition of Hungary into deliberately artificial administrative areas cutting across traditional boundaries – the favourite imperial stratagem of 'redivide and rule' – failed to undermine raised Magyar consciousness. The forcible dispossession of many of the gentry supporters of 1848 increased their sense of grievance and committed the ex-gentry to nationalism as the only means of restoring their lost status. Meanwhile Western public opinion, as sentimental as it was fickle, fêted and lionised the exiled Kossuth, and Western governments were increasingly impressed by the responsible behaviour of the Magyar leadership after 1849. Selecting only public protest and passive resistance as weapons from the political armoury, the Magyar liberals Deák and Eötvös laid siege to the Habsburg establishment in a disciplined, considered campaign which won the respect of Vienna.

With its nationalism actually strengthened by persecution and an appreciative (if uncommitted) Western audience, the Magyar cause needed only a dip in Habsburg fortunes to have a chance of success. That opportunity came in 1866 when the Prussian defeat of the Empire at Sadowa plunged the Habsburg establishment into a period of collapsed morale skilfully and relentlessly exploited by Deák and Gyula Andrássy. With almost nonchalant ease, given the furore of 1848, the Kingdom of Hungary was conceded extensive autonomy by the terms of an *Ausgleich*, or 'compromise', between the Austrians and Magyars. Three governmental spheres were reserved as an imperial monopoly: the dynasty itself, the conduct of foreign policy and the armed forces. But while Vienna retained dynastic, diplomatic and military control, the Empire was divided geographically into Austrian 'Cisleithania' and Hungarian 'Transleithania' for all purposes not specifically reserved for Imperial monopoly (see Map 2). Out of the *Ausgleich* formally implemented in early 1867 was born the

MAP 2 The Habsburg Empire, 1867–1918

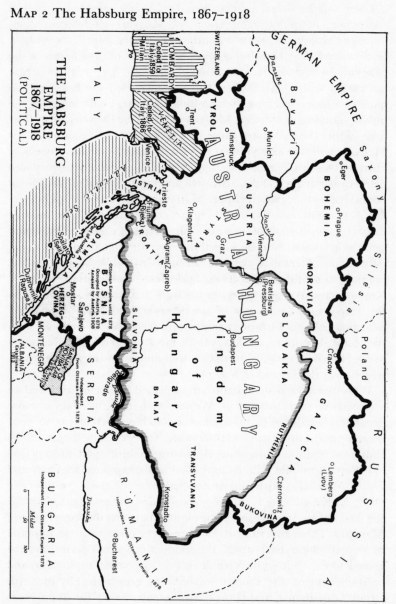

Source: Martin Gilbert, *Recent History Atlas* (London: Weidenfeld and Nicolson, 1966) p.5.

reconstituted state of 'Austria–Hungary'. Although the Magyars had not won (or indeed sought) the national sovereignty proclaimed in April 1849, they had secured within twenty years the restoration of the autonomy so briefly enjoyed in summer 1848.

The *Ausgleich* between Habsburg centralism and Magyar nationalism prompted all the other subordinate minorties to move up one in the queue for similar treatment. Next in line by virtue of demographic weight, cultural development and national self-consciousness were the Czechs. Setting aside what has been called the 'Jacobin nationalism' of the fifteenth-century Hussite period, early Czech nationalism was essentially aristocratic and traditional. Based upon *landespatriotismus* and the concept of 'Historic' Czech territory, this nationalism had much in common with the Magyar variety. A defensive boost to both was provided by the nobility closing ranks against the Germanisation of Josef II and each responded with a cultural revival to broaden the previously restricted class appeal of nationalism.

The 'Prague Spring of 1848' achieved little materially but profoundly influenced later Czech nationalism, albeit negatively. In March 1848, the 'Assembly of St Wenceslas' petitioned Vienna to grant autonomy on the basis of Bohemian historic territory. Under pressure from elsewhere, Vienna made concessions in the 'Bohemian Charter' of April 1848, a modest enough victory in a tentative nationalist campaign. Much more important were two events which served to crystallise Czech ideas about the nature and direction of its nationalist movement.

First came the refusal of František Palacký the eminent historian and nationalist leader, to attend the Frankfurt Parliament. Since Bohemia was a part of the German Confederation, the German nationalist assembly in Frankfurt invited a Bohemian delegate to attend its deliberations: but Palacký declined out of allegiance to the Habsburg Empire. In his famous published letter of refusal, Palacký asserted that 'if the state of Austria had not already been in existence for centuries, we should be forced in the interests of Europe and even of humanity to create it'.[3] To Palacký the Empire was not a political dinosaur mysteriously preserved from a pre-nationalist era and meriting only prompt despatch but the basis of a future federation in which the Slav members would enjoy a demographic majority and political equality. This 'catechism of Austro-Slavism' introduced a political philosophy prevalent among Czechs throughout the lifetime of the Empire: the confidence both that the Czechs were better off within the imperial structure and that the Empire was susceptible to reform and political progress.

The second event was the Prague Rising of June 1848, when students and intellectuals were joined by workers in a five-day occupation of the Czech capital but were efficiently suppressed by the Habsburgs' chief troubleshooter, General Windischgrätz. If Palacký's letter introduced Austro-Slavism as a justification for voluntary Czech membership of the Empire, the Prague Rising represented an isolated and untypical gesture by a mostly unrepresentative group within Czech society to bring to eastern Europe for the first time the heroic spirit of the Paris barricades. Whilst accorded perfunctory honour in retrospect, the Rising served principally to ensure that there was no repetition of such misguidedly open defiance of authority in future.

Over the decades after 1848, Czech nationalism moved into its second phase. The artificially induced cultural revival assumed an independent momentum, the National Theatre became a focus of national sentiment and the compositions of Bedřich Smetana articulated musically the burgeoning pride of the Czechs in their heritage. Cultural nationalism had, in the words of W.V.Wallace, 'to carry the torch for politics' at a time when the Habsburg reaction to 1848 included censorship, trials and close surveillance over Czech society.[1] Although the emphasis of Czech nationalism was shifting away from the aristocratic-traditional variety towards a bourgeois-liberal brand, the political position of the Czechs actually declined. When the imperial 'February Patent' of 1861 offered an ostensibly more liberal constitution which in reality artificially favoured the Bohemian Germans by penalising the Czechs, Palacký organised a half-hearted and ineffectual boycott of the Imperial Diet in protest. Again, when the Poles rebelled against tsarist rule in 1863, Czech opinion polarised between the 'Old Czechs', who could not shake off their Pan-Slavist respect for Russia, and the 'Young Czechs', who refused to condone any imperial repression and applauded their fellow Slav nationalists. The combination of suspicion of Czech sympathy for the Polish insurrection and the Czech leaders' self-defeating boycott served to alienate the Habsburgs at a critical juncture. When the Magyars scored the most striking constitutional coup of the century in 1867, the Czechs were left out in the political cold.

Czech disappointment that the Empire had settled for a squalid deal with the Magyars rather than commit itself boldly to federalism was, of course, coloured by the fury of frustrated self-interest. A Czech campaign of passive resistance, essentially a social broadening of the parliamentary boycott adopted a decade earlier, made little impression and was abandoned by 1878. Partly through their own political shortcomings, the Czechs missed the supreme opportunity for advancement in 1866–7 and no second chance presented itself for the rest of the lifetime of the Empire. Proposals to improve the Czech position were made on a number of occasions, usually on Habsburg initiative, but were invariably defeated by powerful vested interests. The Hohenwart federalist plan of 1871 and the Badeni scheme to grant the Czech language equality with German in 1897 were both scrapped through the combined opposition of the Magyars and the Bohemian Germans, an irresistible political combination.

Given the public failure of the Czech campaign for autonomy to bring tangible results, the wonder is that the Czechs were not driven to seek independence by violent means. The frustration and resentment of the Czechs were profound and almost universal by 1900 yet Czech nationalism still kept within the bounds of general legality and continued to press, dutifully rather than hopefully perhaps, for the conversion of the 'Dual Monarchy' into a tri-partite federation.

Various explanations have been advanced for what may be interpreted as Czech patience. The Czech national character has been explored, noting an inbred reluctance for commitment to drastic or violent courses unless all alternatives have been exhausted. While the Magyars and Poles, it was said, were conspicuously ready to die for their countries, the Czechs preferred to live for theirs. The class character of Czech nationalism has been emphasised: the rapid development of a strong bourgeoisie over the nineteenth century and its takeover of the nationalist movement replaced the aristocratic features of elitism, privilege and pugnacity with more middle-class considerations like pragmatism, security and compromise. Another interpretation stresses the extraordinary economic development of Bohemia over the second half of the nineteenth century. By 1914, Bohemia had become the Habsburg industrial estate, providing for example 85 per cent of Austria's coal and 95 per cent of its sugar. Although most of the investment was Austrian rather than Czech, the prosperity of Bohemia far outdistanced any other area of the Empire. To some nationalities, economic strength fostered ambitions for independence. The Czechs preferred to settle for their more-than-tolerable existence, notwithstanding its political disappointments, rather than risk the dangers of fighting to win independence and then, in all probability, having to fight to retain it. Life for the Czechs even in the early twentieth century was still improving both economically and socially. Disarmed by prosperity, there was no major political group among the Czechs prepared to risk all the nation already possessed to pursue the elusive benefits of national sovereignty.

The Croats were the last of the 'Historic' nations to be situated wholly within the Habsburg Empire. Throughout the nineteenth century, the Croats found themselves sandwiched geographically and politically between the Magyars and the imperial government. The complexions of Croat and Magyar nationalism were not dissimilar, which may in itself explain much of their perennial mutual antagonism. Both constituted taxocentric nationalisms, dominated by the local nobility, confronted by substantial ethnic minorities. By the 1830s, the previously quiescent Croat nobility was being angered by Magyar attempts to substitute their own tongue for Latin as the official language of Croatia. The brief but disproportionately influential period between 1809 and 1813, when parts of Croatia had been consolidated into the Napoleonic colony of Illyria, had launched a protracted, controversial but eventually successful campaign to unite the South Slavs into a single state. Although the Croat nobility was far from sympathetic to the idea of unity with the Serbs, the Magyars tried to impose their 'linguistic imperialism' at just the time when the Croats were conducting a lively debate on their identity and future. The sides were drawn in 1847 when the Croat *Sabor* (or Assembly) unanimously rejected the Magyar language, proposing instead the substitution of Croat for Latin in Croatia.

Under Jellačić the energetic *Ban* (or Governor) of Croatia, the Croatian military intervention of 1848–9 made a major contribution to Magyar defeat. As a reward for its loyalty during the Empire's greatest crisis, Croatia received from Vienna privileged status in the limited sense of milder treatment within the overall Habsburg campaign of reaction. The seditious Hungarian joke that the minorities loyal to the Empire in 1848 received as a reward what the Magyars suffered as punishment was not true in the case of Croatia: by the 'Sylvester Patent' of 1851, for example, Croatia's independence from Hungary was confirmed by Vienna.

However, partly through their class sympathy with the Magyar nobility (which to some degree overrode nationality), the Croat leaders soon found their 'special relationship' with the Habsburgs evaporating. By the time that the *Ausgleich* was being prepared, not even a panic-stricken speeding of a full Croat delegation to Vienna could forestall an arrangement which effectively delivered the Croat nation into the hands of the Magyars. At first, the worst Croat fears seemed exaggerated: the Magyar liberals who had contrived the *Ausgleich* with the Austrians were prepared to concede in 1868 the *Nagodba*, an equivalent local 'compromise' which granted Croatia autonomy in all spheres except the army and finance. But it was not long before the *Nagodba*, always an arrangement fixed to favour the Magyars, came under pressure. On the Magyar side, an accelerating trend towards intolerance culminated in a general policy of Magyarisation of all minorities, threatening the privileged Croat status guaranteed by the *Nagodba*. On the Croat side, as with Czech nationalism, the nationalist leadership shifted from an aristocratic to a middle-class supremacy, shedding its noble personnel *en route* in favour of the more militant intelligentsia.

In 1878, the Congress of Berlin granted Austria–Hungary the right to administer the ex-Ottoman territory of Bosnia–Herzegovina. For the Habsburg Slavs generally, the addition of Bosnia increased the Slav proportion of the Empire, reinforcing their campaign for a renegotiation of the *Ausgleich* to admit the Slavs into full participation in a federal state. The Croats both identified with the broader Slav contention and laid claim to Bosnia as part of medieval 'Greater Croatia'. The issue came to a head in 1883, when the *Sabor* agitated so stridently for possession of Bosnia that the Magyars abolished the *Nagodba* and the autonomous Croat constitution. For two full decades, Croatia was run by the Magyar 'direct rule' of the 'Iron *Ban*', Count Khuen-Hedérváry, who ingeniously allied his Budapest-appointed administration with the local Serb minority the better to oppress the Croat majority. Although the 'Magyar bondage' was frustrating enough to foster the contradictory developments of both a growing commitment to South Slav unity and a stronger Austrian orientation, Croatia continued without an autonomous constitution under a variety of Magyar-imposed *Bans* until the First World War. In retrospect, it is difficult to avoid the conclusions that Croatia almost wilfully sabotaged its relationship with its traditional Habsburg benefactor and that the imperial government was equally to blame for neglecting and then abandoning a nation which was fundamentally loyal through both sentiment and self-interest.

The last of the Habsburg 'Historic' nations was that fragment of

Poland taken by the Empire after the First Partition of 1772, the crownland of Galicia. Until the mid-nineteenth century, the Habsburg Poles were shabbily treated: thereafter they became a relatively privileged minority fully reconciled to 'German captivity'. The essence of the Polish nationalist dynamic lay, as so often, in its class structure. As with the Magyars, it was the Polish gentry (or *szlachta*) which monopolised the early nationalist movement and which the Habsburgs taught an unforgettable lesson in 1846. In peasant risings throughout Galicia in early 1846, the embattled gentry came to appreciate only too vividly that the intercession of the imperial government alone preserved their privileges and protected them from bloody extinction at the hands of the lower classes. Readily taking the point, the *szlachta* deserted the nationalist banner *en masse* to preserve its class privileges. In 1848 and 1863 the Habsburg Poles remained so conspicuously well-behaved that the Empire institutionalised the politico-social deal in 1868, granting effective autonomy to Galicia and specifically the local Polish gentry as a reward for exemplary loyalty. After 1868, the 'Polish Club' became a bastion of the Austrian establishment. Plans by Polish *emigrés* to make Galicia the organising centre for the reconstitution of Poland, a 'Polish Piedmont', were strongly discouraged by the local gentry. The 'Cracow School' of academics publicised the solid material advantages of Poles resting content with membership of the Empire rather than intemperately pursuing the impossible dream of Polish unification and independence. Willing parties to a self-interested 'sell-out', the Habsburg Poles were the most successful instance of a dangerous nationalist challenge being defused by the flexible policies of the imperial government.

The same province of Galicia also demonstrates Habsburg tactics regarding the Ruthenes. Galicia was divided ethnically between the Poles and Ruthenes, officially 58.6 per cent and 40.2 per cent respectively in 1910, although the Poles were largely concentrated in west Galicia and the Ruthenes were the overwhelming majority in east Galicia. The Ruthenes were almost entirely peasant, economically backward and lacking any national consciousness until the early nineteenth century, when they became unwitting pawns in a wider political game. In domestic terms, the Habsburgs artfully favoured Ruthene nationalism in order to keep the Poles in place. Although Polish nationalists claimed that Ruthene nationalism was a cynical Habsburg invention rather than a genuine movement, even the *szlachta* appreciated its usefulness after 1846 in diverting popular

Polish nationalism away from a peasant *jacquerie* directed at themselves. Another reason for the promotion of the Ruthenes became apparent in the later nineteenth century. With the Ruthenes the most westerly sub-group of the Ukrainian nation, the Habsburgs and Romanovs competed for their allegiance: the Romanovs claimed the Ruthenes ethnically and territorially in a spirit of Pan-Slavist expansionism (though running into trouble over their devotion to the Uniate faith): the Habsburgs defensively nurtured the separate identity of the Ruthenes to undermine the appeal of Pan-Slavism and convince the nationality that it was receiving better treatment within Austria–Hungary than it could expect within the Romanov Empire. The Habsburgs won the game in that the improving economic and political condition of the Ruthenes had by the early twentieth century made eastern Galicia the centre for exiled Ukrainian nationalists, a potential 'Ukrainian Piedmont' which could inflict more damage on the Romanovs than on the Habsburgs. An area of Habsburg vulnerability to Romanov attack had been converted into an offensive weapon against Russian domination of the Romanov Empire.

The treatment of the remaining 'Unhistoric' nationalities of the Empire depended largely on whether they fell within the Austrian or Magyar spheres of influence. The Slovenes, an isolated if territorially compact and self-contained Slav sub-group, had the good fortune to find themselves on the Austrian side of the post-1867 political divide. Although Vienna initially resisted the rather faint-hearted attempts by Slovenes to convert their nationalism from a cultural revival into a campaign for political autonomy, the grateful Habsburg response to an evolutionary, non-violent Slovene movement ensured that no crisis of relations ever occurred. As evidenced by the 'Resolution of Ljubljana', a vote of confidence in Austria–Hungary in 1912, the Slovenes were never provoked into ambition for independence, especially not as partners with the hated Orthodox Serbs in a South Slav state.

Other groups were less fortunate in their geopolitical destinies. The Slovaks developed fast from a very low level of national consciousness over the early nineteenth century, partly encouraged by a Habsburg policy for inhibiting the Magyars. Disliking the prospect of racial union with the Czechs almost as much as political union with the Magyars, the Slovaks relied on the Habsburgs to protect their nationality by the eventual concession of autonomy. All hope was snuffed out when the *Ausgleich* permanently deprived the Slovaks of

Austrian protection and abandoned them to the tender mercies of the Magyars. By an act of heavy symbolism in 1875, the institutional centre of Slovak cultural nationalism, the *Matica Slovenská*, was closed down by the Magyar government for 'promoting Pan-Slavism'. Though Slovakia benefited from the Magyar connection economically, the cause of Slovak nationalism was badly damaged by Magyarisation, leaving the Slovaks at a low political ebb by the early twentieth century. Without practical recourse, the Slovaks could do little but hope that a shift to 'Trialism' would improve their position within the Empire.

The Rumanians too suffered from being involuntarily transferred from Austrian to Magyar jurisdiction. From the moment of its emancipation from the Turks in 1691, Transylvania comprised an area under Austrian rule to which the Magyars laid claim. In 1848 the Diet of Pressburg loftily authorised a Magyar takeover of Transylvania, contemptuously ignoring protests from the leaders of the Rumanian community meeting at the Assembly of Blaj. In its own interests, the Rumanian minority supported the Habsburgs against the Magyars over 1848–9, being rewarded with imperial concessions to Rumanian identity which culminated in 1863 with recognition for the first time of the Rumanian political 'nation'. The *Ausgleich* cancelled all the Rumanian gains, handing over Transylvania and its Rumanian population to Magyar jurisdiction. What the Magyars failed to acquire in 1848, they secured in 1868, to the sorrow of the Rumanian minority. Racially distinct from the Magyars but without the numerical weight or looming Great Power patronage which favoured the Slav minorities, the Rumanians suffered greatly under Magyarisation. Little cheered by the growth just across the Carpathian Mountains of Rumania (which together with all the emergent Balkan states will be considered in the next chapter), the Rumanian minority in Hungary could only hope, like the Slovaks, that a move towards federalism within the Empire might ease their future lot.

The Serbs were relatively favoured by both Austrians and Magyars, a rare distinction among Habsburg minorities. The Habsburgs encouraged the Serbs to adopt an anti-Magyar stance, a line for which they needed no prompting over 1848–9, even granting the Serb-dominated Voivodina autonomy from 1849 to 1860. After 1867, the Serbs were promoted by the Magyars as part of their outmanoeuvring of the Croat ascendancy within Croatia. With the Habsburg acquisition of Bosnia in 1878, the Serb population of

Austria–Hungary rose to over three-quarters of the Croat (see Table II), aggravating the internal feud between the South Slavs. Although the Serbs were scattered in settlement, they still comprised 25 per cent of the population of Croatia, making them the natural collaborators with the Magyars. Even so, the growing attractions of the independent state of Serbia to the south fostered a substantial emigration of *prečani* (beyond the frontier) Serbs from Austria–Hungary. The relatively high educational quality of the Habsburg Serbs by comparison with the Serbs within Serbia ensured that the Habsburg migrant loss was Serbia's gain, fuelling the confrontation which was eventually to precipitate the First World War.

The Jews were 'unpersoned' in imperial censuses, being permitted to register a religious but not a national or linguistic identity. The situation of Habsburg Jews varied widely within the Empire. In Galicia, a large proportion of the Jewish population existed in appalling social conditions near or below the bread-line. In the towns and cities however, long-established Jews secured a disproportionately large share of the commercial economy, most notably in Hungary. The Jews became equally prominent among the liberal professions of Vienna and Budapest (with Sigmund Freud and Gustav Mahler perhaps the most celebrated personalities). By the turn of the century, the improved economic situation and greater 'social visibility' of the Jews were provoking a widespread anti-semitism: Karl Lueger regularly swept to office in the elections for Mayor of Vienna by cynically exploiting mass prejudice against prosperous resident Jews. As so often in eastern Europe, the Jews could not win: if confined to squalid ghettos, they were condemned as 'human vermin': if successful, they were denounced as social parasites and – with the surfacing of the ritual murder accusation – as quite literally 'bloodsuckers'.

This survey of the national minorities of the Habsburg Empire should convey an impression of the magnitude of the imperial problem and the nature of the official response. It must not be forgotten that, despite the undoubted trauma of 1848, the Empire survived almost completely intact, through war and peace, for the next seventy years. The only territorial losses were the north Italian provinces of Lombardy and Venetia (in 1859 and 1866 respectively), for which the Empire received some belated compensation and consolation with the acquisition of Bosnia after 1878. The territorial development of the Habsburg Empire was therefore less shrinkage than a slight shift eastward. The demographic effect was to shed a west

European nationality almost entirely – the Italian population of the Empire fell from 5,000,000 to 500,000 through Italian unification – and gain another east European nationality, the Muslim-based Bosnians. The net effect was to make the ethnic complexion of the Empire some 20 per cent more Slav and east European. The mid nineteenth-century process of German and Italian unification confirmed the exclusion of the Empire from western Europe, compelling Vienna to divide its attention between central and east European interests.

It was very broadly the division of the Empire into Austrian central Europe and Magyar eastern Europe that was achieved by the *Ausgleich* of 1867. At the time, the *Ausgleich* was greeted (particularly abroad) as the fateful breaking of the Austrian power monopoly, the crucial breakthrough which would precipitate a struggle for territory amóngst all the national minorities which could only result in the early disintegration of the Empire. The fact that Austria–Hungary lasted a full fifty years after 1867 demonstrates that these contemporary evaluations of the *Ausgleich* were mistaken. By the 1860s, it was appreciated in Vienna that neither the supra-national concept of *Kaisertreue*, personal loyalty to the dynasty, nor the German nationality featured by barely one-fifth of the total population was sufficient to maintain authority over a poly-ethnic territory fired by nationalism. The 'compromise' of 1867 effected a self-serving deal between the two largest minorities of the Empire the better to control (and if necessary to repress) the smaller minorities.[5]

The Magyars received a free hand in Hungary. Without the trouble and expense of creating a dynasty, a diplomatic service and an army formidable enough to defend their territory from a host of enemies, the Magyars could indulge their long-held prejudices. As the generation of liberal Magyar leaders like Deák and Eötvös passed away, they left as a legacy the *Nagodba* with Croatia and a generous Nationalities Law promising non-Magyars fair treatment. Rather more prophetic of the future trend was the transfer of Transylvania from Austrian to Magyar jurisdiction in 1868, accompanied by the cancellation of the special privileges of its Saxon, Szekler and Rumanian 'nations'. The liberal promises were broken in the 1870s as the new generation returned exultantly to the earlier intolerant spirit of Magyar nationalism. Employing the traditional argument of ensuring the survival of the Magyar race against the threat of extinction, the new establishment led by landowners like Kálmán Tisza embarked upon a massive campaign of forcible Magyarisation.

Just how effective the Magyarisation drive proved has been a matter of some controversy, with the balance of evidence appearing to stress its limitations. Passive, dogged resistance on the part of the non-Magyar minorities often thwarted Magyar intentions. A comparison of the Hungarian censuses for 1890 and 1910 (see Table III) shows that the proportion of the population claiming to be Magyar rose only from 42.8 per cent to 48.1 per cent. After twenty years of Magyarisation, even a census which could be relied upon to exaggerate the Magyar hegemony could only register that the Magyar proportion increased by 5.3 per cent and was still under half the population! Although the census figures claim a reduction in virtually all the non-Magyar minorities, there are legitimate grounds for suspicion. An official report of 1902 suggested that while Magyarisation was making headway at the expense of weaker minorities like the Slovaks and Ruthenes, it was failing even to maintain the Magyar position against more determined minorities like the Germans and fast-breeding Rumanians. Many Western observers argued that the dubious material improvement in the Magyar position was massively offset by the stiffened resistance Magyarisation provoked among the minorities. Some Magyars contended that, notwithstanding the disappointingly meagre results of the campaign, Magyarisation stemmed what would have been a much more dramatic deterioration in the Magyar position and was therefore justified as a geopolitical 'holding operation'.[7]

Whatever the shortcomings of the Magyarisation exercise, there was no doubt of the solidity of the Magyar hegemony within Hungary. By the gerrymandering electoral system introduced in 1879, the Magyars occupied 405 seats in the Hungarian Parliament, with the other half of the population expected to rest content with just 8 seats (5 for the Rumanian minority, 3 for the Slovak, none at all for the Germans, Croats, Serbs and Ruthenes). By 1910, the year in which the Magyars (by their own most generous estimate) reached 48.1 per cent of the population, the dominant nationality claimed 92 per cent of all teachers, 93 per cent of academics and 96 per cent of government employees. In broad class terms, the aristocracy prospered (by 1895 one-third of Hungary was owned by 4000 Magyar landowners); the gentry never recovered from a combination of the dispossessions following 1848 and the general agricultural crisis of the late nineteenth century and became the personnel of the post-1867

TABLE III National Composition of Hungary (Transleithania) in 1890 and 1910[6]

Nationality	% in 1890	% in 1910
Magyars	42.8	48.1
Rumanians	14.9	14.1
Germans	12.2	9.8
Slovaks	11.1	9.4
Croats	9.0	8.8
Serbs	6.1	5.3
Ruthenes	2.2	2.3
Others	1.7	2.2

Notes. 1. Official pressure for returns favourable to the Magyar establishment compounded the more familiar crop of 'nominal Magyars' to make the censuses less objective demographic documents than exercises in Magyarisation publicity.

2. The censuses recognised a Jewish religion (see Table IIb) but not a Jewish nationality. In Transleithania, Jews were usually registered—often willingly—as Magyars, with the obvious effect of artificially inflating the Magyar figures, probably by up to 2 per cent.

civil service and the peasantry suffered as aristocratic appetite for land coincided with the ubiquitous population explosion. As elsewhere, nationalism was employed by the Magyar propertied establishment to deflect lower-class grievance away from itself towards the even more disadvantaged national minorities.

The Austrians too came to relish the solid advantages of the *Ausgleich*. Though at first disposed to view the 'compromise' as a dishonourable expedient which must be disavowed at the first practical opportunity, the Habsburgs learned to swallow their hurt pride as the benefits of Austria–Hungary became apparent. The concessions of 1867 were ·the belated response of the Habsburg establishment to the unpalatable but undeniable lesson of 1848: political partnership with the Magyars to bring the 'dominant 'nationalities' up to an impressive 44.1 per cent of the total population was necessary to prevent the Empire from becoming ungovernable. Far from precipitating the fragmentation of the Empire, the *Ausgleich* was the only stratagem capable of postponing the state's otherwise imminent demise.

It became possible for the Austrians to devote more time to the pursuit of dynastic, diplomatic and military objectives. With the most awkward minorities like the sullen Rumanians and touchy Croats foisted upon the Magyars, the Austrians were legally rid of responsibility for their most taxing internal problems. However unsavoury the methods employed by the Magyars within Hungary, the Austrians were grateful to shed accountability for their most troublesome nationalities and consistently turned a blind eye to the east. Withdrawing from their traditional role of protector of all minorities against oppression with cynical speed, the Habsburgs settled down to a less demanding, more *gemütlich* style of government. As the censuses of 1880 and 1910 (see Table IV) demonstrate, the ethnic balance within Austria was stable, the Austrian demographic position was secure (if far from overwhelming) and the more manageable Czech, Polish, Ruthene and Slovene minorities proved easy to contain by fair treatment from an experienced imperial administration. The *Ausgleich* offered the Austrians a longer and quieter existence for the Empire than seemed possible after 1848.

Two developments, both associated with Hungary, spoiled the *Ausgleich*-sponsored stability of the Empire over the last decade of peacetime. The first was the natural progression (or possibly regression) of Magyar nationalism which, having exploited its autonomy to the full, flirted with the idea of pressing for complete independence. Diplomatic pressure to soft-pedal the Magyarisation campaign in the interests of avoiding bad publicity was labelled 'interference by distinguished foreigners' by the Magyar premier István Tisza. The Magyar mood of 1848, indulged in Hungary ever since the *Ausgleich* , shifted inexorably towards the defiant spirit of 1849. Over 1905–6 an activist coalition led by Ferenc Kossuth, son and political heir of the hero of 1848, defeated the pro-*Ausgleich* parties and demanded the seizure of full sovereign powers, starting with the raising of a Hungarian army.

But there was to be no repetition of 1849. Backed by the unanimity of Austrian public opinion and the formidable imperial army, Emperor Franz Josef answered the immediate crisis by dissolving the

TABLE IV National Composition of Austria (Cisleithania) in 1880 and 1910[8]

Nationality	% in 1880	% in 1910
Germans	36.8	35.6
Czechs	23.8	23.0
Poles	14.9	17.8
Ruthenes	12.8	12.6
Slovenes	5.9	4.5
Serbs and Croats	2.6	2.8
Italians	3.1	2.7
Others	0.1	1.0

Notes. 1. Although the phenomenon of the 'nominal dominant nationality' was common, there is no evidence of Austrian pressure on censuses comparable to the Magyar.

2. The Jews were again refused recognition as a nationality, being registered as Poles or Ruthenes in Galicia and Germans in Bukovina. The German, Polish and Ruthene proportions are therefore all slightly inflated, probably by up to 1 per cent each.

Hungarian Parliament by force and ruling by decree. His most effective weapon however was to threaten the Magyar upper classes with the power of the people: a bill for universal suffrage in Hungary was introduced to intimidate the Magyar leaders into submission. Universal suffrage would allow the non-Magyar half of the population and the lower-class three-quarters of the population to overwhelm the existing Magyar governing clique, calling the bluff that they really represented Hungary. Like the Polish gentry in Galicia after 1846, the Magyar militants were instantly brought to heel by this threat to their social privilege, jettisoning the whole issue of independence with indecent haste. Having achieved his object of preserving the territorial integrity of the Empire (and incidentally dramatically enhanced his authority as Emperor), Franz Josef had no need to follow through: the universal franchise plan for Hungary was allowed to lapse and the chastened but grateful Magyar establishment returned to its Magyarisation.

This is not to suggest that the Habsburgs were slavish adherents of the *Ausgleich*: although defending the arrangement stoutly over 1905–6, they were repeatedly tempted to extend the principle of 'compromise' to include the Slavs. The internal debate about imperial strategy may be gauged by comparing the views of the Habsburg royal family. The temperamental Empress Elizabeth pursued a long and passionate affair with Hungary, championed the Magyar cause at court and prized her title as Queen of Hungary above that of Empress. Crown Prince Rudolf articulated a nostalgia for the past glories of the centralised Empire, repudiating the letter and spirit of the *Ausgleich* (before committing suicide in scandalous circumstances at Mayerling in 1889). Franz Josef conducted a conscientious, pragmatic rearguard action over almost sixty-eight years, succeeding in becoming a legend in his own lifetime by encapsulating the principle of *Kaisertreue*. Finally, Archduke Franz Ferdinand was widely known to favour an extension of the *Ausgleich* principle to include at least some of the Slav nationalities which together comprised half the population.

It serves as some kind of tribute to the flexibility of the Habsburgs that they could arrange a political partnership with the Magyars, introduce major constitutional advances throughout Austria over the last decade of peace and regularly entertain plans for Trialism admitting the Czechs or South Slavs into membership of the political establishment. The Kremsier Parliament of 1848–9 and the Hohenwart Plan of 1871 were early examples of the Habsburgs testing the water with federalist schemes. The publication (through the patronage of Franz Ferdinand) of Popovici's book *The United States of Great Austria* in 1906 prompted a spirited official and public debate by its advocacy of an elaborate and ambitious federal state. Within Austria itself, improved (though never equal) representation was extended to the non-German minorities by the cautious Moravian Compromise of 1905, the advanced Bukovina Compromise of 1910 and the judicious Polish-Ruthenian Compromise of early 1914. The Habsburgs were spreading the principle of *Ausgleich* as far and as rapidly as politically feasible until the very outbreak of the First World War.

On each occasion, the opposition to fundamental change came from a coalition of the Magyars and the German minorities. By the late nineteenth century, the original concept of the supra-national dynastic empire had been overtaken by the idea of an empire dominated by its most vigorous nationalities. The Germans were retreating from commitment to the Habsburgs, instead concentrating on nationalistic aims like the defence of privileged German communities, notably the Bohemian Germans. The Magyars had barely secured autonomy in 1867 before Vienna was considering redistributing their territory amongst others. Having only recently gained freedom and land after a long, hard-fought campaign, the Magyars were not prepared to allow less-deserving nationalities to capitalise on their triumph. Federalism, which was the most constructive (as well as the most ambitious) response of a poly-ethnic empire to the force of nationalism, found its greatest enemy not in the ruling imperial dynasty but in the most recent beneficiary of nationalism. The strongest barrier to the full expression of nationalism within the Habsburg Empire was less that all-too-predictable villain, the Emperor, than the self-interested jealousy of the emerging nations.

THE ROMANOV EMPIRE

While the Habsburg Empire was enduring the Springtime of Nations, the Romanov Empire was languishing in bleakest mid-winter. On hearing of revolution in Paris, Tsar Nicholas I recalled all Russian citizens to the Empire, sealed the frontier against the 'Jacobin contagion' and instituted heightened surveillance over an imperial populace now politically quarantined from Europe. The precautions proved quite unnecessary: not a flicker of revolution or hint of subversive nationalism disturbed the domains of the Tsar over 1848.

Just why was 1848 such a non-event in the Romanov Empire? An often-repeated piece of conventional wisdom would have us believe that emigration acted as a safety-valve for Russian grievance, siphoning off malcontents and reducing the social pressure level within the Empire. Although this argument has a place at a later date, until the serfs were emancipated in 1861 there was no mass labour mobility to participate either in colonisation within the Empire or in emigration abroad. Over the period 1801 to 1850, the total migration to non-European Russia was only 375,000 (an average of 7500 a year); of these 250,000 were prisoners and exiles, leaving some 125,000 over half a century as voluntary migrants. The idea of the Siberian safety-valve cannot, therefore, explain away the lack of a Russian 1848.[9] Moreover, until the 1860s the Romanov Empire experienced a greater volume of immigration – typically a steady stream of Germans, sometimes augmented by groups fleeing persecution (like Gypsies and Jews arriving from Rumania) – than emigration, resulting in a net *in* flow of population to add to the meteoric rise in the resident population. In 1848 population pressure was increasing sharply with no major outlets, a situation which could well have been expected to cause demography-based responses to the European '1848'.

Perhaps the favourite explanation for the non-appearance of a Russian 1848 is the repressive 'police state' of Nicholas I. There is no doubt that the Tsar – nicknamed *Nikolai Palkin* (Nick the Stick) by the gallows humour of his unfortunate subjects – went to great pains to create an unprecedented police surveillance system in his empire. Disturbed by the Decembrist Revolt which greeted his accession in 1825, Nicholas set up the 'Third Department of the Imperial Chancellery' to be responsible for internal security, which within a decade had multiplied many times over in personnel and earned a formidable reputation for arbitrary action in the pursuit of its quarries. And yet the evidence would suggest that the well-advertised Third Department was less a necessary security measure against a massive threat than an over-reaction by a gullible and politically inexperienced tsar. Behind the self-confident *persona* of Tsar Nicholas I lurked a frightened, unsure personality who almost literally looked under his bed for a Red each night before retiring. The hanging of the aristocratic Decembrist leaders and the despatch to Siberia of their followers liquidated the only 'revolutionaries' in Russia and intimidated into silence or exile those tempted to emulate them. The Third Department was accordingly superfluous, neurotically searching for non-existent dissidents to justify its continued employment and remuneration. That Nicholas I established a police system for maximum security is irrefutable: but to suggest that the Third Department saved the Romanov Empire from 1848 lacks any credibility.[10]

It was not repression which spared Nicholas I revolution in 1848 but the backwardness of Romanov society. The population of Russia was at so much earlier a stage of social, economic and political development that the Western 'triggers' of 1848 were meaningless. Without the social and political explosive, the detonator of 1848 could have no effect. Aristocratic nationalism was irrelevant where the concept of 'Historic' nations and territories was either absent or antiquarian. Liberal nationalism was impossible in a society yet to produce a middle class. Popular nationalism could not appear when there was no industrialisation to produce an urban population and the abysmally low literacy rate cut off the peasantry from all endeavours beyond subsistence and survival. In all areas of European Russia, the primitiveness of society made an '1848' quite literally anachronistic. Only in the far west of the Romanov domains, in recently acquired territories featuring separate national identities and more modern societies, could 1848 pose any kind of threat.

The Romanov Empire was naturally shielded against the nationalist challenge by the pattern and balance of its ethnic composition, as a comparison with the Habsburg Empire makes clear (see Tables II and V). The first feature is that the 'dominant' nationality in the Romanov Empire comprised 44.3 per cent of the population: the equivalent in the Habsburg Empire commanded only 23.9 per cent. The Russians were therefore demographically almost twice as 'dominant' as the Austrians. Although the Russians were still a minority within the Romanov Empire, they approached the majority figure in a way that the Austrians never could. While the Austrians were driven in self-defence to concoct a 'dominant complex' of 44.1 per cent of the Habsburg population by the *Ausgleich* with the Magyars, they had still only fabricated an artificial alliance of self-interest. What the Habsburgs had painfully to contrive, a near-majority establishment of dominant national minorities, the Romanovs possessed quite naturally.

Relative racial uniformity immensely favoured the Romanovs. Within the Romanov Empire, so many of the larger 'subordinate' nationalities – like the Ukrainians and Belorussians – were Slav that the non-Slav element reached barely 26 per cent of the total. By contrast, the Habsburg Empire incorporated four racial camps: the Germans (23.9 per cent), the Magyars (20.2 per cent), the Latins (8.4 per cent) and the Slavs (47.5 per cent). The divisive political effect of this racial composition was emphasised by the *Ausgleich*, which made the Germans and Magyars 'dominant' (or indeed 'master') races and the Latins and Slavs 'subordinate' races. Meanwhile the Russians in the Romanov Empire mustered not only almost half the population but were the undisputed leaders of a racial camp which numbered 73 per cent of the total.

The challenge to the dominant nationality was weaker in the Romanov Empire. The Austrians had always to face determined

TABLE v National Composition of Romanov Territories in 1890s

(a) *The Romanov Empire (1897)*[11]

Nationality	Population (rounded in millions)	% of total
Russian	55.7	44.3
Ukrainian	22.4	17.8
Polish	7.9	6.3
Belorussian	5.9	4.7
Jewish	5.1	4.0
German	1.8	1.4
Lithuanian	1.7	1.3
Latvian	1.4	1.2
Mordvin	1.0	0.9
Estonian	1.0	0.9
Other Finno-Ugrian	1.5	1.2
Others (mostly Asiatic)	16.4	15.9
Total	122.7	99.9

(b) *The Grand Duchy of Finland (1890)*[12]

Nationality	Population	% of total
Finnish	2,048,500	86.1
Swedish	322,500	13.5
Russians and Germans	9,000	0.4
Total	2,380,000	100.0

opposition from another race: before 1867 it was the large and explosive Magyar nation: after 1867 it was a Slav alliance headed by the Czechs. The Magyars after 1867 were confronted by a mixed racial coalition of Germans, Latins and Slavs. Within the Romanov Empire, the immediate demographic challengers to the Russians were the Ukrainians, only one-third the size of the dominant nationality and with a low level of national consciousness partly attributable to their racial compatibility with the Russians. The non-Slav minorities, together numbering barely 26 per cent of the total, were too small and divided to present any major challenge to Russian hegemony. The national opposition to the Russian establishment was both quantitatively and qualitatively weak.

A final consideration under the heading of demographic composition was the vulnerability of the Empires not only to nationalism but to each other's imperialism. Once again, the Romanov Empire came off best. The Romanov Empire featured only tiny, isolated minorities related to the Habsburg dominant nationalities: with German and Magyar elements running at less than 2 per cent of the total, movements like Pan-Germanism and Pan-Hungarianism which might be exploited by the Habsburgs in the cause of expansionism held no terrors for the Romanovs. On the other hand, although few Russians were resident in the Habsburg Empire, its huge Slav population (47.5 per cent of the total) rendered it susceptible to the appeal of Pan-Slavism. In general therefore, the Habsburg Empire was vulnerable to Romanov 'ethnic attack' but the Romanov Empire was immune to Habsburg pressure.

There was just one respect in which the Austrians within the Habsburg Empire had the advantage over the Russians within the Romanov Empire. However pressed in terms of numbers, the Austrian minority headed the imperial league table in overall quality. For example, the male literacy figures for the nationalities of Austria in 1900 were: Czechs 98 per cent literate, Germans 95 per cent, Slovenes 78 per cent, Poles 55 per cent, Serbs and Croats 33 per cent and Ruthenes 29 per cent.[13] Whatever index of progress is selected – economic, social, cultural, educational or political – the Austrians figured at (or very near) the head of the list. Although significantly below Austrian standards, the Magyars held a similar position within Hungary. The Austrians within Austria and the Magyars within Hungary always comforted themselves with the hope that whatever they lacked in quantity might be remedied by superior quality.

The reverse was true in the Romanov Empire: the Russians needed their demographic weight to offset their mediocre quality. The male literacy figures for the nationalities of the Romanov Empire in 1897 show a very different pattern from the Habsburg: Germans 60 per cent literate, Lithuanians and Latvians 52 per cent, Jews 49 per cent, Poles 35 per cent, Russians 30 per cent and central Asians 0.2 per cent.[14] The Russians were not the poorest educated nationality in the Empire, for all the Asian groups were dramatically worse, but they were the most illiterate in Romanov Europe. Leaving aside the Ukrainians and Belorussians (for whom no reliable separate statistics are available), all the European nationalities were superior to the Russians in quality, making it inevitable that these groups would sooner or later challenge the right of the 'inferior' Russians forcibly to contain them within the Romanov Empire.

The most privileged and in many ways the most advanced of the national minorities under Romanov rule were the Finns. The high quality of the Finns was essentially a legacy of their long-standing Scandinavian connection. Only during the course of the Napoleonic Wars, by the Treaty of Fredericksham in 1809, was Finland detached from Sweden and claimed by the Romanov Empire. Most Finns were appalled by their involuntary change of geographical and political orientation, although Tsar Alexander I went some way towards calming fears by his Declaration to the Diet of Borga (also in 1809), in which he promised that Finland could retain all its traditional institutions as a separate Grand Duchy, associated with but not incorporated into the Romanov Empire. The link between the two territories was to be only that the head of the Romanov dynasty would now combine the offices of Tsar of Russia and Grand Duke of Finland. Fragile though this assurance by the Russian Autocrat may seem, the arrangement was scrupulously observed by both sides for the better part of the nineteenth century.

The arbitrary change in Finland's 'ownership', although without dramatic prejudice to its rights and privileges, stimulated a sense of separate Finnish identity. The patriot-academic A.I.Arwidsson announced shortly after 1809 that 'Swedes we are no longer: Russians we cannot be: therefore we must become Finns'. Cultural nationalism flowered during the second quarter of the nineteenth century; Elias Lönnröt collected the folk myths which were to invest the Finnish national epic, the *Kalevala*: Turku Academy and the University of Helsingfors became centres of 'academic patriotism'; and the Finnish language, previously a despised peasant dialect, rose in status and public usage to match the 'imperial languages' of Swedish and Russian. Although the Finns were sympathetic to the efforts of the co-racial Magyars, nothing resembling a 'Finnish 1848' occurred. Nevertheless, when the Russian army invaded Hungary in 1849, Nicholas I typically covered his Finnish flank: neurotically agitated by the potential propaganda damage of a recent translation into Finnish of *Wilhelm Tell*, the Tsar suppressed the publication of all Finnish books except on domestic and religious themes. As with so many decisions of the 'Nicholas System', the precautions were out of all proportion to the threat: bemused by the tsarist over-reaction, the Finns had still to reach the stage of political nationalism.

The same could certainly not be said of the Poles. Poland's glorious heritage meant that the Poles would always cherish the hope of a revival of the state which had been so unceremoniously partitioned in the late eighteenth century. So disaffected were many Poles that they gave active support to the Napoleonic Empire and showed every sign of becoming the leading troublemakers of eastern Europe. After the defeat of Napoleon, the Congress of Vienna repartitioned the Polish nation but attempted to placate the nationalists by handing the greater part to the Romanov Empire only on the understanding that its traditional customs and liberties were respected by the Tsar. 'Congress Poland' was accordingly 'attached to', not 'incorporated into', the Romanov Empire under conditions similar to Finland a few years earlier, ostensibly a reasonable basis for future accommodation.

While the Finns were meticulous in their observance of legality after 1809 to give their constitutional arrangement a fair trial, the relationship between Poles and Russians soon came under intolerable strain. It is only fair to report that little provocation came from the Russians. Alexander I seems to have been genuinely solicitous about his most recent subjects, permitting his Foreign Minister and personal confidant Prince Adam Czartoryski to promote Polish cultural and social ascendancy in Congress Poland (if only to sugar the bitter pill of their loss of political power). Nicholas I regretted the preferential treatment accorded the Poles, being particularly sensitive to the Russian mock prayer 'O Tsar, Bestow upon your own people what you have already dispensed to the Poles and Finns'. But despite recognising the anomaly of 'colonial' peoples enjoying greater privileges than the 'imperial' nation, Nicholas respected the promise tended by his elder brother at Vienna and made no moves to cancel the special status of the Poles he personally disliked so much.

The Poles could not reconcile themselves to Russian rule. Far from mollifying Polish society, the special status of Congress Poland was viewed as a calculated insult to its legitimate demands for national sovereignty. In November 1830, Polish Army cadets attacked the palace of the Russian Viceroy in Warsaw, precipitating a military confrontation with the Tsar. Following the tradition of aristocratic nationalism, so socially and ethnically exclusive was the Polish Rising that its doom was never in doubt. Contemptuous of non-Polish minorities within Congress Poland (who naturally looked to the Tsar for protection against the local oppressor) and arrogant towards the middle classes and peasantry, the *szlachta* which insisted on retaining the monopoly on Polish nationalism ruined its own cause.

The response of Nicholas I was entirely predictable: in 1832 the separate Polish Army was dissolved and the privileged territory of Congress Poland abolished, to be fully incorporated into the Romanov Empire. To many Polish nationalists, even this plight was more honourable than what amounted to accepting the charity of the Russian Tsar, though less impetuous observers suggested that the Poles had impetuously and gratuitously ruined a situation which might well have been exploited to their further advantage. With the 'Golden Emigration' after 1831, Polish political life was transferred into foreign exile for virtually a quarter of a century. The resulting impoverishment and demoralisation of indigenous Polish nationalism can be seen most poignantly in the 'Year of Revolutions': after a characteristically mistimed and misfired attempt at revolution in 1846, the Poles who were expected to lead '1848' had shot their bolt. Although the Polish 1846 made a contribution to the European 1848, it left the Poles themselves exhausted, with nothing to contribute beyond the 3000-strong 'Bem Legion' which fought alongside the Magyars in 1849.

The next Polish rising had to wait until a new tsar, Alexander II, promoted a fresh attempt at imperial reconciliation. In the early 1860s Alexander magnanimously granted extra constitutional powers requested by the Finns, who erected a statue of the Tsar-Liberator in gratitude which still holds pride of place in front of Helsinki Cathedral. Plans were simultaneously afoot to relax the repression of the Poles: under licence from the Tsar, the Viceroy Wielopolski initiated moves for greater autonomy on the lines of the former privileged status of Congress Poland. What was intended as reform was taken as weakness by the incorrigible Polish nationalists, who in early 1863 mounted a Warsaw Uprising against tsarist rule. The movement had wider social support than in 1830–1, with a middle-class and intelligentsia membership to augment the traditional leadership of the *szlachta*. A half-hearted attempt was even made to enlist the backing of the peasantry by promising land redistribution, but with little response from the (rightly) suspicious lower classes. Yet many of the old faults were still present: the leadership was Romantic and quarrelsome rather than. realistic and remotely democratic: exaggerated reliance was placed upon the patronage of France: and despised national minorities like the Ruthenes and Belorussians were once again alienated by Polish arrogance. After a protracted and bitter campaign, the Russian imperial army was again triumphant.

The reaction of tsarism was vicious and comprehensive. The modest plans of Wielopolski were permanently shelved and repression even fiercer than that after 1831 was inflicted upon the Poles. All Polish public institutions were taken over or suppressed by the Russians. Worst humiliation of all, the holy name of Poland was expunged from the tsarist record: after 1864 what had once been Poland received the official de-nationalised label of the 'Vistula Provinces'. As far as Polish nationalism was concerned, the failure of 1863 bankrupted the Romantic legend of emancipation through defiance. The heroic tradition begun by Kosciuszko in 1794 had run its course without success and his prophecy of doom as he lay wounded on the battlefield of Maciejowic – *Finis Poloniae* – seemed to have received its ultimate endorsement.

Given the proven limitations of Polish nationalism and the impressive military might of the imperial army, the Poles now abandoned the fight. Cultural nationalism geared to the survival of the Polish nation replaced the played-out political nationalism predicated on the military recreation of a Polish state. Only in the late 1880s did a new Polish generation consider returning to the political arena by creating a genuinely popular nationalism: the Polish League after 1893 was novel in the breadth of its social appeal and composition but firmly traditional in its chauvinistic contempt for the non-Polish minorities. Even so, the lesson of 1863 had been learned: no open challenge to Romanov power was mounted ever again. Over the last decade of tsarism, the nationalist leader Roman Dmowski restricted his activities to campaigning for the modest aim of Polish autonomy, in effect the restoration of Congress Poland.

The tsars employed the 'carrot' as well as the 'stick' within Poland. While the ominous presence of the imperial army intimidated Polish society, its economy was allowed to prosper. Alexander II emancipated the Polish peasantry in 1864, thereby earning the gratitude and, more important, the social quiescence of a class permanently alienated from its own upper orders. Agriculture and industry took advantage of the abolition of trade barriers between the 'Vistula Provinces' and Russia to exploit the enormous potential of the under-developed imperial hinterland. Industry grew at a meteoric rate, urbanisation proceeded apace, railway expansion soared and the standard of living of the Polish population rose steadily. The mood of Polish society changed to reflect its material improvement: the past heroic and Romantic values were rejected in favour of 'positivist' occupations within industry, business and education. The fruitless tradition of insurrection was abandoned, replaced by social and economic 'organic work' and political 'triple loyalty'. The combination of military menace, cultural autonomy and economic prosperity effected the sedation of Polish nationalism for the half century following the Rising of 1863.

To assume that a 'dominant' nationality is rendered immune from the appeal of nationalism by its imperial status is of course false; yet the nationalism of a dominant nationality is naturally possessive rather than emancipatory, 'imperialist' rather than 'secessionist'. It is understandable in terms of their differential historical development that Russian nationalism should follow, and in an important sense be a reaction to, Polish nationalism. The Polish debacle of 1863 had as great an impact on the Russians as on the Poles, profoundly shocking official circles and dismaying educated public opinion. It had been demonstrated that the Slav blood relationship was far from being a guarantee of political harmony: while the non-Slav Finns had proved perfectly behaved associates of the Russians, the Poles seemed irreconcilable in their antagonism. As the concept of Slav solidarity was repeatedly revealed as a sentimental rather than a practical proposition, the Russians retreated self-protectively into their own burgeoning nationalism.

Witnessing the self-sustaining upsurge of emotional nationalism within Russian society from the 1860s, tsarism had to integrate the popular dynamic into a coherent, practical and reassuring imperial strategy. Nicholas I and his successors were far too security-conscious to have missed the essential lesson of 1848 for tsarism: if it was fundamentally backwardness which saved the Romanov Empire from nationalist threat in the past, then the tsars could expect a 'Romanov 1848' in the future. The Empire had not escaped its experience of nationalist challenge, only been alerted to the danger looming. It was against a 'Romanov 1848' that tsarism started making its preparations after the 1860s utilising the growing force of Russian nationalism in the construction of a system loosely called 'Russification' which, it was hoped, would spare the Romanovs the tribulations of the Habsburgs.

'Russification' is a vague pejorative term which has for too long been employed as merely an ironic euphemism for bludgeoning ethnic minorities into bruised submission. Although it did on occasion assume that repellent form, the rationale and selectivity of Russification have rarely been objectively considered in the universal rush to condemn the practice.

The Jews were undeniably the targets of the most sustained and often violent 'Russification'. The Jewish problem in Russia was created virtually overnight by the partitions of Poland. Although Catherine the Great and Alexander I had no particular animus against the Jews, it was considered safer to contain the newly acquired minority by limiting residence to a 'Pale of Settlement' on the western borderlands. A harsher line from Nicholas I was, typically, succeeded by an attempt at greater integration of the Jews under Alexander II and the 1860s. Thereafter, partly because of their religious distinctiveness and social visibility, the Jews became the most popular target for the new defensive nationalism of the Russians. The participation of Jews in the terrorist *Narodnaya Volya* group which assassinated Alexander II in 1881 provoked widespread, spontaneous local *pogroms* against Jewish communities. The tsarist government immediately exploited popular anti-semitism to its own advantage, starting with the notorious code of discriminatory legislation known as the 'May Laws' of 1882.

Until tsarism itself came to an end in 1917, a relentless campaign of harassment was waged against the unfortunate Jews. A remark on the Jewish problem in Russia attributed to Konstantin Pobedonostsev, the Procurator of the Holy Synod from 1881 to 1905 and *éminence grise* to both Alexander III and Nicholas II, is always quoted for its cold-blooded callousness: 'A third will be converted, a third will emigrate and the rest will die of hunger'. If this succinct statement was indeed an encapsulation of official policy, the overall failure of the exercise is apparent. There were very few Jewish conversions to Orthodoxy: a figure of 1300 a year (or 3 in every 10,000) has been estimated. A cash incentive for conversion of 15–30 roubles, perhaps deliberately the classic thirty pieces of silver paid for betrayal, brought no significant increase, leaving the proportion of converted Jews grotesquely short of the one-third projected. As an American Immigration Report of 1892 exclaimed: 'Is there in our world of today any spectacle more touching or more rare than this impregnable attachment of millions of unhappy beings to the faith of their fathers, when to desert it, even as a matter of form, would save them from terrible suffering and would ensure them their freedom?'[15] Without legal territory or an unequivocal racial or linguistic commitment, the Jews hung on tenaciously to their religious and cultural heritage as their only irrefutable criterion of corporate identity. Religious 'Russification' of the Jews was an almost complete failure.

Emigration was another option favoured by Pobedonostsev. In 1903 the Zionist leader Herzl and the tsarist Minister of Interior Plehve agreed that mass emigration to Palestine was in both their interests and should be energetically promoted. From the early 1880s, foreign Jews, mostly acquired by the Russian takeover of Bessarabia in 1878, were expelled from Russia. Privileged Jews living outside the Pale were increasingly reconfined, sometimes by such callous operations as the expulsion of 30,000 Jews from Moscow in the winter of 1891, an act of 'purification' of Russia's Holy City. The authorities increasingly envisaged the Pale as an immense embarkation-point for emigration to the west. But although the proportion of the Jewish population which emigrated relative to those who remained was higher than for any other east European nationality, running at an estimated 22 per cent, it was still not high enough. The movement of Jewish emigrants was enormous both in absolute and relative terms but it still did not constitute an exodus: the great majority of Jews remained within the Romanov Empire. The unavoidable conclusion is that emigration even on this massive scale could not solve the Jewish question in Russia. If all or the great majority of Jews had departed and been acceptable elsewhere, a solution pleasing to tsarism might have resulted. If the emigrant departure rate had kept pace with the Jewish birth-over-death surplus, emigration would have prevented the problem gettting worse, acting as a demographic palliative. But in practice the Jewish population grew faster than the emigration rate: at best therefore, emigration acted as a safety-valve, preventing a bad situation from deteriorating as much as it would have otherwise. Emigration, which could not prevent the overall Jewish population growing and their circumstances deteriorating, was not even a Romanov solution to the Jewish problem in Russia.

The last, apocalyptic option of Pobedonostsev was physical liquidation. It is most doubtful that tsarism ever serously entertained the notion of mass murder but 'homicide by culpable neglect' would seem an appropriate charge. By confining the substantial Jewish population in a cramped geographical area and further concentrating it in ghettos and *shtetls* – pales within the Pale –*tsarism ensured that overpopulation would precipitate a collapse in the Jewish standard of living. In a Pale which was being reduced in area but experiencing a population explosion, the rich Jew of anti-semitic propaganda disappeared among the destitute and starving *Luftmenschen* attempting to live on air. To quote a shocked American account of 1894, 'in lieu of a violent and brutal extermination, the persecutors of the nineteenth century have substituted a more lingering method . . . famine and epidemic diseases'.[16] Tsarism was left by the patent failures of conversion and emigration to rely upon making Russian Jewry so vulnerable to hunger and disease that nature would do the Romanovs' dirty work.

It would be quite unhistorical to leave the impression that the Jews alone suffered from 'Russification'. Although the Jews were persecuted by tsarism with a zeal reserved for them alone, all other subordinate minorities received attention in the course of the 1880s and 1890s. In the Baltic provinces, for example, all local nationalities came under Russian pressure. In the mid-nineteenth century, the tsarist government tended to promote Estonian and Latvian self-consciousness to inhibit the dominant German minority, but from the 1890s switched to alliance with the local Germans against the growing nationalist threat. Similarly in Lithuania, the government first encouraged Lithuanian aspirations against the Polish ascendancy, then backed the newly amenable Poles against the Lithuanian menace. Typically however, the cause of Baltic nationalism was monopolised by the emerging middle classes, who set their heights no higher than the grant of greater autonomy within the Empire.

The factor which introduced a new undiscriminating intensity into 'Russification' was the first national census of the Empire conducted in 1897. Censuses in eastern Europe were invariably political events, never neutral bureaucratic exercises. With national self-identification notoriously unreliable, minority under-enumeration was the rule. Citizens entering census information were under implicit political pressure: no member of a dominant nationality entered himself as of subordinate nationality: but in an era of 'Russification' a proportion of members of subordinate nationalities entered themselves as 'nominal Russians'. At the highest level of census administration, no dominant nationality missed an opportunity, if not to falsify the returns, at least to exhibit the statistics in a light favourable to the political establishment. As a result, it may be safely assumed that the 1897 Census exaggerated Russian demographic strength, probably by up to 5 per cent.[17] Until the Census, the tsars had always believed that the Romanov Empire was also, in a purely demographic sense, a Russian Empire (or to follow official terminology, both *rossiiskii* and *russkii*). The Census sensation was that the Russians comprised a minority within the Empire, certainly a very sizeable minority at officially 44.3 per cent (and really around 40 per cent) but still incontestably a minority. The immediate effect was a stepped-up campaign of 'Russification' to retrieve a position worse than the tsarist government and Russian nationalists had believed possible.

The Finns were singled out for frontal attack. The reasons for the souring after the 1880s of what had previously been an almost model relationship were cumulative. Russian nationalists resented the privileged status of Finland (and of Finns within Russia) and claimed to discern security risks in its exposed location and meagre military resources. On the Finnish side, the cultural nationalism of the mid-nineteenth century had become undeniably more political, producing both a Greater Finland campaign for the acquisition of Karelia and Ingria, and a racially based movement for the greater solidarity of the Finns, Estonians, Mordvins and other Finno-Ugrian groups which together comprised some 6 per cent of the total imperial population. The touchy tsarist government started to suspect that the Finns – like their Magyar cousins – were ambitious to proceed from guaranteed autonomy to complete independence. From 1899, the Finns came under a veritable barrage of measures intended forcibly to incorporate the Grand Duchy into the Empire, including the demotion of the Finnish Diet and the abolition of the separate Finnish army. The effect was to intensify the emerging political nationalism of the Finns and divert it from its traditional target, the large and powerful Swedish minority, to the Russians.

The Russian Revolution of 1905 temporarily halted the prosecution of Russification. Many Russian nationalists feared that the minorities would exploit the Tsar's discomfiture in a spirit of 'Russia's difficulty is our opportunity' but although Russification had to be suspended for a few years, 1905 did not turn out to be the 'Romanov 1848' that some dreaded. No major breaks for freedom from the 'Prison of Nations' needed to be countered and the greatest humiliation Tsar Nicholas II had to suffer was the November Manifesto of 1905 cancelling all his recent anti-Finnish legislation. A combination of the backwardness of most national minorities, the intimidating might of the resident imperial army and the prosperity of the leading Polish and Finnish nations saved the Romanovs from a crisis comparable to that afflicting the Habsburgs over 1848–9.

As tsarism recovered from '1905', the policy of Russification was gradually reintroduced. With the granting of a *Duma*, an elected parliament, the minorities hoped they might gain an influential voice in the counsels of government. In the First Duma elected in 1906, the Russians held 59.1 per cent of parliamentary seats, Ukrainians 13.8 percent, Poles 11.3 per cent, Belorussians 2.9 per cent, Jews 2.8 per cent and other minorities some 10 per cent. Though collectively under-represented, the minorities still expected the Duma to defend their positions. It was not to be. From mid-1907 the composition of the later Dumas was fixed by electoral weighting to prejudice the left wing and minorities and favour the right wing and Russian hegemony. By the Fourth Duma, elected in 1912, non-Russian representation was down to 15 per cent. Far from being a champion of national minorities, the Duma first neglected the issue and was then converted into a *claque* for the tsarist govenment in its renewed Russification. Finally, by an act of 'aggressive constitutionalism', in 1910 the Duma voted itself jurisdiction over Finland, entering thereby into a squalid Russifying deal with tsarism.[18]

On the eve of the First World War, all minorities were succumbing to Russification. By his Protocol of June 1908, the Tsar reserved the right to distribute the affairs of Finland as he thought fit between the Finnish and Russian governments, which in practice meant handing over all significant power to the latter. By 1914 the Finns were reconciling themselves to the disappearance in all but name of their autonomous Grand Duchy. The Jews were being subjected to a fresh official campaign of harassment best publicised by the scandalously perverted Beilis Trial in Kiev in 1913. The tsarist government even took the territorial offensive, expanding 'Russia' by absorbing Kholm province from 'Poland' and Vyborg province from 'Finland'.

A principal reason why 'Russification' is such an unhelpful term is that foreign attention was always seized by minorities which either were so different from the Russians that the policy seemed irredeemably iniquitous or fought heroically against its imposition. With the Jews and Finns falling into the first category and the Poles into the second, western public opinion got into the habit of fulminating (uselessly) against tsarist 'Russification'. In reality, the leading targets for Russification were not the minorities most different from the Russians – who were to be forced out or simply crushed – but the minorities which were most similar. Only the tsarist government seemed to appreciate that the survival of the Romanov Empire depended not on the peripheral, often non-Slav nationalities but on the 'Slav brothers' of the Russians. If the other Slav nationalities could be literally 'Russified', that is to say assimilated beyond recognition by the dominant Russians, the Tsar need have no fear for the future security of his Empire. With the Russians already comprising 44.3 per cent of the total population, only the unconditional adherence of the Ukrainians (17.8 per cent) and Belorussians (4.7 per cent) was necessary to provide a uni-racial, uni-national Russian ascendancy commanding almost exactly two-thirds of the entire Romanov population. It is therefore no surprise that no national minorities received closer tsarist attention than the Belorussians and especially the Ukrainians.

The Belorussians were suspect to the tsars as potential traitors to the Russian cause. As Belorussia straddled the cultural and political watershed between Poland and Russia, each neighbour expended considerable effort to strengthen its own position and undermine its rival's by 'recruiting' Belorussians. As part of a quarantine exercise after the Polish Rising of 1830–1, the historic name of 'Belorussia' was officially changed to 'West Russia' because of 'fears that symbols of a historical past might foster secessionist trends'. After 1839 the Belorussian language was prohibited as a 'Polish dialect' and the distinctive Uniate Church which might have fostered a separate Belorussian identity was forcibly incorporated into the Orthodox hierarchy. Though Belorussians were instinctively distrustful of the Poles and rejected all participation in the Risings of 1830–1 and 1863, the Russian government redoubled its efforts to secure their loyalty. As Polish academics attempted to demonstrate that Belorussia belonged with Poland, Russian ethnographers and linguists 'proved' that the Belorussians were brothers to the Great Russian people. The tsarist government deliberately maintained the Belorussian illiteracy rate at its egregious level of probably the highest in European Russia to minimise opposition to Russian assimilation. Even the most innocuous cultural self-consciousness was under official ban until 1906, when Nicholas II, under pressure from revolution elsewhere, lifted the prohibition on the Belorussian language to allow a very modest local literary movement to emerge. It has been estimated that as late as 1914 'the total number òf active supporters of nationalism . . [was only] three to four thousand persons'.[19] The regime had successfully compounded the natural backwardness of Belorussia to retard the development of nationalism and foster a sense of community with Russia. Belorussia was an almost unqualified triumph for the tsarist policy of the Russification of Slavs.

The tsars were somewhat less successful with the Ukraine. The Ukrainians could find national inspiration and political pedigree in the 'first Russian state' of Kiev in the tenth century, a heritage which later nationalists claimed had been shamelessly stolen by the *moskaly* (or 'Muscovites') in their own quest for legitimisation. The action of the Ukrainian leader Khmelnitsky in becoming vassal to Moscow in the seventeenth century was interpreted by nationalists as treason, an historical disgrace which must be expunged from the record. The 'Father of Ukrainian Nationalism', the historian Mikhail Hrushevsky, attempted to play a role similar to that of Palacký for the Czechs, in particular arguing that the Ukrainian *Rada* meeting at Pereyaslav in 1634 had only authorised a 'personal union' with Muscovy and therefore the constitutional position of the Ukraine should legally be analogous to that of the Grand Duchy of Finland.

The historical legitimacy of the Ukrainian nation remained essentially an academic issue throughout the nineteenth century. Although a Ukrainian literary language based on peasant speech was promoted almost singlehandedly by the national poet Taras Shevchenko, the concerted efforts of the tsarist government retarded the natural progression from cultural to political nationalism. So effective were the tsars in removing nationalist troublemakers that after the 1870s it was only by flight to Galicia, the homeland of the Ruthene sub-group of the Ukrainian nation, that political nationalism could be developed (under the cynically benevolent eye of the Habsburgs). There seemed no immediate prospect of the 'Ukrainian Piedmont' posing any major threat to the Romanov Empire. When the First

World War intervened, Ukrainian political nationalism, only a speculative conspiratorial alliance of intelligentsia and peasantry, had still not broken free of tsarist control. The biggest demographic prize of all had been retained by the tsars: apart from a relatively harmless separate cultural identity, the Ukraine had been unable to make significant headway against the dogged Russification of the Romanovs.

With the effective securing of the Ukrainians and Belorussians, the Russified heartland of the Romanov Empire commanded two-thirds of the total population, a numerical dominance which no qualitative inferiority could fundamentally undermine. Russification was most appropriate to, and therefore most successful with, the non-Russian Slav minorities. The great good fortune of the tsars was the combination of an ethnic distribution balance which naturally favoured the Russians and a pre-nationalist society (with the sole exception of 'Poland') which could be inhibited in its historical progress by judicious imperial intervention. Although 1848 meant nothing immediately to their Empire, the Romanovs were alerted to the nationalist implications for their future and embarked upon what might be termed a 'preventative campaign' involving a series of increasingly authoritative 'pre-emptive strikes' against leading minorities. Although 1905 had a certain success as a nationalist consciousness-raising exercise, there can be no argument that the Romanovs had infinitely more victories than defeats in their war against nationalism. No European territory was lost over the century before 1914 (and enormous tracts of Asian territory were added). A precautionary offensive against the mounting threat from nationalism, commonly but misleadingly dubbed 'Russification', was showing more signs of success than failure. With its imperial holding-operation conspicuously more effective even than that of the relatively successful Habsburg Empire, the Romanov Empire was the strongest and most stable in eastern Europe.

4. Fight or Flight?

THE success or failure of a national minority in pursuing social, economic and political advancement in nineteenth-century eastern Europe was determined by the inter-relation of three cardinal factors: the demographic size and nationalist quality of the minority concerned; the availability and strength of support from existing Great Powers; and, perhaps most important, the state of health of the multi-national empire in which the minority was located. The almost infinite variety of local combinations of these factors promoted an expanding range of available options for employment in the developing confrontation between 'nation' and 'empire'.

FIGHT

The most heroic course open to a minority was to fight for its national aspirations. Although it was the Polish example, starting with Kosciuszko's despairing protest at the dismemberment of his country in 1794, which served as the inspiration for most acts of outright defiance of traditional authority, it was the minority nationalities of the Ottoman Empire which proved most adept at implementing the tactic. The failure of the Ottomans to keep pace with the military, administrative and economic advances of the West steadily disarmed the imperial establishment, offering openings to the Balkan nationalities which, despite their small populations, limited resources and cultural backwardness, were able to score nationalist victories, achieve independence and justify the minority course of fighting for freedom. The 'fight option' was conspicuously valid in Ottoman Europe, albeit less a tribute to Balkan nationalist heroism than a symptom of irreversible imperial decline.

The Serbs were the unlikely first national minority successfully to defy Ottoman authority. Campaigning after 1804 not for independence but for imperial redress against the arbitrary repression of the insubordinate local Janissaries, the Serbs under Karadjordje and then Obrenović made such a nuisance of themselves by their guerilla operations that the complaisant Ottoman government in Constantinople was increasingly disposed to turn a blind eye to Serb defiance. Despite ostensibly crippling handicaps – like a backward society without nobility, middle class or intelligentsia– the Serb resistance to oppression developed almost despite itself into the prototype of defiant Balkan nationalism. Appetite came with eating and in 1826 Serbia was formally granted autonomy by Constantinople, establishing a South Slav 'Piedmont' for the territorial expansion which was eventually to be crowned by the creation of Yugoslavia almost a century later.

Infinitely more famous a cause was the campaign of the Greeks for independence. Building upon the Ottoman millet system and acquiring exceptional commercial power through conspicuous loyalty to the Ottomans in the eighteenth century, the Greeks increasingly rejected their past 'collaborationist' tradition in favour of a broad allegiance to the idea of a sovereign Greek nation. Working through the conspiratorial *Filiki Etairia*, nationalist groups already persuaded of the impotence of the Ottoman Empire by its performance during the Napoleonic period made a commitment to armed defiance. In 1821 Alexandros Ypsilanti and his Greek 'Sacred Legion' posted nationalist intent, the signal for a rash of uprisings throughout the Greek peninsula which was bound to attract the reprisals of the Ottoman army. There seems little doubt that the nationalist rebellion would have been savagely crushed but for the mounting intervention of the Great Powers. Although it would be ludicrous to suggest that the Greeks achieved their eventual independence in 1830 purely through feats of Greek arms, the armed defiance of the Greeks served a crucial purpose in the broader campaign, attracting Great Power intervention in a way that nothing else could have.

The fighting option may not have been a guaranteed path to independence, even against the Ottomans, but it became an indispensable component in successful Balkan nationalism. Incapable of scoring victories over Great Power armies, the only military exercises of which the Ottomans became capable were punitive expeditions against recalcitrant national minorities, a consistently counter-productive response which only stiffened national resistance and incurred international censure. Internally, armed defiance fostered a sense of national solidarity, even willing martyrdom, which greatly advanced the general commitment to self-determination against the repressive imperial power. Internationally, armed nationalist rebel-lion became a standard device for winning Great Power patronage: even if a nationality had no hope of securing emancipation by military action, the public demonstration of nationalist 'spirit' was often sufficient to recommend its cause to the Great Powers, attract a powerful patron and secure a diplomatic victory over the Ottomans. All Balkan nationalisms exhibited this shrewd tactic of military defiance to draw the fire of the Ottoman overlord, thereby compelling the Great Powers to intervene in a part-humanitarian, part-diplomatic settlement from which the individual national minorities could be expected to benefit.

The Rumanians exploited 1848 to secure national sovereignty through foreign patronage within the decade. Fired by the revolution in Paris, the substantial French colony of the young Rumanian intelligentsia, already organised into secret societies like the *Fratia* (Brotherhood) and passionate adherents of Latinism, rushed home to detonate the liberal and nationalist revolutions in Moldavia and Wallachia. A radical government led by the historian Nicholai Balcesco survived just three months before the Ottoman army invaded Wallachia, compelling the Rumanian 'apostles of freedom' to flee back to Paris. Although it would be easy to condemn the Ottomans for crushing a promising experimental liberal government, the unpalatable truth was that the Balcesco government was a fiasco of epic proportions. The demands of a desperately poor, land-hungry peasantry soon stripped away the liberal veneer of the privileged 'revolutionary' government. The social conservatives who stood revealed resorted to employing nationalism to deflect criticism from their own self-interested establishment, a stratagem with little immediate success but later consistently employed by successive Rumanian governments. What saved the reputations of Rumanian liberalism and nationalism in 1848 was prompt suppression by the Ottomans: the defeated nationalists back in Paris could profess outrage at the cruel repression of their liberal hopes whilst privately indulging their heart-felt relief that the magnitude of their disgrace had been fortuitously obscured.

The combination of apparently heroic defiance of the Ottomans in 1848 and the strengthening of French patronage brought the Rumanian nationalists prompter results than they either expected or deserved. At the end of the Crimean War, the Treaty of Paris in 1856 sought to block Russian territorial expansion at the expense of the declining Ottoman Empire by ordering the amalgamation of the 'Danubian Principalities' of Moldavia and Wallachia into the autonomous state of Rumania, which secured formal independence in 1878. In Alan Palmer's words, 'by a curious irony, the most ineffectual of the 1848 revolts was the first in east-central Europe to gain general acceptance'.[1] The essence of the victory for Rumanian nationalism was that a gesture towards defiance of imperial authority had attracted Great Power patronage on a scale which rendered further Rumanian military effort superfluous. The fighting option had again proved its worth, not as a means of defeating the Ottomans militarily but as a publicity stunt to enlist all-powerful international intervention.

As Rumania joined Greece and Serbia as independent Balkan states, the competition for the territory remaining to the Ottomans (see Map 3) mounted. It was increasingly the stimulus of rivalry between the newly emancipated states rather than the repression of the Ottoman Empire which forced on the pace of Balkan nationalism. The Bulgars, retarded in their national consciousness by the political domination of the Ottomans and the spiritual subjugation of the Greeks (not to mention the lack of a local nobility, middle class and intelligentsia), only burst upon the Balkan stage in the 1870s. Fired by the examples of the Serbs, Greeks and Rumanians, the Bulgars were confident in their own fighting spirit and the patronage of their co-religious and co-racial mentor Russia. Apostles of liberty like Georgii Rakovsky, the 'Bulgarian Garibaldi', and Liuben Karavelov preached the activist line that 'liberty is not received, it must be taken'.[2] The genuinely popular appeal of nationalism among the Bulgars finally overflowed in an enthusiastic but chaotic insurrection in 1876. The subsequent Ottoman over-reaction, a massacre of 15,000 mainly innocent peasants by the Bashi-Bazouks, promptly dubbed the 'Bulgarian Atrocities' by the outraged West, abundantly repaid the original provocative action by the nationalists. Russia obligingly invaded the Ottoman Empire and, by the Treaty of San Stefano in

MAP 3 The Growth of Balkan Independence, 1822–1913

The Growth of
BALKAN INDEPENDENCE
1822-1913

Dates refer to the year in which independence
was gained from Turkey.
Territory lost by Turkey as a result of
the Balkan War of 1913

RUSSIA

BESSARABIA

AUSTRIA - HUNGARY

Jassy

Moldavia
Autonomous 1822

BOSNIA

Belgrade

1878

RUMANIA

1878

Dobrudja
1878

1913 from
Bulgaria

Sarajevo

SERBIA

ALEKSINATZ
1876
Nish

Wallachia
Autonomous 1822

Bucharest

PLEVNA
1877

Black Sea

1913 from Serbia
1880

MONTENEGRO
Independent since 1389

Durazzo

ALBANIA
1913

KUMANOVA
1912

1913
Macedonia
Ochrid

1878

BULGARIA

Sofia

1885

1913

Burgas

Adrianople

KIRK KILISSE 1912
LULE-BURGAS 1912
Constantinople

Salonika

1913

ITALY

Adriatic Sea

CORFU
English 1814-63
Greek 1863

1881-1897

Aegean
Sea

GREECE

TURKEY

Smyrna

MISSOLONGHI
1826

1830

Athens

NAVARINO
1827

Miles
0 50 100 150

DODECANESE
(Italian 1912)

Mediterranean   Sea

CRETE
(Greek 1913)

Source. Gilbert, *Recent History Atlas*, p. 13.

early 1878, a 'Big Bulgaria' was created between the Aegean and the Black Seas. With a territorial prize considered well worth a massacre, the Bulgars offered effusive thanks to Tsar Alexander II, privileged by history to emancipate Slavs on two separate occasions, the Russians in 1861 and the Bulgars in 1878.

The prompt disappointment of the Bulgars is well known. Suspecting the new Bulgaria as a tsarist puppet-state, a Russian land bridge to circumvent the Ottoman-held Bosphorus and Dardanelles, the West dissolved both the San Stefano Treaty and the bloated territory of Bulgaria at the Congress of Berlin in summer 1878. With Thrace restored to the Ottoman Empire at Western insistence, Bulgaria lost access to the Aegean before it had even glimpsed the sea. In a fury of frustration, Bulgarian nationalism indulged in intemperate pursuit of what it chose to call the 'restoration' of Big Bulgaria. With territorial expansion the touchstone of national honour, almost of neurosis, Bulgaria opted to fight its neighbours: in 1885, Rumelia was snatched from the Ottomans and joined triumphantly to existing Bulgaria; and at the battle of Slivnitsa (celebrated by George Bernard Shaw in *Arms and the Man*), the Bulgarian army had a resounding victory over the Serbs. Arriving late in the competition for Ottoman territory and having to fight harder to secure any share, the Bulgar newcomer proved itself a force in the Balkans more attuned to military action than its predecessors.

The last Balkan nation to claim a share of the Ottoman booty, and consequently having the greatest difficulty in securing territorial recognition, were the Albanians. With topographical, social and linguistic difficulties long delaying national self-consciousness, Albanians were awakened less by Ottoman repression than the awareness that imminent Ottoman withdrawal would mean dismemberment by neighbouring states. Montenegro to the north and Greece to the south laid claim to tracts of Albanian territory whilst Serbia to the east was set on acquiring the whole of Albania as its geopolitical corridor to the Adriatic. Agreeing upon a defensive campaign at an assembly at Prizren in 1878, the Albanians developed their nationalism to the point that a revolt after 1908 proved so ineradicable that even the Young Turk government conceded autonomy from Constantinople in 1912. Having won imperial recognition by its fighting spirit, Albania now attracted the patronage of Italy and Austria–Hungary. Although the independence of Albania was contested by all neighbouring states, the fighting option both secured Albania initial recognition and became an ongoing nationalist commitment to ensure the survival of the state.

None of the new Balkan states was content with its territorial spread. All regarded the territory received at independence as no more than a 'Piedmont', a basis for legitimate national expansionism. The ethnic settlement pattern ensured that national minorities of some description were invariably left outside the boundaries of the 'nation state', encouraging a sustained dialogue between state majority and isolated minority which always favoured territorial expansionism. With the membership of the Balkan states increasing steadily but no single state being large enough to rest content or powerful enough to satisfy its territorial ambitions, the competition for the dwindling Ottoman lands reached fever pitch.

By the early twentieth century, Ottoman territory in Europe that was effectively 'up for grabs' was reduced to the ethnically inert Balkan heartland of Macedonia. All the surrounding nations laid claim to Macedonia, either on the grounds that its national identity was most akin to their own or because it was an identity-less 'geographical expression' which might as well be theirs. The most provocative moves came, as usual, from the Bulgars: a premature insurrection by the Bulgarian-backed Independent Macedonian Revolutionary Organisation (IMRO) in 1903 was countered by the Ottoman authorities with a ferocity which recalled the 'atrocities' of 1876 (though without attracting Great Power intervention).

The logical next stage was reached in the First Balkan War of 1912–13, when Bulgaria, Greece and Serbia allied to oust the Ottomans from Europe (and to partition shamelessly the plundered territory of Albania). By the Treaty of London in May 1913, the Ottoman Empire lost all but the backyard of Constantinople to the Balkan allies. But the disappearance of Ottoman Europe could not stem the land hunger of the new states. If the self-interested alliance of ambitious local states in the First Balkan War was understandable, its sequel was totally predictable: in the Second Balkan War of 1913, the victors quarrelled over the Ottoman spoils. The eventual Treaty of Bucharest in August 1913 saw territorial losses for Bulgaria and gains for Rumania and even the Ottomans but there could be no doubt that the treaty constituted not a permanent definitive settlement of the Balkans but only another temporary breathing-space in the nationalist quarrel.

The 'fight option' played a prominent role in Ottoman Europe. A

nationalist legend of 'fighting for independence' was revered throughout the Balkans, although in practice the fighting was intended not to
defeat the Ottomans – an impossible military task for an unaided
Balkan nationality – but to attract Great Power patronage for the
purpose of benefiting from a diplomatic intervention in the 'Eastern
Question'. But if there was a bogus element about 'fighting the
Turks', there was none about defending oneself against ambitious
neighbours. The idealistic Mazzini-style nationalism of universal
emancipation was revealed in the Balkans as a political 'law of the
jungle', in which the 'survival of the fittest' was the principal theme
and 'cannibalistic nationalism' was the general rule. Far from solving
the national problem, the shrinkage and eventual disappearance of
the Ottoman Empire in Europe only created a Balkan zone of fiercely
competitive new states, each motivated by an exclusive and intolerant
nationalism geared to self-interested expansionism. A valuable
ingredient in the drive for independence from the Ottomans, the fight
option became an indispensable component in the nationalisms of the
newly emancipated Balkan states.

For all its growing authority through the nineteenth century,
nationalism was no irresistible force. The principal lesson to be drawn
from continental experience, steadily reinforced as the century
progressed, was that nationalist success depended less on *who* you
were than *where* you were. In 1830, 1,000,000 Greeks won from the
Ottoman Empire what 5,000,000 Poles could not wrest from the
Romanov Empire. In the Romanov Empire, the fight option was
unsuccessful to the point of becoming totally discredited: as the
numerically formidable and culturally advanced Poles were repeatedly chastised by the imperial army, finally convincing even head-
strong Polish nationalists of the pointlessness of the exercise, the lesser
Romanov nationalities reconciled themselves to the inefficacy of
tackling the tsars head on. In the Habsburg Empire, the lesson was
more equivocal: although the only nationalist successes of the century
in the Empire – the Italians and Magyars – had earned respect by
fighting for their causes in 1848–9, they owed their eventual victories
primarily not to military heroism but political expertise and Great
Power patronage. Not a single clear-cut success for the nationalist
fight option was registered in the Romanov and Habsburg Empires
throughout the nineteenth century.

Unfortunately for the heroic tradition, independent developments
in government and society served to undermine the classic fight

option. The civil powers of the political and social establishment underwent dramatic reinforcement. As government bureaucracies expanded in size, recruited superior personnel, raised their horizons of ambition and invented more sophisticated methods of social control, it became increasingly unlikely that a subordinate nationality would catch imperial authority unawares. The raising of modern police forces to patrol the social interface between the rulers and the ruled, and the creation of secret political polices as intelligence agencies, information-gathering organs and disciplinary instruments, were just the more obvious means by which modern governments protected themselves against the threat of rebellion.

The role of the army was traditionally to provide the ultimate force to defend the state against foreign enemies but protection of the political establishment against internal threat loomed larger with each passing decade. Over the century after 1848, only some ten years were spent in hostilities involving east European states so the routine function of the army was in practice more domestic than external. For every one year fulfilling the duty of guardian against the foreign invader, the army spent nine years acting as police auxiliary within the confines of the state. Although a lesson of 1848 was to demonstrate the need for police to cover the contentious social divide between the civilian population and the armed forces, the promotion of police forces over the late nineteenth century by the Romanov and Habsburg Empires in no sense rendered the disciplinary role of the army redundant. The army was more often kept in reserve, under normal circumstances intimidating violent opposition into more peaceful or constitutional channels by simply 'maintaining a military presence'. Although by the early twentieth century social control techniques had improved to the point where the army needed only to exist rather than to take action, the peacetime importance of the army was never underestimated by the Habsburg and Romanov establishments.

In times of peace and domestic calm, the army was an invaluable institution of imperial government. Despite a growing commitment to general (although never universal) conscription which raised some spectres, the reliability of the armies of the Habsburgs and Romanovs in peacetime was never seriously in doubt. Conscription itself was employed as a de-nationalising process. Individuals who would otherwise be the most likely recruits for nationalist causes were instead forcibly ripped from their supportive cultural environment and isolated in an authoritarian hierarchical system designed at very least to ignore their ethnic identities. Given that the safest technique for survival in a Procrustean mechanism like the army was anonymity, conscripts from minority nationalities were impelled to pursue conformity and uniformity; the sheer exercise of naked power forced a substantial degree of self-interested surrender of identity on the part of the minority conscript. Though much of the conformity might be relatively superficial, even the process of 'nominal assimilation' brought tangible advantage to the empire. With the most promising raw material for nationalism, the healthy adult male, instead conscripted into the army, the imperial establishment lost no opportunity of intimidating its would-be nationalist heroes into resignation to their fate through necessary acquiescence to overwhelming force. In wartime, the armies were reserved for action against the foreign enemy; in peacetime, they mounted continuous offensives against nationalism.

There was a positive as well as a negative aspect to the conditioning process administered by the army: military service was intended not only as a de-nationalising treatment but as a device for implanting supra-national solidarity. By a combination of stick and carrot techniques, the minority-nationality soldier was regimented or seduced into collaboration with the existing regime. 'Stick' measures included harsh discipline and draconian punishments. 'Carrots' included regular pay, clothing and shelter – no derisory offer in an era of chronic overpopulation and underemployment – a sense of purpose and camaraderie, and the prospect of regular windfalls in the form of booty, alcohol and the attentions of the female populace. In the Habsburg imperial army, conscripts were entitled to substantial bounties at the completion of their terms of service, enabling many to buy farms or start businesses (usually taverns).

The nineteenth-century evidence would suggest that the attempt to foster a supra-national allegiance in the Habsburg and Romanov armies encountered a high degree of success. National 'out-groups' were often more than reconciled to the imperial establishment, developing their own *esprit de corps* which more than matched nationalism in its combined romantic and self-serving appeal. Regiments raised on a national or regional basis to minimise language problems and foster an immediate sense of corporate solidarity were employed against other nationalities within the state and (if the need arose) against other regiments within the army. When in 1848 certain

Magyar regiments of the imperial army entertained ambitions for becoming a Hungarian army, other nationality regiments were brought in which could be relied upon to possess an anti-Magyar prejudice to reinforce their loyalty to the dynasty. The Croat regiments under Jellačić played a major part in defeating both the Italian and Magyar causes over 1848–9, motivated as much by their intense dislike of the rebel nations as obedience to a vacillating Habsburg establishment. To quote Francois Fëjto, 'the Austrian Council of State did its utmost to avert disaster by a most skilfull application of the "Divide and Rule" principle: order was maintained in the Italian provinces by Hungarian and Croat garrisons, in Hungary by Czechs and in Poland by Austrians and Italians. Thus a natural antagonism towards an army of occupation was turned by Vienna against the different nationalities composing her empire'.[3]

However perhaps the most remarkable feature of the Habsburg 1848 was that the imperial army remained so impervious to the blandishments of nationalism that the stratagem of setting one nationality against another was generally unnecessary. While some Magyar regiments deserted to the nationalist cause of Hungary, the remainder stayed almost immune to the 'contagion of 1848'. For example, almost two-thirds of the imperial infantry employed against the Italians and Magyars in 1848–9 were, respectively, Italian and Magyar, an eloquent testimonial to the inherent military strength of the Habsburg position. The Habsburgs were most successful at manipulating smaller nationalities still at an early stage of national consciousness, like the various Slav groups which made up almost half the total population of the Empire and substantially more than one-half of the rank-and-file of the imperial army. Marx and Engels remarked bitterly in 1848 that the real Slav Congress was not the assembly bickering in Prague but the Habsburg army, composed of Slav soldiers hoodwinked by national immaturity and short-sighted self-interest into being the prime instrument of imperial repression.[4]

Put on their guard by 1848, both the Habsburg and Romanov establishments were thereafter sensitive to the nationalist challenge, in particular employing their armies to mount precautionary campaigns which contained the threat. Instead of being allowed to stand apart from society as the bluntest instrument of either self-defence against foreign menace or repression of domestic rebellion, the army was mobilised by the Habsburgs and Romanovs as a regular, perhaps an indispensable, weapon in the social and political arsenal of peacetime. The imperial armies proved most effective agencies of the political establishment, bastions of the status quo and the last institutions to succumb to either the pressure or the appeal of nationalism. As armies grew in size, improved in quality and developed more elaborate technology and devastating weaponry, the chances of minority nationalities successfully challenging an imperial army dwindled away. Imperial armies became too formidable either to attack or to resist. National minorities could not contemplate direct defiance of authority unless the imperial army had dramatically and demonstrably failed to keep pace with modern military and political developments. In Ottoman Europe, a nationalist show of fight could reap the ultimate reward of independence; but in Habsburg and especially Romanov Europe, the fight option was little short of suicidal.

FLIGHT

Among the options available to national minorities, 'flight' is conventionally represented as the opposite extreme to 'fight'. One could speculate that 'fight' and 'flight' were mutually differential: where prospects were optimistic enough to make 'fight' feasible, there was little need for 'flight'; conversely, where it was impractical to 'fight', the pessimistic option of 'flight' became supreme. This historical scenario would anticipate that 'flight', or mass emigration, was least marked in the Balkans, much more common in Habsburg Europe and most prevalent in Romanov Europe. But while there is some truth in this interpretation, the phenomenon of emigration from eastern Europe proves in practice too complex for easy generalisation.

To claim a scientific approach to nineteenth-century migration, especially from eastern Europe, is needlessly foolhardy. The wildest statistical discrepancies appear in authoritative accounts. Although the United States was by far the most popular destination, the lengthy list of receiving states makes a cumulative immigrant total elusive. Statistics normally recorded only the volume of legal immigrants while the illegal traffic, believed to be substantial for west European destinations, can only be estimated. Official immigration statistics were until relatively late concerned only with the 'state of origin', neglecting the question of nationality: as a consequence, Jews, Lithuanians and Ukrainians were, for example, frequently indiscriminately bracketed as 'Russians'. Hard-pressed immigration officials, especially those at the American receiving centre at Castle Garden, confronted by hordes of non-English-speaking immigrants, could be pardoned for being less than meticulous about the accuracy of their returns. Nationalist historians have tended to exaggerate the emigrant outflow to emphasise the sufferings of pre-emancipation society. Finally, the 'return-rate' of emigrants back to their home-lands varied by nationality from between almost nil to 90 per cent, posing the demographic historian the dilemma of whether to count these 'birds of passage' as emigrants or not.[5] And yet, fully acknowledging that methodologically the exercise smacks of attempting 'to quantify the unquantifiable', the phenomenon of mass emigration was so significant that some attempt at gaining even a general impression of the pattern of 'flight' from eastern Europe must be hazarded. With no migration statistics being totally reliable, the lowest figure from a variety of reputable estimates has been taken to produce a national league table of emigration by volume and percentage (Table VI) to illustrate the varying commitment to 'flight' among the east European minorities.

As so often in eastern Europe, geographical location proved a cardinal factor. In Ottoman Europe, the viability of the fight option in achieving national independence dissuaded the minority nationalities from abandoning their homelands. But once independence was secured, emigration increased markedly in three ways. The ex-imperial nationality, now vulnerable and disliked in an ex-colony, opted to quit in large numbers: as the Ottomans surrendered sovereignty to a new state, the Turkish minority began to withdraw, an untidy process of demographic retreat and relocation in Asia Minor which continued until the late 1920s.

The new dominant nationalities viewed temporary emigration as a means of enriching themselves (and indeed their new states). The ambitious brash new Balkan nationalities abandoned thoughts of permanent emigration but appreciated the value of short-term migration. America was seen as the get-rich-quick prospect for the energetic young man: for all dominant Balkan nationalities, the typical 'emigrant' was an unmarried male in his twenties anxious to make as much money in as short a period of time as possible in America, in order to return home, marry and use his dollars to buy land or invest in a business. Of all Greek emigrants, for example, 96 per cent were male and 89 per cent of the total returned to Greece. For the new masters of the Balkans, America remained the land of

TABLE VI Emigration from Eastern Europe by Nationality, 1850–1914[6]

Nationality	Minimum emigrant population (millions)	Indigenous population, 1900 (millions)	Emigrants as %
Jews	1.6	7.5	21.0
Slovaks	0.4	2.0	20.0
Croats	0.5	2.5	20.0
Romanov Germans	0.3	1.8	17.0
Slovenes	0.2	1.25	16.0
Lithuanians	0.22	1.7	13.0
Poles	1.8	15.0	12.0
Czechs	0.5	6.5	7.7
Greeks	0.3	4.0	7.5
Finns	0.15	2.1	7.0
Ruthenes	0.2	4.0	5.0
Serbs	0.15	4.0	3.7
Magyars	0.25	10.0	2.5
Latvians	0.03	1.45	2.1
Rumanians	0.15	9.0	1.7
Bulgars	0.04	4.0	1.0
Ukrainians	0.2	23.0	0.9
Belorussians	0.05	6.0	0.8
Russians	0.06	56.0	0.1
Habsburg Germans	0.01	12.0	0.08
Total	7.11	173.8	average 4.1

opportunity but did not figure as a permanent commitment, only a trans-Atlantic means to a European end.

For the small nationalities of the Ottoman Empire which were converted overnight into substantial minorities within the new Balkan states, emigration not only continued but increased. As discrimination from the new nation states became worse than under the Ottomans, without even a millet system to afford minimal protection, there was mounting pressure to leave. The Jews in Rumania furnish the clearest instance: the very low Jewish emigration rate before the 1850s was succeeded by an accelerating response to Rumanian persecution thereafter. By the first decade of the twentieth century, almost 90 per cent of all emigrants from Rumania were Jewish, amounting (as one American authority suggested) to 'so large a part of the Roumanian immigration as to be practically synonymous with it'.[7]

Within Habsburg Europe, the very territorial stability of the regime sponsored a very different emigration pattern. Emigration operated at a low level until 1867, when the imperial government for the first time permitted unrestricted right of departure. Within Austria, the dominant German minority's established political and economic position made emigration unattractive and unnecessary. The Czechs, by contrast, supplied a steady and substantial outflow of emigrants, motivated by a combination of the 'push' factor of limited economic prospects in Bohemia and the 'pull' factor of America's much-vaunted opportunities for men of talent, energy and application. Of all the nationalities arriving in America over the period 1899–1910, the Czechs showed the highest proportion of skilled occupations (67 per cent) and the second lowest illiteracy rate (2 per cent). In Galicia, the Poles, Ruthenes and Jews increasingly (though not dramatically) resorted to emigration from the 1880s. The typical Polish emigrant from Galicia was an unmarried unskilled worker in his twenties, often an illiterate younger son with little prospect of paternal inheritance, essentially forced off the land by rural over-population. The Ruthene emigrant was similar, with his only dubious distinctions being the highest average illiteracy of any east European nationality (63 per cent) and the second lowest 'return rate' to his homeland (12 per cent). The typical Jewish emigrant was (like the Czech) skilled, literate and travelling as a member of a family, for reasons of economic ambition. The relative contentedness of Jews in Austria was demonstrated by a low emigration rate (74 per 10,000) and a high return rate (14 per cent, twice the rate of Russian Jews and three times that of Rumanian Jews). No accurate statistics are available on the Slovenes as a result of the American immigration commission being unable to distinguish them from Croats and therefore 'amalgamating' the two nationalities for official purposes.

Within Hungary, economic and also political 'push' factors were in operation. That the Magyar establishment after 1867 was both nationalistically and socially repressive was shown by the incidence of high Magyar emigration. The typical Magyar emigrant was again an unmarried male in his twenties from a rural background, unskilled but with enough education (illiteracy rate only 11 per cent) to take advantage of American opportunities and stand a good chance of making his fortune and returning home in triumph. Never forgetting their native Hungary, the Magyar emigrants always intended to return: before 1914 their return rate of 64 per cent was the highest outside the Balkans; and on the complete (if territorially reduced) independence of Hungary after 1918, they returned from America in droves.

The subordinate nationalities of Hungary had, of course, Magyarisation to reinforce the economic incentive for emigration. The Rumanians were divided between those who wished 'their' land of Transylvania to be united with Rumania, those who emigrated to America and those who migrated to Rumania. All but one-sixth of the ethnic Roumanians emigrating to America between 1901 and 1920 were from Hungary. The average Roumanian return rate of 50 per cent rose much higher in 1919 when Transylvania was transferred from a reduced Hungary to an expanded Rumania. The residual German minority in Hungary suffered little from Magyarisation, partly out of diplomatic regard for Austrian sensibilities, partly through disproportionately strong German influence within such vital institutions as the army officer corps. The Jews too were sufficiently integrated and economically valuable to the Magyar establishment to avoid serious harassment: of Jews emigrating from Habsburg territory, only 20 per cent were from Hungary. Slovak emigration became prodigious by the early twentieth century. The Slovak emigrant again tended to be a single male of unskilled agricultural occupation but with a fair education (illiteracy rate of 24 per cent) and a high return rate (59 per cent). The Croats too (or the Croat-Slovene monstrosity concocted by American immigration practice) were unskilled rural labourers but although worse-educated (with 36 per cent illiterate) featured a high return rate of 56 per cent.

A salient feature to emerge from the emigration pattern of Austria–Hungary was the high and persisting commitment of most emigrants to their national homelands. Only a few nationalities, like the backward Ruthenes, entered into a permanent and irrevocable commitment elsewhere; even the Jews had a much higher return rate to Austria–Hungary than to anywhere else in eastern Europe. Probably a majority of emigrants were 'birds of passage', forced out by mainly economic pressures and hoping to return once America had provided the capital for a new start in their homeland. Emigrants who were materially successful sometimes returned in triumph but often chose to stay with their adopted benefactor. Those who failed sometimes drowned themselves in the ethnic ocean of American society; others preferred to seek solace by ending their days in a supportive traditional community rather than suffer in a brash new civilisation geared to success. While conditions in their Habsburg homelands remained unchanged, the average return rate of 50 per cent maintained a regular traffic and sustained relationships between 'residents' and 'emigrants'; once national states were created after 1918, a significantly larger proportion of the new dominant nationalities flocked back to eastern Europe.

Romanov Europe had a different 'flight pattern' again, with the state assuming a more authoritative and strategic role. Until the 1860s, the Romanov Empire was an area of net inflow, with immigrants usually outnumbering emigrants. The volume of migration was relatively small, with a steady inflow of (mainly German) settlers more than balancing the occasional dramatic outflow prompted by such events as the failure of the Polish Risings of 1830–1 and 1863. The very notion of permanently abandoning jurisdiction over any of its citizens was repellent to the Romanovs: in an empire of relatively low population and density, the tsarist authorities found manpower resources in short supply and passed restrictive legislation against mass emigration.

From the 1880s, tsarist policy shifted from general prohibition to selective release. The manpower shortage of fifty years before had become an embarrassment of bodies, making overpopulation a prime reason for revising emigration practice. The essence of the new policy was to combine an emigration made necessary by demographic pressure with the current imperial preoccupation: if the non-Slavs were allowed to depart and the Slavs constrained to remain, state emigration policy could become a major instrument of Russification. The differential rate of emigration between the Romanov nationalities was consequently a product both of the individual minority's sense of persecution or disadvantage and of discriminatory imperial policy. Over the period 1899–1910, emigration from Romanov

Europe was 43.8 per cent Jewish, 27.0 per cent Polish, 9.6 per cent Lithuanian, 8.5 per cent Finnish, 5.8 per cent German and 4.4 per cent Russian. Even more revealing is the proportional emigration rate: the Jewish figure was 1 emigrant per 79 of the Jewish population, the Finnish figure 1 per 191, the Polish 1 per 200, the German 1 per 205, the Lithuanian 1 per 212 and the Russian 1 per 11,552. It is this table which comes closest to providing an index of discrimination within the Romanov territories.[8]

The Jews were undeniably the prime target for adverse nationality discrimination: while the Jewish proportion of the total outflow averaged 43.8 per cent for the period 1899–1901, it rose to well over one-half in the pogrom season of 1904–6. Even so, it was in the 1880s and 1890s that the Jews almost monopolised emigration from the Empire, reaching 91.6 per cent of the total in the peak year 1891. Jewish emigration was characterised by a high proportion of entire families, the highest figure for skilled occupations of any immigrant nationality to America (67 per cent) and a determination never to return to Russia. The relatively high illiteracy rate testified to the high incidence of female participants and the effects of discriminatory tsarist educational policy. Even so, the emigrant illiteracy rate of 26 per cent compared favourably with the resident rate of 51 per cent (in 1899), revealing the Jewish practice of despatching the most vigorous of their community abroad when in danger. It was for promoting a Jewish exodus that the tsarist administration first relaxed its traditional embargo on emigration: in 1891 a government spokesman announced to Russian Jewry that 'our western borders are open to you Jews'. And yet, although the Jewish emigration reached astronomical proportions, it never approached an exodus. Acting at best as a safety-value for the Jewish problem, mass emigration was no 'final solution'. The overwhelming majority of Jews remained, a tacit demographic defiance of Russification.

For the Finns, the Russification of their Grand Duchy after 1899 served to reinforce the established economic motive for extensive emigration. The typical Finnish emigrant seems to have been a young married man, often accompanied by his wife, generally an unskilled agricultural labourer with a burning ambition to become a prosperous farmer. With an illiteracy rate of under 2 per cent, the lowest of any nationality entering America over 1899–1910, the Finns were almost ideal immigrants from the point of view of the receiving country. Committing themselves readily to their adopted country,

Finnish emigrants were not conspicuous for their attachment to a motherland whose autonomy was under attack and their return rate in the early twentieth century was relatively low.

Polish emigration rose dramatically after the 1880s, reaching its peak of 174,000 in the year 1912–13. For the one year 1910, Polish emigration even topped the Jewish. Once again, although Russification undeniably played a part in demoralising the nation into emigration, the underlying cause was economic. As with the Finns, the Poles who emigrated were generally forced off the land by rural overpopulation. The typical emigrant was an unskilled agricultural labourer but his illiteracy rate of 36 per cent was dramatically better than the 75 per cent average for the total population of Romanov Poland. The Habsburg Poles were twice as likely to return as Romanov Poles (with return rates of 41 per cent and 22 per cent respectively). Since the difference in the economic conditions of Habsburg Galicia and the Romanov 'Vistula Provinces' was marginal, one may assume that it was the political climate which largely governed the Polish emigrant's attitude to returning 'home'.

Settling originally at the invitation of Catherine the Great, the German minority was scattered in almost 200 peasant communities, with the greatest concentrations on the middle Volga and Black Sea coast. Two factors accounted for the emigration of this prosperous and best-educated of all Romanov nationalities. First was the fear of religious persecution. It was no coincidence that the pacifist Mennonites were the leaders of the movement to quit Russia. The overwhelmingly Protestant Germans feared that Russification would include an Orthodox crusade against all other faiths. Closely connected in German minds was their new liability to military service. The original conditions of settlement in 1762–3 had specifically included exemption from military service, a privilege scrupulously observed by the tsarist government until the Military Reform of 1874 flatly cancelled all categories of exemption. To the German minority, the arbitrary abolition of its guaranteed privileged status was the first step on the road to Russification. The response was a steady and eventually substantial emigration of whole families from Russia, with little practical or sentimental notion of returning.

The last of the principal emigrant minorities, the Lithuanians were attracted to emigration through geographical proximity to embarkation-points to the west like Memel and Riga, an instance of ready supply stimulating demand. Like the neighbouring Poles, the Lithuanians were concerned by the religious dimension of Russification as the Orthodox hierarchy threatened the position of Catholicism. As usual, the unskilled male adult was the typical emigrant, with a high level of illiteracy (at 49 per cent the second highest of all east European nationalities migrating to America – and yet very close to the resident Lithuanian illiteracy average of 48 per cent). With a return rate of only 14 per cent, the Lithuanian emigrant had little commitment to his natal land, although the surprise foundation of an independent Lithuania after 1918 sponsored a certain revival of *emigré* self-consciousness.

The exceptionally low emigration rate of the Russians merits fuller explanation. There were certainly entirely 'natural' reasons for the low level of Russian emigration: Russian settlement in the interior of the Eurasian land mass made the journey to America more protracted, arduous and expensive than for the peripherally located national minorities; the low level of literacy among Russians made them less aware of alternatives and less likely to risk leaving the land they knew; and the almost mystical Russian love of country (which made their *toska*, or home-sickness, almost unendurable) inhibited any commitment likely to estrange them permanently from Mother-Russia.

Even so, state intervention was probably the paramount factor. Since the whole purpose of the emigration aspect of Russification was to export Romanov minority problems, for the tsars to have let their own people go would have ruined the exercise. Ideally, the ultimate operation would have been to move the expanding Russian population into those areas recently vacated by the mass emigrations of the minorities, resulting in a homogenised, truly Russian Empire. But with emigration falling short even of removing the excess population of the minorities, the problem of the nationalities remained. Moreover, although the Russians were not subjected to persecution or harassment on the grounds of national identity, there was no relief from the relentless pressures of overpopulation. If the excess Russian population could not replace the emigrating minorities and was not permitted to emigrate itself, where could it go?

The tsarist answer lay not with emigration but migration: an increasingly massive, state-sponsored and subsidised Russian colonisation of Siberia. From the 1880s and especially the early 1900s, the surplus agrarian population which elsewhere in eastern Europe comprised the staple of emigration was in Russia channelled into

Siberia. A migratory 'watershed', part natural, mostly artificial, separated the western minorities looking towards America and the Slav groups of the interior directed east towards Siberia. Turning their backs on one another, the two migrant streams followed opposite directions: 3,000,000 were carried by the westerly current to America, 7,000,000 by the easterly torrent to Siberia. It has been estimated that the colonists of Siberia were some 50 per cent Ukrainian, 35 per cent Russian and 15 per cent Belorussian. By 1911, the indigenous population had been swamped and the Russian-Ukrainian-Belorussian demographic dominance reached 89 per cent of the total. Siberia became a melting-pot for the three Slav groups, with biological, cultural and even linguistic miscegenation producing a composite 'Russian' identity. The Russian eastern frontier had been secured: Siberia was to be not another poly-ethnic society like European Russia but an eastward extension of the Slav heartland. Great Russia was becoming Greater, and the various Russian groups could not be spared for emigration elsewhere.[9]

This is not to suggest that no 'Russians' emigrated, although it is safe to assume that the majority were actually Ukrainians, whose nascent national consciousness was starting to chafe under Russification and whose proximity to ports like Odessa made escape more feasible. The typical Russian-Ukrainian emigrant was the familiar unmarried adult male, unskilled and ill-educated (although his 38 per cent illiteracy compared favourably with the 70 per cent average for indigenous Russians). Having spent everything on the long passage west, typical 'Russians' arrived in America destitute and 'among the most unskilled and economically insecure of all the newer arrivals'. Substitute Ukraines were established in the prairies of America and Canada to counter the notorious *toska*. Threatened in their loneliness and cultural isolation as much by Americanisation as they had once been by Russification, many Slav emigrants were unable to resist the call of their homeland.[10]

Romanov Europe witnessed an infinitely more ambitious strategy, blending imperial and emigration policies, than anywhere else in eastern Europe. The impact of the tsarist Grand Design in demographic engineering was very variable: the Siberian venture, an undeservedly little-known triumph for tsarism, decanted the excess 'Russian' agrarian population eastwards from Europe; the less successful but more publicised policy towards non-Russian minorities foundered on the fact that emigration at its most extensive could do no more than siphon excess population westward towards America. For the nationalities and for the tsars, the limitations of the 'flight option' proved at least as significant as its opportunities.

The variety of the emigration pattern from eastern Europe in the later nineteenth century was impressive. The conventional wisdom that emigration represents a vote of no-confidence in the homeland was far from universally applicable. Members of the dominant nationalities of the Balkans emigrated to enrich themselves and their new nation states, a motive which totally undermines the usual sense of emigrant 'flight'. The subordinate nationalities of Austria–Hungary were almost invariably forced into emigration by economic pressure, felt little antagonism for their imperial masters and retained a strong interest in their homelands (to which a very large proportion returned). Emigrants from the Romanov Empire were typically fleeing a combination of natural economic pressure and deliberate adverse discrimination, quitting their homelands rarely to return. Imperial attitudes to emigration differed greatly, especially over the role of the state: the Ottomans followed an 'open border' policy throughout; the Habsburgs were converted to an open border as overpopulation reached critical proportions; and the Romanovs converted a one-way border permitting only immigration to a selective half-open border designed to encourage their minorities to 'escape' in the interests of a stronger Russian hegemony.

A broad correlation between the subordination and emigration of minority nationalities may therefore be advanced. Even more indisputable is the correlation between dominance and lack of emigration: the Austrians did not emigrate because they did not need to, the Russians because they were not allowed to. The demographic result was that, almost literally, the New World redressed the imbalance of the Old: the dominant nationalities of eastern Europe were greatly under-represented in emigration and became the minorities among emigrant society; the subordinate minorities of eastern Europe were grossly over-represented in emigration and became the dominant nationalities of emigrant society.

As emigration assumed epic proportions, patently affecting the national minorities more than the dominant nationalities, eastern European society attempted to resolve its very mixed feelings about the phenomenon. The natural American-orientated outlook of the West tends to stress the universal benefits of emigration. The most famous short exposition (appropriately from the Jewish poet Emma

Lazarus) is inscribed on the Statue of Liberty past which the migrant ships sailed into New York:

> Give me your tired, your poor,
> Your huddled masses yearning to breathe free,
> The wretched refuse of your teeming shore.

The poem implicitly suggests that emigration benefits migrants and the despatching and receiving countries. At the demographic level, moving people from an area of European overpopulation to an area of American underpopulation could only benefit both, distributing population more evenly and economically, cutting unemployment in the former and ending manpower shortages in the latter. The emigration of the pre-1914 era could be seen as logical and natural: what constituted a political, economic and social safety-valve for eastern Europe provided a healthy head of steam in America. Everyone gained in the population shift, including the shipping agents; there were no losers in international emigration.

Many nationalists argued that emigration could positively favour nationalities disadvantaged in Europe. One of the lessons of nineteenth-century nationalism was that Great Power patronage was a desirable, and often an indispensable, ingredient of victory. The difference between success and failure among Balkan nationalisms was commonly attributed to the degree and quality of external support they enjoyed. As a result, the idea of exploiting emigration to establish abroad a political lobby, pressure group or even publicity exercise was a favourite *emigré* nationalist preoccupation. Time was to strengthen the argument: during the First World War, the efforts of Czech, Slovak and Polish migrant groups in America to influence official policy were crowned with success when Woodrow Wilson became converted to fostering self-determination in eastern Europe, a principle somewhat eccentrically implemented in the Paris Peace Settlement. Even the presence of a celebrated personality could do wonders for a nationalist cause abroad: the lionising of Kossuth as the Hungarian Martyr-Hero throughout Europe and America after 1849 was a triumphant propaganda exercise. In a nation's extremity, 'ambassadorship' abroad might be more rewarding and productive than suffering uselessly at home in an act of moral solidarity with the motherland. For the most functional of reasons, *emigré* nationalists could claim to be

> True patriots we; for be it understood,
> We left our country for our country's good.

Practicality went hand in hand with self-sacrifice in furthering the national cause abroad. By this interpretation, emigration was not 'flight' but transferring the 'fight' to more favourable ground.

With the passage of time, national minorities became more dubious about the benefits of emigration. More 'developed' minorities with a robust self-consciousness might indeed preserve their identities abroad or fabricate a 'dual allegiance' which enabled the emigrant community to influence its host state. The Czechs, Slovaks and Poles were cases in point. But 'developing' nationalities with less assertive self-awareness frequently lost touch with their motherlands, relinquishing their fragile cultural identities in unsympathetic alien environments. Minorities like the Ruthenes, Belorussians and Macedonians disappeared as corporate identities beneath the relentless Americanisation they encountered. While the stronger nationalities could on occasion turn their foreign location to their homelands' advantage, the weaker nationalities tended to lose their identities far quicker abroad than they did at home. Even for the more resilient emigrant nationalities, the chances of materially aiding their homelands' cause were remote. *Emigrés* were fond of recounting the rare occasions when their influence had been discernible; they conveniently forgot the hosts of occasions when even the most articulate and persuasive intercession with foreign governments proved totally fruitless. Successful emigrant lobbying of a host state was demonstrably the exception, not the rule.

Another defence of the emigrant nationalist which came under increasing fire was that, to quote Lord Acton, 'exile is the nursery of nationality'. At its most simplistic, the argument suggests that as dynamic nationalism can only be generated by awareness of the alternatives, so temporary deprival of one's homeland is the only way that its real value can be appreciated. The 'cradle of nationalism' view of exile and emigration, thrown up by the young idealists of the early nineteenth century, quickly grew stale and untenable. As a brave attempt at whistling in the dark the idea may have served some transient purpose, but the commonest effects of extended or permanent exile were far from healthy. General symptoms of the *'emigré* mentality'were a breakdown of communication with the mother country, extravagant territorial claims (as if to point up political impotence), self-indulgent nostalgia, a progressively evaporating sense of reality, gullibility about History turning one's way and living in a permanent state of apocalyptic expectancy.

The most dreadful warning of the dangers of the *emigré* mentality was the Polish experience after the Rising of 1830–1. In exile in the West, the Polish nationalists of the 'Golden Emigration' confirmed their past reputation for believing what they wanted to believe rather than what was demonstrably true. Practical politics were abandoned in favour of a preposterous exercise in self-congratulation. Having sacrificed itself as the 'Christ of Nations', Poland would emerge through suffering to redemption, resurrected in divine form, purified by its experiences to find ultimate apotheosis. Other persecuted nations would benefit from Polish martyrdom by a mystical ceremony usually portrayed as communicants partaking of the eucharistic body of Poland. The messianic, chiliastic excesses of the Polish exiles are difficult to comprehend except as an intuitive, collective morale-boosting therapy, the deliberate creation of a fantasy world in which to dwell because the real world had become too painful to endure. The fact that most of the exiles had taken no active part in the Rising of 1830–1 may have added an element of guilt to their Romantic protestations. But the effect of the *emigré* retreat from reality was indisputable: having already missed 1830, the Polish leadership then missed 1848, as eloquent a testimony to the dangers of the exile mentality as could be imagined in nineteenth-century Europe.

With mass emigration increasing dramatically in volume towards the end of the nineteenth century, fears grew that the continuous heavy outflow would permanently damage the despatching nations. The 'dustbin theory' of emigration now became applicable: if emigration were compulsory, the destinations became the dustbins of society, filling up with transported criminals, exiled agitators, religious dissidents and unruly relatives, presumably to the purification and betterment of the mother country; but if emigration were voluntary, the destinations might attract the more valuable members of society, especially the young, the talented and the determined, leaving the mother country as the social dustbin. Given that emigration throughout eastern Europe was (at least technically) voluntary, it seemed possible that the emigrant motherlands would become the losers. Emigrant homelands might become demoralised societies of 'those left behind', socially unbalanced communities dominated by the old, the female and the very young. The continuous creaming-off of the mature male generation of society would cause economic retardation, social dislocation and political enfeeblement. The vital new generation earmarked to become the activists of nationalism would instead be diverted into emigration, to the inevitable impoverishment of the motherland and the emasculation of its nationalism.

Croatia offers an illuminating and not untypical example of the growing alarm about mass emigration. Although the Croat *Sabor* introduced emigration control as early as 1883, legal and then illegal traffic grew so astronomically that in 1903 the historian Smičiklas warned that 'the best of our people have emigrated to America. Should we continue this way, Croatia will perish'. In 1911 further restrictions on emigration were implemented and a fund for re-integrating returned migrants established on the basis of fees levied on current emigrants; the only effect was massively to increase the proportion of illegal over legal emigrants.[11] As the issue became emotionally charged throughout eastern Europe, nationalists began to regard emigrants not as heroes but, depending on whether they appreciated the damage they were inflicting on their homelands, as at best deserters from, and at worst traitors to, the nationalist cause.

There was some truth behind the alarmism. The effect of the emigration of a disproportionately high number of adult males, often of above-average education and drive, was to differentiate nationalities according to the stage of development attained. The larger, developed nationalities absorbed the effects of emigration with relative ease: a sizeable population with a thriving culture and sense of identity could weather protracted emigration without serious damage to either homeland or nationalist movement. Developing smaller nationalities proved more vulnerable: a nation in its suscepti-ble infancy could be irreparably stunted or deformed as the resources necessary for its healthy development were withheld. In terms of both the fate of emigrants in their destination country and the effect on their homeland, the overall result of emigration was to polarise the 'developing' and the 'developed' minorities. Developed nations like the Poles and Czechs suffered little damage and benefited from the acquisition of influence and publicity abroad. Developing nationali-ties like the Ruthenes and Slovenes were retarded at home and lost their emigrants forever through assimilation. On balance, emigration marginally favoured the developed national minorities while penalis-ing the still-developing groups.

The social, economic and political impact of emigration upon the minorities of eastern Europe was exaggerated by emotion at the time and has remained over-rated ever since. No nationality showed a marked collapse in health as a result of the regular 'transfusions' or indeed continuous 'haemorrhages' of emigration. In the Balkans, a return rate averaging 80 per cent meant that the overall loss in personnel was slight, more than compensated by the high birth rate and the extra wealth brought into the new states by emigrant traffic. To quote a recent historian of the Croat experience: 'the improvements and the general rise in the standard of living were to a great extent the result of American dollars sent by immigrants to relatives and of the financial resources of those who returned to stay'. It has been estimated that Croat emigrants in America sent home 13,000,000 dollars over the 1890s alone.[12] Within Habsburg Europe, the average return rate of some 50 per cent dulled the impact of permanent emigration, together with a similar inflow of emigrant earnings from America. For the bulk of eastern Europe, typical emigrant-fodder was so unarguably excess population that its loss could only be seen as the welcome removal of a social, economic and political liability on society. Whilst recognising therefore that the impact of emigration was differential, favouring the stronger and handicapping the weaker national minorities, it is probably judicious to conclude that the overall effect of 'flight' was both healthier and slighter than appeared at the time. Immigration may have made America; emigration made relatively little difference to eastern Europe.

NEITHER FIGHT NOR FLIGHT

By the turn of the nineteenth century, the fighting option seemed to be running its course in the Balkans but to be suicidal elsewhere; and the flight option had prompted a broad public reaction which was shifting towards outright disapproval of emigration. As nationalists appreciated that neither fight nor flight could solve the problems of most minorities in eastern Europe, a new determination to stand by their nations became pervasive. The homeland had the moral right to expect, even to exact, loyalty in the past, commitment in the present and faith in the future. In this deterministic spirit, the Magyar poet Mihaly Vörösmarty appealed earlier in the century:

Be faithfully devoted to your fatherland,
O Hungarian . . .
Nowhere in the wide world
Is there room for you but here.
Blessed or cursed by fate,
Here you must live and die.[13]

Although the present circumstances of one's nation might demand suffering and sacrifice, there could be no gainsaying the value of the experience in forging the unity of the community and deepening its sense of purpose and dedication. Of the eventual triumph of nationalism, there could be no doubt: while the dynastic empires mounted defensive rearguard actions, the force of nationalism was gathering irresistible momentum. With the scale of the confrontation between nation and empire still mounting, the inevitable victories (and defeats) of the future would be all the more resounding and cataclysmic.

In the light of the impracticality of 'fight' and the discrediting of 'flight', an intermediate area of manoeuvre was opened up between empires and nationalities. By the late nineteenth century, subordinate nationalities were seeking new options, previously undiscovered or undervalued weapons to advance their cause. One possibility was 'social infiltration' of the imperial establishment. Empires traditionally recruited for their bureaucracies on the basis of talent, a policy which might be turned to advantage by a nationality with above average quality to acquire a large representation in the imperial civil service. Unfortunately, hopes of bureaucratic infiltration by minorities (a prospect replete with profound political implications) were almost invariably disappointed. Successful individuals of minority origins usually played down their 'parochial' backgrounds and became at least nominally assimilated by the dominant nationality in order to rise in the state hierarchy and become acceptable to the imperial establishment. The career of a successful personality from a minority nationality typically passed through a 'de-nationalisation' to an 'imperialisation' phase, with negligible benefit to the nationality from which he sprang.

'Economic infiltration' was no more successful. The hierarchy of nationality was commonly reflected in a popular pecking-order of occupation. In Vienna, for instance, nationality–occupation stereotypes included Czech tailors, Polish cobblers, Jewish doctors and Austrian army officers. Although minorities might by accident or design secure disproportionate economic importance, which they sought to convert into political influence, concessions on these grounds were rare. The economic boom in the Polish, Finnish and Latvian territories of the Romanovs over the late nineteenth century coincided with a period of Russification, not conciliation. Bohemia became so valuable to the Habsburgs that they could not contemplate putting it at risk by concession to the Czechs. The Jews had exploited the disdain indulged by the landed gentry of the 'Historic' nations for trade and industry almost to monopolise the middle classes in Poland and Hungary; but their economic power in Vienna, Budapest and Warsaw, although utilised less for political advancement than for protection against persecution, provoked a growing anti-semitism which the Habsburg and Romanov governments employed in their traditional tactic of 'divide and rule'. Far from leading inexorably to political improvement or promotion, economic value tended to stiffen resistance to compromise on the part of the imperial establishments. If national minorities possessed little economic clout, they were contemptuously ignored; if they developed economic muscle, they attracted suspicion as potential troublemakers on property too valuable to lose.

What may be termed 'biological infiltration' made no headway either. The incidence of bi-nationality marriages producing ethnically mixed offspring needed to be large-scale to make any major demographic impression, and in practice proved relatively rare. The traditional endogamous practice was reinforced in an age of nationalism, making ethnic divisions actually sharper than in the past. 'Half-breeds' tended (as usual) to constitute not a social bridge between parent nationalities but a low-status, isolated caste despised by all parties. The imperial establishment took care to marry within its own class and nationality, with occasional exceptions favouring high-status foreigners. With no perceptible blurring of the ethnic divide through marriage and reproduction, this last variety of infiltration was as unproductive as the others.

The search for an 'outflanking force' powerful enough to bring down the empires either independently or in alliance with nationalism was a favourite preoccupation with minorities. Socialism was a natural magnet for those minorities lacking confidence in nationalist emancipation. A glance at the leading personnel of socialist movements in eastern Europe reveals the over-representation of national minorities, particularly the smaller ones. The leading echelon of the Bolshevik party is a celebrated example, featuring a number of Jews (Trotsky, Zinoviev, Kamenev and Sverdlov), Georgians (Stalin and Ordzhonikidze), Poles (Dzerzhinsky) and individuals of mixed nationality (notably Lenin). As the Russian premier Witte complained to Herzl in 1903, the Jews who constituted only 4 per cent of the population of the Romanov Empire 'produced fifty per cent of its revolutionaries'.[14] It does not seem to have occurred to Witte that tsarist persecution was creating the very problem he described or, to repeat Metternich's aphorism, 'every country gets the Jews it deserves'. Although it would be trespassing beyond the scope of this survey to pursue the subject of minority membership further, it may be suggested that while right-wing movements were generally staffed by majority nationalities and dominant minorities, left-wing movements commonly featured a disproportionately high level of subordinate national minorities.

A sustained campaign of 'direct pressure' on imperial authority was another recourse. An empire might win all the pitched battles yet still lose a war of attrition. The most successful example of the application of direct pressure was the Magyar campaign of the 1860s. The threat of another 1848 was continuously dangled before a Habsburg establishment already harassed by the problem of retaining its Italian territories. The advantages of a self-interested political bargain from which both Austrians and Magyars would benefit were persistently pressed upon a Habsburg government which increasingly conceded the force of the argument. Magyar political pressure was demonstrably no bluff: although they had been defeated in 1849 (but only with great difficulty and Russian intervention), the Magyars cogently argued that the volatile situation in Hungary threatened to boil over into nationwide insurrection at any time. Representing themselves as interceding between the Habsburgs and an inflamed populace, the Magyar leaders led by Deák urged the *Ausgleich* as the only alternative to anarchy, revolution and the disintegration of the Empire.

As a blue-print for minority action however, the Magyar campaign proved a disappointment: 1867 marked the last (and in a sense the only) victory for 'direct pressure' in nineteenth-century eastern Europe. Within decades, minorities were reconciling themselves to mainly moral gestures of defiance and complaint, without any great confidence in their efficacy. An early failure was the tactic of political boycott or abstention. Within the Habsburg Empire, nationalities employed boycott to protest at the various rigged constitutions introduced by the government to mollify them. The Magyars had boycotted the Imperial Diet in the early 1860s, though only as a salient in a much broader campaign. The Czechs in the 1860s and 1870s, and the Slovaks and Rumanians in the 1880s and 1890s, attempted to shame the Austrians and Magyars respectively into concession by political boycotts which, unsupported by any wider or deeper backing, had absolutely no effect. Within the Romanov Empire, there were no opportunities for political boycott until the granting of the Duma in 1905. During the subsequent career of the imperial parliament, at no point did the progressively shrinking representation of the non-Russian nationalities ever attempt to employ boycott as a political weapon. The policy of boycott was useless as a weapon for subject nationalities against imperial authority: its employment simply played into an empire's hands by granting the dominant nationality the monopoly of power which it naturally always preferred.

It was with the tactic of 'civil disobedience' or 'passive resistance' that the minorities found their greatest (though still limited) success in the early twentieth century. The idea of organising wider society into unarmed yet forceful resistance to authority places 'civil disobedience' below 'direct pressure' but well above 'political boycott' on the scale of effectiveness. At the political level, all official and constitutional links were repudiated while various means of thwarting the operation of imperial authority were evolved within minority society. A number of arenas of conflict between minorities and empires appeared over the last decades of peacetime.

The streets were an obvious social arena, with minority nationality youth playing the most prominent role. On the more exalted plane, university students were among the first publicly to demostrate their national commitment. A good example were the *corsos* in Prague, regular Sunday parades of the rival Czech and German student fraternities, each asserting its national identity as provocatively as possible and frequently inciting outbreaks of real or ritual violence. At a humbler social level, the periodic absence of the paternal generation through emigration and the lack of prestige of the substitute, predominantly old and female authority brought predictable social repercussions. Ill-educated, unemployed youths of minority national-ity, maturing without acceptable authority, formed gangs to reinforce their identity. Providing protection in a hostile world, with a strong investment in a territorial 'patch' to possess and defend, the youth 'tribes' claimed the monopoly of rites of initiation to manhood and paraded as the champions of nationality. The line between legality and criminality became controversial as the minority's conception of legitimate action overlapped the establishment's definition of law-breaking. In mixed nationality areas, street confrontations between police and minority youth became a principal social interface between the dominant and subordinate nationalities.

Civil disobedience was not always so overt or youth-orientated. The Finnish campaign of resistance to Russification after 1900 involved broad sectors of society in an orchestrated but entirely passive protest: youths neglected to answer the conscription summons, public officials went on indefinite strike, citizens omitted to pay their taxes and the populace declined to communicate in anything but its well-nigh incomprehensible language. Sibelius's *Finlandia* was just the most enduring of various propaganda exercises to enlist international sympathy and liberal support. Almost garrulous towards the West, Finns maintained a dumb insolence towards their Russian masters. By 1903, a frantic tsarist government was advertising for Finnish, Swedish and German speakers to recruit as official interpreters in Finland. The nuisance and embarrassment caused the harassed Russian occupying forces was prodigious, graphically demonstrating the hitherto untapped and undervalued power of the ordinary citizen to frustrate authority. The Finnish campaign was a profound influence on Gandhi's elaboration of the tactic of *satyagraha* (or 'soul-struggle') in British India.

With the most influential social group in the campaigns of passive resistance being the intelligentsia, public education became a leading bone of contention. The universities were seen as staff colleges for the imperial bureaucracy by the empires and as training colleges for the leading cadres of the nationalist movement by the minorities. In the late nineteenth century, appreciating the susceptibility of the universities to minority penetration, the Habsburg and Romanov Empires launched campaigns to protect the position of the dominant nationality. A notorious example was tsarist introduction of the *numerus clausus* in 1886–7, which specifically limited Jewish representation among students of universities of the Romanov Empire to fixed quotas. The Jewish response was that the quota system was an indefensible breach of the principle that education must be open to talent and blatant discrimination against the Jewish minority, with its long record of proven aptitude in academic pursuits. The tsarist counter-argument assumed a number of forms. Firstly, the Jews only swamped the universities because an academic degree brought entitlement to quit the Pale; the government was therefore indirectly plugging the biggest leak from the Jewish Pale. Alternatively, the superior educational level of the Jewish minority–49 per cent literate as against the Russian 30 per cent even in 1897, after over a decade of discrimination – lent an unfair advantage in boosting that proportion to an unacceptably high figure in the future. A more persuasive defence was that the quota levels broadly matched the Jewish proportion of the total population. The 1886 law specified maximum quotas of 3 per cent at the Universities of St Petersburg and Moscow, 5 per cent otherwise outside the Pale and 10 per cent within the Pale (figures raised in 1909 to 5 per cent, 10 per cent and 15 per cent respectively). The official statistics record that the Jews constituted 13 per cent of the population of the Pale and 4 per cent of the total population of the Empire, figures which undermine the accusation of grossly unfair discrimination. Tsarism could have claimed to be implementing a policy which would now be termed 'positive discrimination': to retard the better-educated minorities and peg their education level to a figure consistent with their share of the population; while promoting the poorer-educated nationalities, most notably the Russians, to a level appropriate to their demographic importance. To the Jewish minority, the policy was anti-semitic and anti-educational. To the modern observer, the tsarist policy could be seen as 'affirmative action' to enable the previously disadvantaged nationalities to assume their rightful share of university education, a long-term educational strategy which was less anti-semitic than pro-Russian.[15]

School education was similarly controversial. With mass education a decisive factor either in the empires retaining the loyalty of their subjects or in the nationalists mobilising 'troops' for their campaigns for independence, the political future was seen as being determined in the classrooms. Battle was joined as the nationalist press, playing a crucial role in both fostering and reflecting wider popular commitment to the nation, agitated for the expansion of primary education and local control over school curricula, staff and text-books. On the other side, a leading component of Russification in the Romanov Empire and Magyarisation in Hungary was centralised control over school education and the imposition of the language and culture of the dominant nationality as an integral part of compulsory state education.

A final arena for minority civil disobedience was over land. The relatively homogeneous ethnic composition of the German Empire persuaded the ebullient Prussian government to repress the Polish minority in its eastern province of Poznania. Bismarck's *Kulturkampf* of the 1870s was in part a disguised attack on the Catholic Polish minority but in 1886 he openly issued a Colonisation Decree authorising the expulsion of Poles from Poznania and their replacement by German settlers. Polish passive resistance was so effective that in 1894 an *Ostmarkverein* was set up to revive the flagging Prussian offensive against the Poles. The Polish minority countered with a stubborn exercise in civil disobedience whose highlights were the school strikes of 1901 and 1907. Desperate to avoid losing face in a welter of adverse international publicity, the Prussian authorities shifted from a policy of German colonisation at the expense of the Poles to compulsory expropriation of Polish-owned land: in 1908 the Dispossession Act declared open war on Germany's Polish subjects. And yet, over the remaining years of peace, little material progress was made. Although the Polish minority comprised barely 5 per cent of the total population of the German Empire, its self-consciousness and solidarity were sufficient largely to frustrate a sustained and occasionally ferocious Prussianisation. It has even been asserted that 'after twenty years, the area occupied by the Poles was actually larger than it was before.' The only indisputable product of decades of confrontation was that 'the Prussian Government was even more hated by the Poles than the Russian Government'.[16]

In the last period of peace before 1914, only in the Balkans had the political pendulum swung decisively in favour of nationalism. Elsewhere, the futility of 'fight' and the irrelevance of 'flight' encouraged a search for new techniques of political warfare on the part of both the challenging nations and the defending Habsburg and Romanov Empires. The offensive capabilities of nationalism and empire proved limited: the various attacks launched by national minorities on authority were uniformly disappointing; but the Magyarisation, Prussianisation and Russification campaigns by dominant nations had no greater success. On the other hand, the defensive capacities of nationalism and empire were impressive: national minorities developed what has been called the 'hedgehog reflex', a prickly passivity against which even the most ruthless authority seemed powerless; while the empires mobilised all their resources after 1848 to create bastions against which nationalism made little impression. Nationalist revolution may have been crushed by superior force in 1848–9 but over the subsequent half-century the 'cold pogrom' was countered by the 'cold rebellion'. There was a frustrating sense of the nearly irresistible force confronting the almost immovable object. Over most of eastern Europe, nationalism and empire were in stalemate.

5. External Intervention

OVER the century following 1848, eastern Europe became less and less sealed against extraneous influences and the incidence of external intervention in the affairs of its national minorities became progressively more frequent and ambitious. In the often confusing welter of historical instances of intrusion from outside the immediate relationship between minority and indigenous authority, four distinct (though occasionally overlapping) categories of intervention may be identified. *Trans*-national 'partnership' can be defined as joint action by two or more national minorities acting out of a sense of community of interest to further the individual or collective cause. *Extra*-national 'patronage' covers political, economic or military promotion of a minority by an existing state for reasons ranging from pure humanitarianism to territorial aggrandisement. *Multi*-national 'partition' describes territorial intervention by two or more foreign states, usually Great Powers, acting in a spirit of businesslike consensus to promote the general good. Finally, *inter*-national 'protection' signifies intercession by philanthropic or peace-keeping institutions standing apart from or (more ambitiously) above narrow national self-interest.

PARTNERSHIP

The initial manifestations of solidarity between national minorities in eastern Europe were racially based, with the Slavs taking the initiative. As the smaller backward Slav nationalities began to raise their heads in the early nineteenth century, they were immediately struck by the repressive capabilities of the dynastic empires but also the potentially sinister inequality of the various national minorities. On the assumption that the doctrine of nationalism was to become the new legitimacy, the ethnic map illustrated that some ethnic minorities were better placed than others: the older-established 'Historic' nations like the Poles and Magyars had advantages ranging from population size to superior literacy over 'Un-Historic' groups such as the Slovaks and Ruthenes. Well before 1848, many observers would only accept the 'Historic' entities as 'nations', relegating the 'Un-Historic' to the infinitely inferior category of 'nationalities'. Marx and Engels, for example, could only bring themselves to recognise the 'nations' of eastern Europe, dismissing the backward Slav nationalities as both counter-revolutionary and doomed to assimilation by their more modern and vigorous neighbours.

The issue came to a head in March 1848 when the Slovaks and Croats on the northern and southern extremities of Greater Hungary found themselves in identical positions: both were being driven into greater national self-consciousness by the Magyars' efforts to foist the Hungarian language on all their minorities. Activated by the Magyar threat, the Slovaks and Croats allied with the culturally advanced Czechs to convene a congress of all Slav nationalities in Prague. Representatives from all the Slav groups, many self-appointed, so eagerly accepted the invitations to attend that the Congress was clearly fulfilling a universally felt need.

Although lasting only ten days, the Slav Congress had abundant time to demonstrate the disunity of the Slav camp. The Czechs led by Palacký wanted the Congress to endorse Austro-Slavism and the ambition of federalising the Habsburg Empire against the threat from German nationalism. The Poles despised all other Slav groups, denounced all the dynastic empires (whilst reserving their saltiest comments for the 'treacherous' Russians) and intrigued to convert the gathering into a trans-national pressure-group to demand a congress of the European Powers to recreate the state of Poland. The Slovaks were suspicious of their Czech neighbours, the Croats scorned the nearby Serbs and the Ruthenes demanded autonomy from the Poles in Galicia (a project rejected by the Czechs). Substantial agreement was only possible between groups geographically remote from one another but sharing a common enemy, like the Slovaks and Croats. The greatest divide, predictably, was between the Slav 'Historic' nations – the Poles, Croats and Czechs – and the 'Un-Historic' nationalities like the Slovaks, Ruthenes and Serbs.

So much disunity was on display that it was inevitable that whatever the Slav Congress produced would either be strong but divisive or unanimous but vague. The 'Manifesto to Europe' drawn up by Palacký on behalf of the Congress was deliberately imprecise, rather desperately accentuating general points of consensus. A European congress of nations both great and small must be convened to discuss the general Slav question and the particular issue of Polish independence. A permanent organisation to foster Slav self-consciousness and solidarity would be established, which could also promote and publicise the Slav cause in the wider world. Finally, the Pan-Slavist concept of the racial, linguistic and perhaps eventual political community of Slavdom must be assiduously fostered.

On 12 June the Slav Congress was dissolved as part of the overall Habsburg suppression of the 'Czech 1848', leaving barely a historical trace. No European congress on Poland ever materialised, revealing the failure of the Slav Congress as a trans-national political lobby. The proposal of a 'Slav International', a permanent trans-national racial institution, came to nothing. Even Slav unity as viewed by Pan-Slavists foundered on the jealousies of the leading participants. Pan-Slavism served in practice as a normally submerged, primarily emotional sense of racial camaraderie which generally broke the political surface only when a Slav nationality was experiencing particular misfortune. The leading Slav nations, however, saw Pan-Slavism as an expedient doctrine to bolster the supremacy of the great over the small: the Russians attempted to persuade all lesser Slavs to accept unconditionally the patriarchal authority of the Tsar; the Poles insisted that the Slav Congress condemn the RussianEmpire as a disgrace to the Slav 'family', then expected the smaller Slav nationalities to fall obsequiously into line as the grateful disciples to the 'Christ of Nations'. The transparent attempts by the Russians and Poles to exploit Pan-Slavism for the advancement of their own sectional interests only alienated the smaller Slav groups, which increasingly clustered about the Czechs as their 'champion of the weak'. Each Slav group viewed Pan-Slavism in an essentially egocentric way, as a legitimisation of authority, a rationalisation of expansionism or a group insurance policy against repression. All things to all Slavs, the doctrine of Pan-Slavism in reality only accentuated the chronic disunity of the Slav camp.

Pan-Slavism had a greater practical impact upon the non-Slavs than upon the Slavs. Nations like the Magyars and Germans had their worst suspicions about the Slav majority ganging up on them confirmed: Pan-Slavism was an organised racial conspiracy to overwhelm those nations whose qualitative superiority had enabled them to survive in the past. The spectre of Pan-Slavism was enough to sponsor a rash of racial copies: the Magyars promoted Pan-Hungarianism, the Germans Pan-Germanism, the Rumanians Latinism and the Turks Pan-Turanianism as counter-blasts to the Slav threat. Very often the Pan-Slav threat was cynically exaggerated by non-Slavs to justify authoritarian government and racial suprema-cy, rather in the manner in which the bogey of Bolshevism was exploited throughout Europe in the 1920s and 1930s to 'legitimise' fascism. Both fundamentally ineffectual trans-national organs, the Komintern was the natural heir of the 'Slavintern'.

The pan-racialist movements were without exception taken more seriously than they deserved. Many were guileless, almost neurotic exercises in bluff, pandering to the new racially based fears about group survival or extinction aroused by an age of rabid nationalism. The gross result was to sharpen racial awareness, ruin any prospect of co-operation across the racial divides and break eastern Europe down into impermeable racial camps. A racial chain-reaction had run its course: the Germanisation plans of Emperor Josef II had provoked the Magyars into assertive nationalism; the Croats and Slovaks who were on the receiving end of early Magyarisation took the initiative (together with the Czechs) in promoting Pan-Slavism; and all other races, alarmed by the 'Slav conspiracy', closed ranks to concoct their own pan-movements. The first moves to create a trans-national solidarity of the oppressed achieved nothing: far from furthering the cause of national minorities, the new emphasis on race only exacerbated local jealousies, promoted new divisions and played into the hands of the resident empires and dominant nationalities.

It was not until the early twentieth century that fresh attempts to organise trans-national partnership were launched, based not on racial membership but on the strategic alliance of all minorities within an empire against imperial authority. The First World War offered a real opportunity for national minorities to make their voices heard at a time when the world was for once prepared to listen. The minorities of the Romanov Empire, who had organised an 'Oppressed Nationalities' conference in Paris as early as 1904, repeated the exercise in 'Peoples of Russia' conferences in neutral Stockholm and

Lausanne in 1916, though without any extravagant hopes of becoming an effective trans-national pressure group. The Romanov minorities proved less successful than the Habsburg minorities. In April 1918 a 'Congress of Oppressed Peoples' representing all the subordinate minorities of Austria–Hungary met in Rome. The timing of the Congress lent it exceptional authority in the West. The Allies had already abandoned their pre-war commitment to the Asian integrity of the Ottoman Empire and, since the rejection (under German duress) of their peace proposals by Vienna in February 1918, were seriously reviewing their attitude towards Austria–Hungary. Appreciating that its voice could be uniquely persuasive, the Congress disassociated itself from the Central Powers, advertised its allegiance to the Allied cause and demanded full independence for all the nationalities of the Habsburg Empire. It is more than possible that Allied policy would have switched from tacit support for the continued existence of Austria–Hungary to open endorsement of its dismemberment without the slightest prompting from Habsburg minorities, but the impression of the Congress winning a fateful diplomatic victory was irresistible. The Congress earned the reputation of being the first successful concerted action by national minorities to influence their own destinies, the first victory for trans-national partnership in eastern Europe.[1]

The combination of the 1918 Congress's famous victory and the opportunities for continued political lobbying opened up by the Paris Peace Conference and then the League of Nations inspired a rash of experiments in trans-national co-operation in the 1920s. By establishing regular procedures by which minorities might appeal for inter-national intervention, the League of Nations indirectly encouraged the growth of trans-national organisations anxious to get their wrongs redressed. A Congress of Minorities was convened annually from 1925 to 1938 to compare notes on how 'host states' with minority obligations were behaving and to make representations where necessary to the League. Unfortunately, the Congress never succeeded in winning formal recognition from the League (or indeed any member government) as official spokesman of the minority interest. Minorities were dealt with by the League individually and the principle of trans-national minority solidarity could not be officially entertained. In the last analysis therefore, the Congresses failed as a trans-national lobby and increasingly settled for annual expressions of complaint directed as much against the League as against offending host states: at the Fourth Congress in 1928, the League was unceremoniously censured for failing to provide adequate protection for the national minorities of eastern Europe.[2]

As the Congress of National Minorities, the most responsible and constitutionally minded of the trans-national minority organisations, grew increasingly frustrated, more militant movements sprang up. Revisionist organisations geared to uniting (or re-uniting) separated national minorities were common, with the German and Magyar leagues predictably being the most fanatical. Perhaps the best known of the conspiratorial trans-national phenomena was the Prometheus Movement, essentially a projected alliance of all the national minorities currently within the jurisdiction of the Soviet Union against the Russian and Bolshevik 'tyranny'. Ukrainian, Belorussian, Finnish, Polish, German and even Caucasian *emigrés* converged on Warsaw and Berlin in the 1930s for regular conferences on the imminent repartition of the Soviet Union. Minority nationalism and anti-Bolshevism produced an explosive (if unstable) mixture. It was soon apparent that the Prometheans had no realistic prospects of overthrowing Soviet authority and represented another of those morale-boosting exercises indulged in so obsessively by exiles to pass away the time without conceding their irrelevance to their home-lands. The only possibility of Prometheus being more than a profitless divertissement by powerless *emigrés* lay in securing backing by an established state. The Polish, Finnish and even Japanese governments showed close interest in the movement but it was eventually left to Nazi Germany to become most committed to the strategy (if not the original personnel) of Prometheanism.

The record of a century of attempts at trans-national intervention in favour of east European minorities was incontestably poor. In the nineteenth century, the racially based movements merely imposed fresh barriers on eastern Europe rather than breaking down old ones. After 1918, no trans-national organisations proved powerful enough either to impress the new institutions of inter-national intervention or to restrain the territorial appetites of the Successor States (let alone Germany and the Soviet Union). Nationalism and trans-national collaboration were fundamentally incompatible: the growth of nationalism exacerbated existing ethnic, linguistic and religious heterogeneity to the point where individual nationalities were incapable of overcoming their mutual dislike and mistrust, no matter how beneficial the cause. The nationalism that made minorities so obsessed about their identities simultaneously prevented effective partnership for the achievement of joint or individual advancement.

PATRONAGE

The responsibility for introducing the modern practice of extra-national intervention by a Great Power on behalf of an east European minority must lie with Napoleon Bonaparte. As the principal victims of the greed of the dynastic empires, the Poles sought a mutually advantageous deal with Revolutionary France and then Napoleon from the very instant of Poland's demise in 1795. The Poles supported Napoleon not out of a Pauline conversion to the revolutionary ideals of liberty, equality and fraternity but out of respect for his power of political patronage: Polish allegiance was transferred in the expectation that Western patronage might return what Eastern ambition had seized. After the Treaty of Tilsit in 1807, which drew a line across eastern Europe between the Napoleonic and Romanov spheres of influence, Napoleon created a Grand Duchy of Warsaw out of the Polish territories of conquered Austria and Prussia. The Grand Duchy was Napoleon's down payment on a future state of Poland, a practical demonstration of good faith upon which the Poles were expected to act. On the strict understanding that extra territory for the Grand Duchy must be won by deeds, the Polish nationalists had the greatest possible incentive for fighting for Napoleon. The *Grande Armée* which invaded Russia in 1812 included almost 100,000 Poles, the largest national contingent of any but the French. Unfortunately for the Poles, although the invasion served the double purpose of promoting Poland and getting back at Russia, the disastrous Moscow campaign led inexorably to the defeat of Napoleonic Europe and the automatic collapse of its constituent Grand Duchy of Warsaw.

The second area of Napoleonic political intervention in eastern Europe was 'Illyria', in the far north of what was to become Yugoslavia over a century later. In contrast to Poland, there was no self-conscious local nationalism for Napoleon to utilise, only an area of mixed Croat, Slovene and Dalmatian settlement with no sense of unity or common identity. By the Treaties of Pressburg (1805) and Schönbrunn (1809), a French client state of Illyria was created out of Habsburg territory. There can be no dispute that Illyria gained enormously from the Napoleonic system wished upon it: a modern

public educational system was introduced; the *Code Napoléon* replaced
the ancient feudal law; cultural contacts to the south and west were
encouraged; and a primitive society became suddenly aware of the
currents of the wider world. Although Napoleon was motivated less
by solicitude for the well-being of the South Slavs than the political
desirability of undermining Habsburg authority, the fleeting existence of Illyria from 1807 to 1813 proved seminal. Although Illyria,
like the Grand Duchy of Warsaw, died with the rest of Napoleonic
Europe, the briefest of direct contacts with the West granted an
isolated Balkan society a distinctive historical experience, the folk
memory of which could never be erased by subsequent Habsburg
repression.

The division of eastern Europe into Napoleonic and Romanov
spheres of influence after 1807 initiated the nineteenth-century
phenomenon of the rivalry of the Great Powers of East and West for
the patronage of national minorities. While Napoleon was promoting
the Grand Duchy of Warsaw and the Kingdom of Illyria (and toying
with the idea of sponsoring a Hungarian client state), Tsar Alexander
I was elaborating schemes for the patronage of the Serbs and Greeks.
Interpreting the Grand Duchy as an act of undeclared war against
Russia, Alexander moved to outflank Napoleonic Europe by raising
the Balkans. At war with the Ottoman Empire from 1806, the
Romanov Empire invaded the northern Balkans in a succession of
campaigns which finally yielded the acquisition of Bessarabia by the
Treaty of Bucharest in 1812. In the process of conquest, the tsarist
government sought allies in the Balkans to join a Russian crusade
against both the Napoleonic and Ottoman Empires. Of all the Balkan
nationalities, only the Serbs responded to Russian overtures, partly
because of their religious and racial kinship with their Orthodox Slav
'big brothers', but principally through their unique popular nationalism, which neither Ottoman repression nor Western neglect could
dim. Although tiny, backward, landlocked Serbia seemed a poor
investment for tsarism in wartime (and was increasingly neglected
after 1815), the tentative initial commitment by Russia to Serbia was
the beginning of the long road which led eventually to Sarajevo in
1914.

Russia's second *protégé* was Greece. The Orthodox faith provided a
religious community of interest between Greeks and Russians which
was increasingly reinforced by tsarist awareness of the far-ranging
strategic implications of gaining a grateful Greek client state.

Intriguing for unrestricted naval access to the Mediterranean since the 1790s, Russia saw in the patronage of the Greeks its most promising prospect for intervention in favour of a minority nationality. On the Greek side, nationalist confidence in the intercession of Russia was boosted by the appointment as tsarist foreign minister in 1816 of the Greek Capodistrias. Although Alexander I was fast declining into a state of mystical conservatism which made him reluctant to undermine any existing authority, even when the authority was Muslim Turkish and the challengers Orthodox Greeks, tsarist self-interest in encouraging the Greek nationalist cause became irresistible.

It was the open championship of Greece by Russia that almost involuntarily drew in the rival influence of Britain and France. The awakening of the West to tsarist ambitions at the expense of the Ottoman Empire converted the Balkans into an arena of constant competition between eastern and western Great Powers for patronage of its increasingly ambitious national minorities. Greece became the first issue in the 'Eastern Question' which was to dominate nineteenth-century European diplomacy. Starting as fashionable Philhellenism (crowned by the glorious death of the Romantic ideal, Lord Byron, 'for Liberty's Battle' at Missolonghi in 1824) and developing into a conscious strategy of 'balance of power' to prevent local Russian hegemony, British commitment to the Greek cause eventually matched the Russian. It was the combination of British action at sea, the destruction of the Ottoman fleet at Navarino in 1827, and Russian action on land, the invasion of the Danubian Principalities in 1828, which clinched the independence of a Greek state through the Treaty of Adrianople in 1829. More by good luck than good management, the Greeks had secured extra-national intervention that finally took the gratifying form of two Great Powers competing to free them forcibly from the clutches of a third. The extent of Great Power involvement in the cause of Greek independence was an immediate inspiration to all other national minorities in Ottoman Europe to follow suit.

The picking of sides by the Balkan minorities held no surprises. The racial doctrine of Latinism alone suggested that the Rumanians would look to France as their extra-national patron. Within the Danubian Principalities, the greater production of grain for the west European market in the 1820s and 1830s substantially improved economic, social and political intercourse with France. In Wallachia, the nobility and emerging commercial bourgeoisie despatched their sons to Paris for their education, a socially privileged group which became the nucleus of the Rumanian nationalist intelligentsia. Although 1848 was a profound disappointment to the nationalists, it served to cement the relationship between France and the Rumanians, a reinforced commitment which bore surprisingly early fruit through the intercession of the Crimean War and subsequent Peace of Paris.

Pan-Slavism dictated that the Bulgars would expect promotion from Russia. From early in the nineteenth century, Bulgars looked to *Diado Ivan*, their Russian 'Uncle', for political and military support on the basis of common race and religion. It was in the *emigré* Bulgar colonies of Bessarabia and Odessa that an embryonic nationalism impermissible within 'Bulgaria' itself was fostered by the tsarist government. As Bulgars were stimulated by the precedents of the successful emancipation of other Balkan nationalities, exile in Russia became insupportable. The effect was to incite a particularly militant brand of nationalism, which took for granted unconditional backing from Russia for its provocative enterprises. The chaotic Bulgar uprising of 1876 and its prompt and bloody Ottoman repression forced Russia's hand, compelling Tsar Alexander II to order an invasion of the Ottoman Empire. So unacceptable was the 'Big Bulgaria' created by the resulting Treaty of San Stefano that the other Great Powers overturned its more extravagant provisions at the Congress of Berlin in mid-1878. Although the Bulgar cause had made enormous progress, with Russian backing securing territorial autonomy for Bulgaria, the Bulgar nationalists felt cheated of their full victory.

The Congress of Berlin testified to the diminishing efficacy of extra-national intervention as the nineteenth century wore on. Although French patronage of the Rumanian minority rather fortuitously paid off in 1856, Russian promotion of the Bulgar minority suffered a controversial, not to say ignominious, fate in 1878. Increasingly, the Great Powers were implicitly down-grading self-interested promotions by individual states in favour of joint action over the Eastern Question. Extra-national intervention was becoming subordinated to the rising concept of multi-national legitimisation of change. The traditional sport of individual Great Power patronage of a national minority naturally did not disappear overnight: the Albanians, for example, received support in the early twentieth century both from Italy, which entertained ambitions for employing an independent Albania as a bridgehead for its own Balkan expansion, and Austria – Hungary, which saw Albania as conveniently blocking Serb access to the Adriatic. Even so, the overall tendency was a decline in the incidence and scale of extra-national patronage.

After the First World War, state patronage of minorities elsewhere underwent a dramatic revival. The greater number of east European states after the Versailles Settlement briefly offered the reassurance that national minorities were becoming both fewer in number and smaller in size; but the nationalist expectations aroused by Versailles and the increased number of potential patrons effectively promoted extra-national intervention into a major phenomenon of the 1920s and 1930s. The great divide between the victims and beneficiaries of Versailles predetermined their interventionist stances. Britain, France and America naturally supported the new states they had legitimised at Paris in 1919 and were not disposed to favour disruptive minorities. The Powers ignored or penalised by Versailles, like Germany, the Soviet Union, Hungary and Bulgaria, set out deliberately to exploit the national minorities of eastern Europe for the purpose of undermining the Versailles Settlement. Motivated by the doctrine that ethnic self-determination furnished the only political legitimacy, 'revisionist' states agitated for the reincorporation of their national minorities separated from their homelands by the 'Versailles *diktat*'. German promotion of the Sudeten Germans within Czechoslovakia and the 'Corridor Germans' of Poland was echoed by Hungarian incitement of Magyar minorities in Rumania, Czechoslovakia and Yugoslavia.

Conventional extra-national intervention on behalf of a minority of a nationality different from its patron was reduced to mischief-making by one state at the expense of a neighbour: Hungary fostered Slovak discontent in the hope of fragmenting Czechoslovakia; Italy encouraged Croat separatism in the interests of disrupting Yugoslavia; Bulgaria promoted Macedonian agitation also to undermine Yugoslavia; the Soviet Union sponsored Belorussian and Ukrainian self-consciousness to undercut Poland, Czechoslovakia and Rumania; and Germany sponsored the Prometheus Movement as a weapon against the Soviet Union. In each case, the primacy of self-interest was incontestable, with one state blatantly exploiting a minority within another state for the exclusive purpose of territorial aggrandisement. If a minority benefited from such patronage, it was incidental to the exercise; the most common result for a minority was either increased repression or an exchange of masters. Although Great Power patronage had never been conspicuous for its altruism in the nineteenth century, the extra-national intervention of the inter-war period was remarkable for its narrow self-interest and expansion-ist *realpolitik*.

Even in its heyday in the early nineteenth century, effective Great Power patronage was strictly limited to areas where traditional authority was already collapsing, which in practice meant Ottoman Europe. In Habsburg and especially Romanov Europe, intervention-ism had little chance. French patronage of the Italian minority within the Habsburg Empire in the mid-nineteenth century was the exception that proved the overall rule. Within the Habsburg Empire, the announcement of the *Ausgleich* sent shocked Czech leaders rushing first to Paris and then to St Petersburg for support but although Napoleon III and Alexander II made sympathetic noises, nothing could be done for the Czechs. Within the Romanov Empire, the Poles nursed hopes of French patronage from the time of Napoleon. When the Golden Emigration reached Paris after the suppression of the Polish Rising of 1830–1, the French government disbursed generous grants to the defeated Romantic heroes, but there was never any realistic prospect of direct French intervention on behalf of the Poles in the Romanov Empire. The Poles fretted under the ineffectual French aegis for a full century before the First World War destroyed Russian imperial authority and enabled France to play the role of patron of Poland. In the meantime, Polish nationalists repeatedly went down to superior Russian force while the West could do nothing but wring its hands in regret and congratulate the survivors. Where authority was secure, in the Romanov Empire throughout the nineteenth century and in Austria – Hungary after 1867, neither local minority nationalism nor Great Power patronage could make any major inroads. Over the bulk of eastern Europe, extra-national intervention was permitted no constructive role.

After 1919, the universal lack of a sense of political legitimacy and therefore of state authority invited extra-national intervention to rally after its eclipse in the later nineteenth century. Whether promoting their own 'expatriate' minorities or national groups of a totally different nationality, the revisionist camp was seeking the restitution of lost property or the acquisition of unjustly denied territory through the disruption of the settlement imposed upon eastern Europe by the

'Versailles camp'. The patent instability and impermanence of inter-war eastern Europe could only sponsor a revival of the extra-national patronage of minorities. It was the failure of resident authority to command respect and legitimacy, and the evaporation of Great Power consensus over the settlement of volatile eastern Europe, which combined to return the minorities issue to the forefront of international diplomacy in the 1920s and 1930s.

PARTITION

Multi-national partition largely superseded extra-national patronage to dominate diplomatic activity with regard to eastern Europe in the late nineteenth century. The conventional exercise of multi-national action was partition, the power-based apportionment of territory, usually at the conclusion of hostilities, a political arrangement which traditionally took little account of the population concerned. But as nationalism started to stir, disturbing the almost hermetic deliberations of the Great Powers, concessions were made to local sentiment in the interests of overall stability, which commonly took the form of the protection of minorities within a larger entity under guarantee from the Great Powers. The blend of territorial partition and minority protection promoted the development of multi-national intervention in the overall pursuit of peace and stability in eastern Europe.

By the Congress of Vienna in 1815, the dynastic empires repartitioning Poland were constrained to swear to respect Polish nationality within their jurisdiction, an action which has been seen as 'the first explicit recognition and international guarantee of the rights of a national minority'.[3] Although the Greek War of Independence started as a national revolt backed by Russia, its extra-national nature soon became multi-national, setting a clear precedent for Great Power action in the future. As the Ottoman Empire withdrew from Europe, typically conceding first autonomy and then independence to its emerging nationalities, the Great Powers intervened to legitimise the process, inserting clauses guaranteeing religious toleration for minorities into successive treaties. In practice, the threat to religious minorities came not from the Ottomans, whose millet system had always provided an acceptable minimum measure of protection for Christian communities, but from the ebullient new states, which distrusted any and all minorities within their domains. The toleration clauses reluctantly accepted by the new states of Serbia, Greece, Rumania, Bulgaria and Albania as the price of their diplomatic recognition were inserted to protect minorities not against the faltering authority of empire but the raw power of nationalism.

Recognising a joint responsibility in ensuring an orderly territorial withdrawal by the Ottomans and an equitable distribution of released territory among the competing Balkan nations, the Great Powers also endorsed the practice of regulating major change by periodic meetings attended by all the Powers. This procedure was a continuation, or perhaps a development, of the informal arrangement for the Great Powers to meet to discuss projected amendments to the Vienna Settlement of 1815, usually dubbed the 'Congress System'. The concept of the 'Concert of Europe' has often been under-rated as a diplomatic phenomenon: between 1830 and 1890, for example, twenty conferences of the European Great Powers – eighteen ambassadorial and two ministerial – met to discuss a wide-ranging agenda of pressing issues, many of which were settled amicably and permanently. Leading instances of multi-national action by the Great Powers in concert include recognition of the neutrality of Switzerland (Vienna 1815), rules for maritime warfare (Paris 1856) and the abolition of slave traffic (Berlin 1885).

Another manifestation of multi-national intervention was that of the 'Holy Alliance', the concept of a self-interested compact of Powers to defend the status quo against nationalist or liberal challenge. The alliance was at its most explicit when the Polish Rising of 1830–1 prompted Russia, Austria and Prussia to agree at Münchengrätz in 1833 to strengthen their joint stand against revolution. When the 'Year of Revolutions' struck, Nicholas I issued an open warning in March 1848 that he would not tolerate foreign interference in Romanov affairs 'on the pretext of reconstructing nations which have ceased to exist'. Far from remaining on the defensive, Nicholas I exercised his chosen function as the 'Gendarme of Europe' to intervene decisively, by invitation of other Great Powers, to crush insurrectionary challenge: in July 1848 he co-operated with the Ottomans in suppressing the Rumanian Revolution (such as it was) and in mid-1849 came to the aid of the Habsburgs by smashing the Magyar Revolution. By far the most effective of all forms of multi-national intervention in eastern Europe in the mid-nineteenth century was joint imperial suppression of the aspirations of leading national minorities.

Even so, the defeat of Russia shortly afterwards in the Crimean War compounded the unsettling effect of '1848' on the east European empires to transfer the emphasis in multi-national intervention to the legitimisation of change rather than its automatic suppression. After the Peace of Paris of 1856, the traditional pastime of extra-national intervention – the unilateral patronage of a nationality by a Great Power – had to cede place to the Concert of Europe practice of collective authorisation for change. When the Romanov Empire pursued, or was stampeded into, extra-national intervention in the Balkans on behalf of the Bulgars, the resulting San Stefano Treaty was instantly repudiated and replaced by the other Great Powers at the Congress of Berlin. The tsarist method of promoting change was humiliatingly condemned and cancelled. The diplomatic lesson of 1878 was that extra-national patronage had been definitively replaced by multi-national consensus as the new prevailing political legitimacy. Within Habsburg and Romanov Europe, a defensive multi-national compact defied the disruptive attempts at extra-national patronage hazarded by the West; within Ottoman Europe, a progressive multi-national consensus withstood the traditional (but increasingly unrealistic) moves at extra-national intervention attempted by the Romanovs.

The most ambitious manifestation of multi-national intervention in eastern Europe was the Paris Peace Settlement of 1919. Since it is all too easy to drown in the oceans of ink spilt by critics and apologists of what is generally called the Versailles Settlement, all that can be attempted here is to chart its principal repercussions on the national minorities. The predicament of the Allies in Paris in 1919 was essentially the same as that of the Great Powers in Berlin in 1878: following a war in which imperial authority suffered collapse, a highly competitive nationalist campaign to divide the territorial spoils posed a potentially explosive situation which drew in the Great Powers as arbitrators and peacemakers. As over the Eastern Question, that diplomatic training-ground in multi-national intervention, it was above all the downfall of traditional authority that sucked in both competing nations and concerned Powers. The Ottoman Empire had already withdrawn from Europe by 1914 and the effect of the First World War was essentially to loosen its hold on remaining Asian territory. The Habsburg Empire had finally succumbed to the military, social and political pressures of war and disintegrated over the last months of 1918, leaving its constituent nationalities to squabble over their shares and forcing the Allies to intervene to tidy up the territorial mess. The Romanov Empire had disappeared in 1917 through a combination of unprecedented wartime strain and dynastic ineptitude, to be followed by a power vacuum so colossal that a four-year civil war could only begin the recovery of Russian power. All the empires of eastern Europe had collapsed under the impact of the First World War, posing a succession problem of continental proportions.

The national minorities which had been contained, controlled or repressed by imperial authority had an unprecedented (and many believed unrepeatable) opportunity for what was now called 'self-determination'. With 'Historic' nations claiming their maximum historical territories and 'Un-Historic' nationalities demanding ethnic unification, a squabble over land on a literally continental scale ensued. As with the Eastern Question, there could be no reliance on the self-restraint or even commonsense of the rival national groups: the appetite for land and mania for national expansionism reached levels almost unimaginable before 1914. Within eastern Europe, the popular insistence on the maximum possible advantage at this (very probably) unique juncture was fuelled by the conviction that those nationalities which lost out now might never be allowed a second chance. As nationalist hysteria reached a climax, there was no possibility of concocting a territorial partition of eastern Europe which would satisfy and engage the allegiances of all its national minorities.

In 1919 the Allies found themselves in the familiar Great Power position of attracting criticism and abuse from minority nationalities whatever they did or neglected to do, only now the stakes were higher and the players more numerous and excitable. The Allies were compelled to assume responsibility for territorial partition and minority protection by a variety of interlocking considerations. As in the nineteenth century, their principal concern was for European stability, to create a new arrangement built upon general consensus which would prevent a repetition of the recent appalling war. The minority problem of eastern Europe had at very least furnished the pretext for the First World War; to solve that problem might well forestall another world war. A sense of moral duty was also in evidence among the Powers, the belief that rank imposes its obligations and privilege must be accompanied by responsibility. And yet the Allied statesmen in Paris were still responsible only to themselves. For all the fine talk of self-determination, the nationalities were entitled (as in the late nineteenth century) to lobby the Powers but then expected to submit to their *diktats*, without complaint or right of appeal. The partition exercise produced by the Allies in 1919, on traditional nineteenth-century lines, was still a select multi-national settlement by the Great Powers, not inter-national intervention.

There were, however, unprecedented features to the Paris Peace Conference. Not since the Congress of Vienna in 1815 had the Great Powers assembled with a brief to redraw the entire map of eastern Europe. At Vienna, the intention had been fundamentally reactionary: to restore as much of the *ancien regime* overturned by the French Revolution and Napoleonic Empire as was consistent with practicality. In 1919, the empires which had dominated eastern Europe for centuries had evaporated, with no hope of restoration. Whatever succeeded them was bound to be novel and contentious. The task was therefore exceptionally intimidating for the Allied statesmen in Paris: the First World War had presented them with a political puzzle decidedly not of their liking, on the solution of which depended the welfare of all Europe and the critical judgement of History. With hardly more political, administrative and technical resources than were available in 1878, the peacemakers of 1919 were expected to achieve so much more. Confronted by historical accident with a task beyond their experience and capabilities, the Allied statesmen knew that their chances of overall success could only be slim.

The much publicised moral basis of the partition also raised popular expectations too high. With the announcement that national self-determination would be the guiding principle of the Conference, nationalism was at last universally recognised as the new legitimacy. In two distinct senses, this approach was practical rather than ideological: the disappearance of the dynastic empires made national states the only conceivable and viable replacements; and the Allies had employed a 'nationalities game' of encouraging the aspirations of the Habsburg minorities over the last year of war and were now under pressure to honour their wartime pledges. All nationalities persuaded themselves that the acquisition of independent statehood was their automatic, unalienable right. But if every nationality were granted sovereignty, the result would be a preposterous patchwork quilt of mini-states, politically and economically unviable, and a standing invitation to takeover by an ambitious predator like a recovered Germany or (worse still) a fanatical Bolshevik Russia. The Allies consequently felt compelled by the threat of 'Balkanisation' to introduce a variety of reservations to, and compromises on, the original principle. Agglomerations of nationalities were promoted in the hope of fostering federal states, with Czechoslovakia and Yugoslavia as the leading examples (see Map 4). The brooding and unpredictable menace of Bolshevism persuaded the Allies to inflate the size of those states bordering on Russia – Poland and Rumania – to create bastions of the West in eastern Europe, necessarily at the expense of smaller nationalities. As the much-trumpeted principle of national self-determination conjured up an impossible nationalist dream, so the compromises deemed necessary by Allied perceptions of practicality and strategy made disillusionment among the minorities all the keener.

And yet, in one sense at least, there is no doubt that the Versailles Settlement, whilst incapable of solving the minority problem, certainly improved the situation. In 1914 about one-half of the population of eastern Europe suffered what may be defined as 'minority status': in the Habsburg and Romanov Empires around 60 per cent of the population were subordinate minorities; only in the ex-Ottoman Balkans was the proportion of minorities well below one-half. By the substitution of smaller political units for larger, ostensibly on the basis of self-determination, the leading subordinate minorities of the pre-1914 empires (like the Poles and Czechs) became the dominant nationalities of the post-1919 states. The effect of Versailles was to reduce the numerical scale of the eastern European minority problem by about one-half: whereas one-half of the population were minorities in 1914, only one-quarter were in 1919. Just how contemporaries evaluated this advance varied widely. Optimists applauded the measurable progress, the constructive improvement through human agency and, by the dramatic halving of an intractable problem, the promotion of one-quarter of the entire population onto a new plane of political privilege and responsibility. Pessimists regretted that an unsolvable question had only been reduced in scope, that one-quarter of the population – almost 30,000,000 people – were still members of subordinate minorities and, perhaps most worrying, that the limits of political ingenuity through partition had now been reached. With the uncomfortable realisation that the Versailles Settlement had probably created as many problems as it solved, the belief grew that multi-national intervention could go no further in the solution of a reduced but still explosive issue.[4]

MAP 4 Versailles Eastern Europe 1919–38

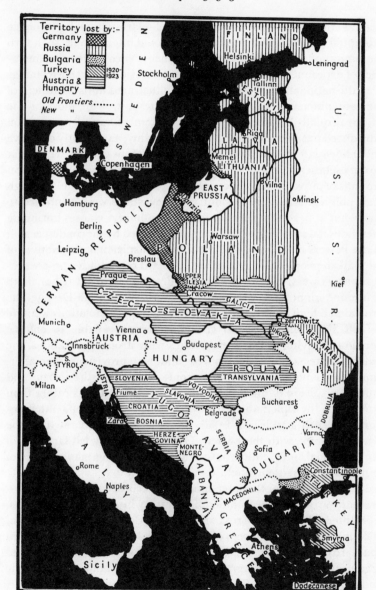

Source: Gilbert, *Recent History Atlas*, P.43.

PROTECTION

Just as the dangerous opportunism of extra-national patronage prompted the development of multi-national intervention, so in turn the limitations of multi-national settlements encouraged the emergence of experiments in inter-national intercession. The shortcomings of multi-national intervention are well illustrated in its treatment of the late nineteenth-century Eastern Question, with most of the features equally evident in 1919. The 'system' of minority protection introduced has been described, a touch harshly, as 'patently defective and inadequate, but the deficiencies were obvious enough. The Great Powers set themselves up as custodians of international justice not on grounds of proven competence or unimpeachable probity but through their political and military clout. The new states were compelled to sign what appeared to them impertinent minority clauses infringing their national sovereignty and were antagonised by the condescension of the Powers in building into the treaties suspicion of the motives of the Balkan peoples. There were no standard consultative procedures between Powers, nations and minorities, no impartial tribunals to determine right and wrong, no avenues of appeal. Despite the proclaimed high morality of the new system, most violations went by default since there was no collective body available to enforce decisions. Having signed their treaties with strong reservations, the Balkan states commonly ignored minority provisions thereafter, almost as a point of national honour, trusting to the inertia and mutual suspicion of the Powers to let the violation pass rather than attempting the diplomatic task of organising multi-national intervention over such a trifle. All in all, the procedures elaborated by the Powers to cope with the Eastern Question not only fell far short of inter-national intervention but revealed the glaring inadequacies of multi-national settlements.[5]

In the meantime, the later nineteenth century was witnessing a dramatic growth in the number of genuinely inter-national agencies. The International Red Cross and Geneva Conventions of 1864 and 1868 introduced the concept of international consensus on minimum standards of conduct, promoted if not enforced by inter-national organisation. The trend gradually involved the political, economic and diplomatic spheres. The International Commission of the Rhine, set up as early as 1815 and often described as the 'doyen of international institutions', was followed in 1856 by a comparable

European Commission of the Danube. Attempts to establish inter-national arbitration to prevent war dominated the early twentieth century. International Peace Conferences were convened on Russian and American initiative at The Hague in 1899 and 1907. The resulting Hague Conventions covered procedures for fostering com-pulsory neutral arbitration to prevent war as well as the more well-known rules for the conduct of hostilities. A Permanent Court of Arbitration was established (although in reality the 'permanence' of its functions and personnel was limited). As more and more increasingly ambitious institutions for the promotion of humanita-rian aims developed, the concept of inter-national intervention became steadily less fantastic, progressively more 'real' and well-supported.[6]

But however influential the proliferation of such regulatory agencies in pre-1914 Europe, it was the combination of the horrific carnage and moral trauma of the First World War and the unprecedented responsibility weighing upon the victorious Allies to produce a permanent peace that forced the pace of inter-national development. It was the belief that, aside from minor border revisions to improve local anomalies, the traditional multi-national recourse of territorial partition could go no further in answering the continuing minorities problem that prompted two experimental exercises in inter-national intervention. Both were associated with the League of Nations, an entirely novel institution which marked a conceptual and political leap forward in the direction of inter-national government (or at least international regulation). The League was envisaged as a permanent inter-national authority whose unimpeachable objectivity would serve as an irresistible moral force to solve (and preferably to forestall) political crises and thereby constitute a universally recog-nised peacekeeping agency worldwide.

Population transfer seemed to many despairing politicians the most definitive, if undeniably the most drastic, solution to the abiding minority problem. If it was demonstrably impossible to concoct frontiers which simultaneously *in*cluded all members of one national-ity and *ex*cluded members of all other nationalities, then the Gordian knot might be cut by moving the people rather than the frontiers. What may be collectively regarded as the pilot scheme for the idea were the 'population exchanges' between Greece, Bulgaria and Turkey over the course of the 1920s. More than 2,000,000 people were transferred over the decade by joint government action under the auspices of, and supervised by, the League of Nations.

By the Treaty of Neuilly in 1919, reciprocal and voluntary transfer of minorities between Greece and Bulgaria was agreed and, as a result, some 46,000 Greeks left Bulgaria (constituting virtually the entire Greek minority) and some 92,000 Bulgars left Greece (about one-half of the Bulgar minority). The immediate point is, of course, that because the populations were allowed to 'transfer' rather than being 'exchanged' in the strict numerical sense, Bulgaria was rid of its Greek minority but Greece had to be content with only having its Bulgar minority halved (with most of those remaining settled in the contested territory of Macedonia). The exchange element was far from perfect, and would have been even less complete but for considerable political, economic and social pressure from both governments, particularly the Bulgarian. What had seemed in 1919 to be a promising trial run in population transfer turned out to be neither truly reciprocal nor voluntary, confirming the view of many League officials that to consider transfer as a 'general prescription' for the minority problem was nothing less than 'outrageous'.

The point was mercilessly rammed home by a convention of the Treaty of Lausanne of 1923, which stipulated quite baldly the compulsory exchange of minorities between Greece and Turkey. There was never any doubt that the convention was a cynical attempt by Turkey to legitimise the forcible expulsion of its Greek minority. It was accepted by Greece only because the alternative was the mass murder of its expatriates: Turkey had demonstrated that it was no bluffer where genocide was concerned by annihilating 1,000,000 Armenians in 1915 and massacring tens of thousands of Greeks at Smyrna in 1922. Over 1,000,000 Greeks were, to follow the contemporary euphemism, 'repatriated' from Turkey to Greece, reducing the Greek minority to almost nil. Simultaneously, some 380,000 Turks were transferred from Greece to Turkey, reducing the size of the Turkish minority in Greece from 13.9 per cent (in 1920) to 1.6 per cent (in 1928). Unfair treatment, most notoriously on the Turkish side, exacerbated the already enormous social and economic problems: a favourite practice was to seize property from outgoing 'transferees' without compensation, to the cynical enrichment of the despatching state, leaving the now destitute evacuees to burden the resources of the receiving state.[7]

The net result of the population transfers was at best very mixed. The Greek-Bulgar transfer involved a relatively small-scale 'exchange' of minorities comprising low proportions of the total populations of both states, but even this more promising of the transfer experiments exhibited a wide range of problems. When the minorities being exchanged were not similar numerically and qualitatively, economic dislocation was inevitable.The state receiving the greater number of transferees suddenly had a larger population than the economy could readily absorb. The sequel was typically a massive drain on the existing resources of the state, impoverishing (and therefore embittering) the established population in order to provide welfare for the incoming transferees. The transferees became almost unavoidably a social, economic and even political liability from which the host state took decades to recover. The Greek government was bankrupted by its refugee problem: the enforced acceptance of over 1,300,000 Greek expatriates from Turkey (to add to the 46,000 from Bulgaria) into a society numbering only 5,000,000 people forced the government to appeal to the League of Nations to arrange massive and repeated loans to enable Greece to survive the experience of population transfer.

The impression left by the 'experiments' in the transfer of east European minorities was unrelievedly gloomy. The League personnel supervising the transfers had four conclusions impressed upon them. Population transfer only had a net beneficial result under almost unattainable conditions of equal and voluntary exchange, and even then the side-effects of large population shifts invariably included a major degree of economic dislocation, material impoverishment and human suffering. Any element of compulsion, lack of parity (whether quantitative or qualitative) between the minorities concerned or failure of goodwill on the part of the participant governments dramatically increased the scale of all attendant problems. Since it was common for both states involved to lose by the transfers, especially in economic terms, it could well be argued that the price-tag attached even to generally desirable national homogenisation was always high, probably unacceptably so. Finally, the League reluctantly recognised that its own role of inter-national supervisor had been ineffectual through lack of experienced staff and blatantly exploited to lend a gloss of legitimacy to enterprises which were at best controversial and at worst deliberate and inexcusable affronts to humanity.[8]

The glaring shortcomings of the 'Balkan trials' persuaded the League of Nations to abandon any general commitment to population transfer in favour of its role (shared with the Permanent Court of International Justice after 1921) as inter-national arbitrator and guarantor of minority rights. As in the case of the new Balkan states in the nineteenth century, the east European states after 1919 were all persuaded, cajoled or intimidated into signing Minorities Treaties as a condition of their diplomatic legitimisation by the Allies. The intention of the League was subsequently to act as inter-national guarantor of the signed Treaties and, if necessary, intervene to reprimand or even discipline 'host states' which defaulted on their minority obligations. The essential failure of the machinery for minority protection became the most disappointing feature of this ambitious attempt at inter-national regulation.

The host states resented the League from the outset. At a time when the new states were understandably hypersensitive about their independence, they were accorded international recognition only on condition that they signed minority treaties which clearly infringed their sovereignty. Why should sovereign states be compelled to submit to the jurisdiction of the League of Nations and Permanent Court of International Justice? More pertinently, why were the Great Powers and other states outside eastern Europe exempt from such minority treaties? League justice seemed to most host states to be partial from its inception, with no universal or even general application of the principle of minority protection. This alienation from the League only incited host states (as in the Balkans in the nineteenth century) to discriminate against minorities as a matter of national bravado, a continuous declaration of independence. It must be conceded that the Allies were generally correct to suspect the proclivities of the new states but to institutionalise that suspicion only exacerbated the problem. The host states collectively advanced the 'clean hands doctrine', the view that mischief-making minorities who refused to accept the Versailles Settlement were outside the jurisdiction of the League and should be punished by the state concerned; only loyal minorities unreasonably or gratuitously persecuted by a state exclusively on the grounds of nationality came under the League guarantee. At heart, the host states saw the League not as a genuine inter-national authority but as a multi-national Great Power agency for maintaining stability, in essence more nineteenth than twentieth-century. Their attitude was all the more unfortunate since, with no inter-national force at its disposal, the League system for minority protection depended absolutely on the goodwill of the host states.

The national minorities of the 1920s and 1930s were equally aggrieved about their treatment. Most never forgave the Powers for denying them independence in 1919 and were therefore, implicitly at least, revisionist and anti-Versailles. If the minorities who had failed to secure promotion to statehood were discontented, those who found their circumstances deteriorating because of Versailles were naturally incensed. The most intransigent minorities were former privileged groups who found themselves 'marooned' inside alien states by the repartition of eastern Europe, like the Magyars in Rumania and the Germans in Czechoslovakia and Poland. As the 'victims of Versailles' such minorities felt no allegiance to their host states and frequently agitated to put an early end to their grudging hospitality. Viewing ethnic solidarity as the only political legitimacy, they excused, sometimes even demanded, disloyalty to their host states, usually provoking a vicious circle of repression and protest which was impossible to break. Whilst demanding the abandonment of the Versailles Settlement, some minorities which had been privileged in the past attempted to exploit the League to secure exemption from change: a favourite ploy was for landowners of minority nationality to claim immunity from egalitarian agrarian repartition pursued by the host state on the grounds that reduction of their position constituted discrimination against a minority. At the other extreme, minorities with more legitimate grievances were infuriated by the appeals procedures of the League, whose Byzantine obsession with confidentiality was interpreted variously as deliberate procrastination to avoid offending a host state and anachronistic, offensively paternalistic behaviour by the Powers which dominated the League. With time, most minorities saw the League not as a judge but as a policeman, far less concerned with justice than the maintenance of law and order. The bitterest critics, totally disillusioned with the League as the 'Protector of Minorities', saw only the 'Jailor of Versailles'.

The cause of minorities was naturally taken up by their 'kin states'. The German minorities within Czechoslovakia and Poland looked to Germany to champion their cause just as the Magyar minorities in Rumania, Yugoslavia and Czechoslovakia looked to Hungary. It was no coincidence that the Magyars in Rumania 'presented more petitions to the League than any other minority except that of the Germans in Upper Silesia'. The very fact that Germany, Hungary and Bulgaria considered themselves grossly victimised at Versailles, making them avowedly revisionist in intent, only underlined their commitment to their 'lost' minorities, mislaid but not forgotten. Underwriting the disloyalty of their minorities to their current host states, the kin states supported irredentism in order to provoke a complete breakdown of the Versailles partition. Host states generally (and in most cases quite correctly) suspected such minorities of being at very least 'states within the State' and at worst 'Trojan Horses' for a hostile foreign power. Claiming that the League procedures disadvantaged the minorities, the kin states campaigned for procedural 'bi-lateralism' so that they could act as official sponsors of minority complainants. The refusal of the League to entertain the suggestion only increased the frustration of both the kin states and the minorities they wished openly to champion.

The attitudes of the Great Powers also tended to foster minority discontent. The United States returned to isolationism with almost indecent haste after 1919. The Soviet Union, disregarded at Versailles and therefore not bound by its provisions, was too engrossed in its own daunting domestic problems to become deeply involved in minority politics for much of the inter-war period. Germany was the leading kin state and proponent of minority direct action. France was the principal military ally and political guarantor of the east European host states and consequently assumed an automatic anti-minority stance. Britain found itself, as the only Great Power which was neither isolationist nor *parti pris*, forced to take the lead in the League over the minorities question, albeit cautiously and unenthusiastically. The Allied solidarity at the end of the First World War which had enabled the Versailles Settlement to be agreed and the League of Nations to be established soon disintegrated, leaving a general sense of lack of Great Power consensus and commitment which could only aggravate the already chronic minorities problem.

The League of Nations itself must accept a share of the responsibility for the failure of minority protection. The procedures of the League were convoluted and bureaucratic, ostensibly to enable the Minorities Committees set up in 1920 to exert discreet pressure on offending host states out of the glare of publicity, but the reaction of the minorities was understandably suspicious. Another decision of the League Council in 1925 emphasised the impartiality of the Minorities Committees by excluding from membership delegates from either host or kin states relevant to a minority petition. Although the laudable intention was to provide more objective, inter-national justice, the effect was more often to produce unsympathetic or downright ill-informed judgements which did nothing to defuse the crises. More generally, public pressure for unanimity in international action kept League intervention in practice to a very low level, consciously or unintentionally allowing the status quo to continue by default. At base however, the chief accusation flung at the League must be that its chief function, by accident or design, was that of gendarme rather than judge: the rights and wrongs of a particular minority issue were always firmly subordinated to the broader preoccupation of keeping the peace by maintaining the Versailles Settlement.

There are convincing mitigating factors in the indictment of the League. It was unrealistic to expect an entirely novel inter-national institution run on a shoe-string budget and staffed by a tiny permanent bureaucracy to avoid failing to measure up to early expectations. Like earlier inter-national authorities (such as the Papacy), the League had no readily mobilised divisions to enforce its rulings and had to rely almost exclusively on the universal acceptabil-ity of its moral stature. Granted the limited resources available to the League and the magnitude of the problems faced, it was inevitable that its sanguine early ambitions should prove unrealisable. In the climate of horror of war in which the League operated, it was understandable that the maintenance of law and order should carry a higher priority than abstract justice. Even if a minority were being scandalously abused, was it justifiable to endanger the peace of the overwhelming majority so soon after the last war?

The very existence of the League, with its imposing guarantees and procedures, keeping the minorities situation constantly under review before an international audience, probably had an inhibiting effect on would-be repressive host states (though it also encouraged the agitation of minorities and kin states). It has even been argued that the League's greatest contribution to easing tensions was in attracting universal criticism. Pablo de Azcarate, Director of the League Minorities Section, asserted that 'insufficient justice has been done to the wide though hidden service ,which the League of Nations has afforded the cause of peace by diverting to itself the many currents of irritation, ill-will and disappointment which would otherwise have done increasing harm to inter-state relations'. It may be that the League's unforeseen greatest service was as an international light-ning-conductor, attracting and rendering harmless the storms of the 1920s. The League also seems to have been treated as a convenient universal scapegoat, perhaps even as a whipping-boy, for the sins and deficiencies of all the other parties in the minorities issue.[9]

In September 1934, Poland unilaterally repudiated its minority obligations before the League. The shock announcement was not necessarily shameless advance notice of the future repression of the Polish minorities as much as an expression of Poland's exasperation at what it regarded as the League's repeated infringement of its national sovereignty. Although Poland saw the action as a belated declaration of real independence, the failure of the League to produce any constructive response revealed its impotence more shamefully than ever before. Unable to discipline or punish member states except by their own masochistic permission, the League died as a minority-protection agency from that moment. With too much expected of the League, inter-national protection of minorities proved as disappointing as all earlier varieties of external intercession in eastern Europe.

It is the limitations of external intervention over the minorities of eastern Europe that are historically most striking. Trans-national partnership was always politically ineffectual, unable to transcend the sectional jealousies which nationalism itself fostered. Extra-national patronage was only operable in areas where existing authority was already demonstrably unacceptable and moribund. Multi-national partition played a significant role if permitted by the collapse of traditional indigenous authority but could never provide anything resembling a totally satisfactory solution. The League of Nations, a regulatory international institution of modest resources in which exaggerated hopes were invested, attempted new answers but made little headway against the inflated expectations of twentieth-century national minorities. Outside authority proved unable to force its attentions on eastern Europe; it had to be admitted by the failure of local authority. With the impact of external intervention markedly less impressive than most standard works on diplomatic history would lead one to believe, only eastern Europe itself could hope to produce long-term solutions to its minority problems.

6. A New Europe?

At the end of the First World War, eastern Europe was territorially repartitioned and politically refashioned. The nationalism of peacetime had already secured the states of Serbia, Greece, Rumania, Bulgaria and Albania from the wreckage of Ottoman Europe, all of which experienced territorial adjustments through the Versailles Settlement. The wartime downfall of tsarism and the inability of its successors to maintain Russian authority over their nationalities led to the fragmentation of the old empire of the Romanovs and the emergence of independent Finland, Poland, Estonia, Latvia and Lithuania. Finally, the collapse of the Habsburgs at the end of the war promoted the formation of new states like Czechoslovakia and Yugoslavia as well as the drastic reduction of traditional entities like Austria and Hungary. With ample evidence that the world of the dynastic empires had departed, never to return, one could have been pardoned for assuming that the new states of eastern Europe represented a complete break with the imperial past and introduced democratic principles into societies which had never had the opportunity before to determine their own futures.

A first surprise comes with the realisation that every one of the new states arrived with a significant proportion of its population still composed of minorities. Just what level constitutes a 'significant' percentage is obviously debatable but a list of the east European states with their minorities expressed as a proportion of the total population (Table VII) is instructive. With between 20.1 per cent and 29.2 per cent of the population of eastern Europe counting as national minorities in the sense of subordinate status, the limitations

TABLE VII National Minorities in the East European States, 1919–38[1]

State	Census Year	Minorities as % of total population	
		By census	By estimate
Albania	1930	22.3	24
Bulgaria	1934	13.3	16
Czechoslovakia	1921	undiffer-entiated	52
Estonia	1934	11.8	13
Hungary	1920	10.4	15
Latvia	1930	26.6	28
Lithuania	1923	16.1	18
Poland	1921	30.8	35
Rumania	1930	29.2	34
Yugoslavia	1931	undiffer-entiated	57
Average		20.1	29.2

Note. With official censuses tending to underplay the representation of minorities, whether innocently or (increasingly) by design, statistics from the appropriate state census and estimates by reputable contemporary authorities are both cited for purposes of comparison.

of the Versailles partition exercise become glaringly apparent. Although the minorities problem had been quantitatively halved, the minorities population was still one-quarter of the total, and the average east European state had minorities comprising one-quarter of its population. Of the major states, Rumania came closest to the average, Hungary was relatively minority-free and Czechoslovakia and Yugoslavia featured by far the highest minority proportions. Despite all the fashionable talk in Paris, the empire had not really yielded to the nation state: although the trend was clearly in the direction of the nation state, in not one instance had it been fully realised. The poly-ethnic or multi-national political unit had not died with the Habsburg Empire in October 1918. The First World War and Versailles Settlement together only converted eastern Europe from an area dominated by a select number of extensive empires to an area quarrelled over by an extensive number of select empires.

At the same time, there was a significant shift within each 'mini-empire' towards creating a 'majority nationality'. Among the dynastic empires before 1914, there existed not a single example of a nationality enjoying a numerical majority: the Russians reached just 44.3 per cent, the Austrians after 1867 only managed 36.8 per cent and even the Magyars, who came closest, strained to touch 48.1 per cent. The over-riding question within the empires had always been not the identity of the majority nationality but whether a minority nationality was dominant or subordinate. After 1919, every state featured a nationality with a numerical majority or, in the cases of Czechoslovakia and Yugoslavia, a near-majority, which automatically rendered it 'dominant'. Among the major states, the most dominant numerical majorities were the Magyars and Bulgars (approaching 90 per cent), in the middle range with healthy majorities around 70 per cent were the Poles and Rumanians, and by far the weakest, falling just short of majority status at all, were the Czechs in Czechoslovakia and the Serbs in Yugoslavia. The traditional imperial phenomenon of the 'dominant minority' had ceded place to the 'dominant majority' feature commonly associated with the nation state, a plain indication of the direction in which political organisation was moving in eastern Europe. None of the new states had either shrugged off the imperial heritage or achieved the ideal of the nation state. Given that the 'Successor States' were political hybrids, exhibiting features of both empire and nation state without falling definitively into either category, what were the repercussions upon the national minorities remaining within the 'New Europe'?

CZECHOSLOVAKIA AND YUGOSLAVIA

The artificiality of the entirely novel states of Czechoslovakia and Yugoslavia was most striking. Expedient agglomerations of territory attached at Allied insistence to the supposedly more mature 'cores' of (respectively) Bohemia and Serbia, their total lack of organic development got the new states off to a shaky start. The frontiers of the states were so arbitrary, with the scantest regard for national identities or the opinions of the resident populations, that quarrels over territory were unavoidable. Within each state, the largest nationality failed to reach majority status, weakening its overall authority and offering the various minorities considerable scope for opposition (whether constitutional or illegal). The combination of undeniable artificiality, the antagonism of neighbouring states and the numerical weakness of the leading nationality made Czechoslovakia and Yugoslavia the most vulnerable of the east European states.

The manner of their creation threw the gravest doubts on their political legitimacy. The concept of a political union between Czechs and Slovaks was never submitted to the democratic vote. In wartime, a referendum on union between the Austrian Czechs and the Hungarian Slovaks would have been suppressed as, at very least, a breach of the *Ausgleich*. In peacetime, a referendum could only embarrass a state which had already been concocted and approved by the Allies under circumstances rather less than democratic. The political duo who 'created' Czechoslovakia, Tomaš Masaryk and Edvard Beneš achieved their remarkable success by a well-orchestrated but almost clandestine campaign of back-stage lobbying of the Allies. Assuming that the Czechs would not mount any rebellion against the Habsburgs – and indeed the underground nationalist movement in Bohemia (quaintly styled the *Maffia*) maintained the lowest of profiles until 1918 itself – Masaryk and Beneš gambled boldly on Allied victory in the First World War. Masaryk was particularly adroit at exploiting his academic contacts in the West to meet and eventually to convert the principal Allied statesmen, especially that other professor-turned-politician, Woodrow Wilson of America.

Perhaps the strongest ploy to 'legitimise' Czecho-Slovakia before it existed was Masaryk's series of undertakings to emigrant communities. Forcibly deprived of a mandate from the Czechs in Bohemia and the Slovaks in Slovakia, Masaryk struck deals with the only Czechs and Slovaks who were available to him. By late 1915, the Czech National Association and the Slovak League in America had agreed to campaign for a federal Czecho-Slovak state. In May 1918 Masaryk signed the 'Pittsburgh Agreement' with the leaders of the largest *emigré* Slovak settlement in America, guaranteeing Slovakia's autonomy within a future Czecho-Slovak state. The mobilisation of the *emigré* communities was necessary to provide the Czecho-Slovak movement with essential financial resources and a popular psevdo-mandate. Great credit must go to Masaryk and Beneš as organisers, tirelessly lobbying the influential, perceptively exploiting the political moment and determinedly employing all the resources accessible. Regrettably, the opinion of the inhabitants of the projected Czecho-Slovakia was unavailable and became a matter of little political account. To a remarkable extent, Czecho-Slovakia was manufactured in the West, by Czech refugees under licence from the Allies in co-operation with emigrants out of touch with the opinion of their homeland, and then presented to the indigenous Czech and Slovak populations as a *fait accompli* for their rapturous applause. Critics of Czecho-Slovakia could claim with some truth that the new state was a preposterous confidence-trick pulled by an unrepresentative clique on both the Allies and the unsuspecting populations of Bohemia, Moravia and Slovakia.

The demographic composition of Czechoslovakia compounded all the other weaknesses of the state. The only common factor among the heterogeneous territories of Czechoslovakia was the Habsburg inheritance but even here there were significant complications: while the western regions of Bohemia and Moravia had been part of relatively benevolent and prosperous Austria after 1867, the eastern areas of Slovakia and Ruthenia had languished under Hungarian jurisdiction. The result was a contrast in political, economic and social development between east and west which imposed an almost schizophrenic identity and its own separate challenge to the integrity of the state.

The national composition of Czechoslovakia (see Table VIII) was ethnically complex. Sensitive to its demographic weakness, the Czech establishment stubbornly adhered to the fiction of an official 'Czecho-Slovak' identity, which mustered an imposing 64.1 per cent of the total population. By refusing to allow a distinction to be drawn in official censuses and statistics between Czechs and Slovaks, the establishment attempted to conceal the fact that the Czech nation constituted less than one-half of the population. Independent evidence would suggest that the Czech population reached around 7,250,000 or some 48 per cent of the total. Even so, the Czechs were numerically dominant, commanding over twice as many bodies as their nearest rivals, a clear advantage reinforced by their qualitative superiority over all other groups.

There was never any doubt that the German minority would prove the most troublesome. Over the late nineteenth century, the Germans of Bohemia had been the most obstinate of all Habsburg nationalities in the almost fanatical defence of their privileged position. An

TABLE VIII National Composition of Czechoslovakia and Yugoslavia[2]

(a) *Czechoslovakia (Census of 1930)*

Nationality	Population	% of total
Czecho-Slovaks	9,750,000	64.1
Germans	3,318,000	22.5
Magyars	720,000	4.9
Ruthenes	569,000	3.9
Jews	205,000	1.4
Poles	100,000	0.7
Gypsies	33,000	0.2
Others	35,000	0.2
Total	14,730,000	98.9

(b) *Yugoslavia (Census of 1931)*

Nationality	Population	% of total
Serbo-Croats	10,731,000	77.0
Slovenes	1,135,000	8.1
Albanians	505,000	3.6
Germans	500,000	3.6
Magyars	468,000	3.4
Rumanians	138,000	1.0
Turks	133,000	0.9
Gypsies	70,000	0.5
Jews	18,000	0.1
Others	236,000	1.8
Total	13,934,000	100.0

example of nationalism being most vigorous on the ethnic frontier, the over 3,000,000 Germans were settled sufficiently compactly in Prague and the Sudetenland to make boundary revision in favour of Germany seem both practical and desirable. Their change in fortunes in 1919 further radicalised the Germans: demoted overnight from being the local agents of the dominant nationality of the Habsburg Empire to being a national minority in a Slav state ruled by the hated Czechs, the Germans were alienated from Czechoslovakia irremediably by their collapse of status. Some tactless moves by the government still further antagonised the German minority, although complaints to the League of Nations about Czech victimisation were usually only the squeals of the wealthy at having their disproportionately large share of the general wealth eroded by government economic policies of redistribution and egalitarianism. With so many problems of local reconciliation to diminution in power, prestige and wealth, the Sudeten Germans under Konrad Henlein were easily exploited by Hitler to provide a pretext for territorial takeover in autumn 1938.

The Slovak minority, estimated at 2,500,000 or 16 per cent of the total population, had a different cause for complaint.[3] Czech insistence on bracketing the Slovaks into a corporate (and entirely bogus) 'Czecho-Slovak' nationality both denied the Slovaks a separate identity and served as a cover for Slovak subordination. When in the course of the 1920s 'Czechoslovakia' entered into official usage, the Slovaks were incensed by the further reduction in their status that 'de-hyphenisation' implied. The Pittsburgh Agreement of 1918, by which Slovakia was promised a separate Diet and autonomy within a federal state, was never implemented. Czech officials flooded into Slovakia on a scale bound to provoke local resentment. The Czech explanation was that the backwardness of Slovakia could only be remedied by a programme of accelerated economic and social development, staffed by Czechs only because of the natural but temporary shortage of qualified Slovak personnel. The jaundiced Slovak view was that the Czechs were imposing colonial-style rule on Slovakia and maintaining a monopoly on the most powerful and best-paid jobs. In economic terms certainly, although the standard of living in Slovakia improved in the 1920s, there was no sign of any dramatic benefits of the Czech 'crash programme'. Indeed, over the whole inter-war period, the Czech standard of living rose more than the Slovak, actually increasing the gap between the Czechs and Slovaks which had been inherited from Austria–Hungary. In these circumstances, a sense of legitimate grievance fostered the recovery of a Slovak nationalism almost crippled by Magyarisation before 1914. A cultural revival soon gave Slovaks a more developed sense of national identity and an autonomist Slovak People's Party headed by the populist priest Monsignor Hlinka attracted wide support despite its extremism. When in 1928 the Slovak Professor Tuka claimed that the validity of the agreements contracted in 1918 was limited to ten years and therefore Slovakia now had both the right and – considering its recent treatment – the reason to secede from Czecho-Slovakia, he was tried for treason and sentenced to 15 years' imprisonment. By such acts of political folly are nationalist martyrs made! Czech insensitivity to Slovak nationalism was the principal cause of the separatist trend which became increasingly well-supported in the course of the 1930s.

A Magyar minority of some 700,000 persistently pursued an irredentist policy, spurred on by a combination of self-interest (like the Germans they had suddenly lost their local dominance to become an isolated minority in a Slav state) and active incitement by the Hungarian government. The compactness of Magyar settlement along the southern border of Slovakia made a minor local revision in favour of Hungary seem feasible and ensured that the discriminatory, ethnically indefensible boundary and the close proximity of the Magyar kin state would prevent the Magyar minority ever reconciling itself to forcible incorporation into Czechoslovakia.

The Ruthene position was somewhat similar to the Slovak. In religious terms, the Catholic Slovaks and Uniate Ruthenes were innately suspicious of the 'Hussite' Czechs. In constitutional terms, the 'Philadelphia Agreement' in October 1918 between Masaryk and Žatković, the spokesman of the Ruthene emigrant community in America, had promised – like the Pittsburgh Agreement for the Slovaks – autonomy within a federal state. Moreover, the Treaty of St Germain specifically stipulated autonomy for Ruthenia, a condition repeated in the Czecho-Slovak Minorities Treaty. The promise was never kept by the Czechs. An attempt by Hugh Seton-Watson to explain away the Czech action sounds lame: 'the country was so backward and the people so lacking in political feeling that it is highly questionable whether autonomy would have been possible . . . the Czechs can therefore to some extent be pardoned for breaking their word'.[1] Although Ruthene nationalism was at an early stage of development, the cavalier and unprincipled breach of faith on the part of the Czechs contributed nothing to fostering a general allegiance to a state which was perilously contrived territorially.

For all its democratic reputation in the (gullible) West and comforting undertakings from Beneš in 1920 to make the new state into 'a kind of Switzerland', Czechoslovakia was never a federation of nationalities. The very heterogeneity and artificiality of Czechoslovakia were taken as justification for a firmly unitary state policy, an attitude perfectly comprehensible to a Habsburg. In operating what was in practice a Czech empire, the Czechs broke all their early promises to their 'subordinate minorities' in a manner almost calculated to antagonise them. With the national minorities in definably compact settlements, with a relatively low incidence of the kind of territorial inter-mixing that erodes ethnic loyalties, the task of either assimilation or cultivation of supra-national allegiance was complicated by the menacing proximity of powerful and historically well-established neighbours. In terms of composition, setting and policy, the long-term prospects for Czechoslovakia were far from promising.

The responsibility for the creation of Yugoslavia must also be divided between the victorious Allies and *emigré* activists advancing views untypical of public opinion in their homelands. As with Czechoslovakia, there could have been no Yugoslavia without the collapse of Austria–Hungary. Self-appointed 'ambassadors' for the Yugoslav ideal, Frano Supilo and Ante Trumbić lived in London from 1915, performing as effective (and deceitful) a job of persuading the Allies as Masaryk and Beneš Just as Masaryk, with his Czech-Slovak parentage, was the ideal personality to promote 'Czechoslovakia', so the Dalmatians Supilo and Trumbić (and later the Croat-Slovene Tito), with no personal stakes in the traditional Serb-Croat rivalry, were the natural publicists for 'Yugoslavia'. Once again, the absence of any democratic mandate for the ambitious and controversial scheme being advanced was shrugged off as a misfortune of war and proved little impediment to Allied recognition of the 'Kingdom of the Serbs, Croats and Slovenes' which announced its own creation in December 1918. Unlike the Czech lands, however, the South Slav area in general (and Serbia in particular) had been so harshly treated by the First World War that the Allies felt an extra moral responsibility to provide some recompense for the carnage suffered by the local population. The greater the damage inflicted on a nationality by the war, the firmer was its determination to secure some substantial reward, a conviction which the Allies were prepared to indulge provided that the torment had been incurred for the winning side.

As another totally new state with only the most tenuous medieval antecedents, Yugoslavia found its patent artificiality (and constitutionally irregular origins) so undermining its general legitimacy as to provoke the hatred and competitive acquisitiveness of longer-established neighbours. Hardly a single frontier of Yùgoslavia could be termed settled and uncontentious throughout the 1920s and 1930s. To the north-west, the Istria area with the ports of Trieste and Fiume were claimed by Italy under the provisions of the Treaty of London of 1915, despite a Slovene majority and the considerable embarrassment of the Allies. Arguments with Austria to the north were shrill until calmed by the Klagenfurt plebiscite of 1922. The long frontier with Hungary was bitterly disputed by the Budapest government as isolating substantial settlements of Magyars in the Banat area of Yugoslavia. In the south, Albania complained about the large Albanian colony included in the Kosovo area of Yugoslavia. To the south-east, the acquisition by Yugoslavia of Macedonia, the traditional prize of Balkan victory in the last decades of peace, incited the Greeks to advance ambitious claims and galvanised the Bulgars into a sustained campaign of cross-frontier provocation and terrorism. By ethnic consensus, only in the north-west was Yugoslavia too small: the collective opinion of its neighbours was that on every other compass point Yugoslavia was too large.

In ethnic composition, Yugoslavia was even more diverse than Czechoslovakia (see Table VIIIb). With eight nationalities numbering over 100,000 people, the threat of internal fragmentation could never be ignored. At the same time, the national balance of Yugoslavia offered some grounds for hope. Racially, the Slavs together polled 85.1 per cent of the population, leaving the non-Slav nationalities deeply divided and numerically unimpressive. Yugoslavia's non-Slav minorities level of only 14.9 per cent made it racially stronger than Czechoslovakia, with a level of 32 per cent. Moreover, while the leading non-Slav challengers within Czechoslovakia were the Germans, numbering over 3,000,000 people (or 22.5 per cent of the population), the equivalent challengers within Yugoslavia were the Albanians, mustering only 500,000 people (or 3.6 per cent of the population). In racial terms, therefore, Yugoslavia had a clear advantage over Czechoslovakia.

The Serbs intended to dominate the new state. Like the Czechs, the Serbs obscured their demographic weakness by officially introducing a composite 'Serbo-Croat' nationality, an ethnic bracketing even more preposterous than the 'Czecho-Slovak'. The 'Serbo-Croat', a statistical monstrosity if ever there was one, included not only the unarguably distinct Serbs and Croats but Macedonians, Montenegrins and even Bulgars. The most accurate definition of a 'Serbo-Croat' was really that of any Slav in Yugoslavia who was *not* a Slovene. Independent evidence suggests that the Serbs probably numbered about 6,000,000, or around only 43 per cent of the total, a slightly weaker position than that of the Czechs within Czechoslovakia.[6] Although almost one-half was an intimidating proportion of the total, the Serb position was in reality much weaker than the Czech: while Czech quality was the highest in 'their' state, Serb quality lagged behind that of both the Croats and Slovenes: and while the Czechs had come through the First World War relatively unscathed, the Serbs had been decimated by the experience. Notwithstanding these disadvantages, the Serbs saw hegemony in the new Yugoslavia as their natural right after a century of fighting and suffering for its creation. The constitution of the Kingdom of the Serbs, Croats and Slovenes was proclaimed on the Serb national holiday of Vidovdan in 1921, emphasising with the bluntest symbolism possible that the new state would be, in effect, a Serb empire.

The 'Vidovdan Constitution', with its unitary concentration of power in the Serb capital of Belgrade, provoked immediate and sustained resistance from most of the non-Serb minorities. As the largest minority by far – probably mustering up to 3,500,000 people or 25 per cent of the total – the Croats assumed the leadership of a broad campaign against Serb domination, agitating from their capital Zagreb for a federal constitution. Throughout the 1920s the political storm threatened to spill over parliamentary confines and become a general civil war. The shooting of the Croat leader Stjepan Radić in the *Skupština* (Parliament) itself in 1928 was prevented from becoming the trigger of Croat insurgence only by the intercession of King Alexander. Suspending the contentious Vidovdan Constitution, Alexander promoted a new administration claiming a supra-nationality, South Slav rationale. The divisive-sounding 'Kingdom of the Serbs, Croats and Slovenes' was rechristened 'Yugoslavia'. Novel administrative units called *banovine* deliberately cutting across traditional frontiers of nationality were established, with unemotive topographical names, in the hope that a genuine sense of South Slav unity might begin to grow.

The Croats were not mollified. As a more prosperous people, the Croats were taxed at a higher rate than the Serbs, adding economic to political grievance. Many minorities suspected Alexander of cynically exploiting the Croat crisis to justify his own dictatorship, a prejudice buttressed by his refusal to tackle the Croat question directly once in power. When Alexander was assassinated by a Macedonian terrorist in 1934, the Croat issue was primed to explode. Thereafter, Alexander's successor Prince Paul, acting as Regent, attempted to find a *modus vivendi* with the Croats in the teeth of the hostility of the Serbs (who saw any concession as prompting general disintegration) and the misgivings of other minorities (who suspected a sell-out to the Croats would leave them worse off than before). The smaller minorities were not altogether wrong. In August 1939, a *Sporazum* between Serbs and Croats established a separate, territorially generous *banovina* of Croatia, with virtual autonomy for the Croats except over certain specified state functions. It is tempting to see the *Sporazum* of 1939 as the Yugoslav equivalent of the *Ausgleich* of 1867. In both instances, the dominant nationality conceded junior partnership to its leading challenger, creating a more stable political establishment the better to resist the nationalist threat from the remaining minorities. The new partners (Magyars and Croats) undoubtedly got the best of the deal, the senior partners (Austrians and Serbs) were more dubious and the lesser minorities (now led by the Czechs and Slovenes respectively) realised with dismay that they were the greatest losers. Whether the *Sporazum* would have turned out as effective an instrument of minority control as the *Ausgleich* remains problematical, since the advent of the Second World War all too quickly disrupted Yugoslavia. The Croat campaign of sustained and often violent 'direct pressure', like that of the Magyars before 1867, secured a victory over the Serb establishment, even though it may have been a classic case of 'too little, too late'.

The Slovene minority was too small to contemplate the frontal attack adopted by the Croats but its tactic of quiet infiltration brought considerable success. The Slovene language was sufficiently different from Serbo-Croat to make Serb takeover of Slovenia difficult, while the Serb-Slovene linguistic barrier was lower for the better-educated Slovenes. The happy chance that included Slovenia in Austria rather than Hungary after 1867 made the Slovenes the best-educated nationality in Yugoslavia and allowed them to acquire disproportionately high employment and influence in the state administration and bureaucracy. The Slovene Clerical Party led by Monsignor Anton Korošec patiently fostered the separate identity of the Slovenes and raised hopes that their undramatic penetration of the civil service would eventually secure autonomy for Slovenia. In Habsburg terms, the Slovenes were the Czechs of Yugoslavia. While the Serbs and Croats were locked in exhausting and often bloody conflict, the Slovenes were tip-toeing away with their clothes.

The remaining small minorities were divided between 'collaborators' and 'provocateurs'. The Muslim Bosnians, led by Dr Spaho, followed the line that support for the government, whatever its complexion and policy, would always bring greater benefits to a small minority than pointless defiance. By contrast, the Magyars and Germans assumed a nuisance value out of all proportion to their small size as their kin states employed them as 'Trojan Horses' to try to bring down the Yugoslav state (although in the Banat the Serbs were quite adroit in the traditional imperial tactic of fomenting quarrels between minorities). In Kosovo, the Albanians gave double cause for concern through holding the records for the highest birth-rate in Europe and the highest proportion of expatriates of any east European state. The combination of these factors made Yugoslavia's south-western border seem extremely vulnerable, expecially as the ominous patronage of Albania by Fascist Italy raised the spectre of Great Power intervention.

The principal reason for the fair success of the minorities' opposition within Yugoslavia was less the strength of their nationalism (even the Croat) than the temporary and uncharacteristic weakness of the Serbs. In 1915, Serbia may have lost as much as 1,000,000 of its population, a quarter of the total, sacrificing almost an entire generation of male adults to the First World War. Already labouring under a qualitative handicap, the Serb numerical loss allowed the demographic initiative to slip to the minorities. Had it not been for its wartime casualties, subsequently propounded as an extra justification for Serb leadership of the South Slavs, the Serb proportion of the total state population would have been nearer two-thirds than one-half, a demographic hegemony too emphatic for the minorities to resist. In the brutally realistic world of South Slav politics, Serbia's calamity became the minorities' opportunity. With the natural demographic dominance of the Serbs temporarily impaired, Yugoslavia became a major arena for competition between nationalities in the inter-war period.

Czechoslovakia and Yugoslavia were both artificial, multi-national states with a dubious legitimacy in an age of nationalism, a description which would serve equally well for the defunct Habsburg Empire. The Habsburg dilemma lived on in post-1918 Czechoslovakia and Yugoslavia. At the most trite yet revealing level of personality, resonant Habsburg echoes made themselves heard: in his last years as elder statesman of Czechoslovakia, President Masaryk enjoyed an almost mystical reverence comparable only to that surrounding the Emperor Franz Josef: and both King Alexander and later Marshal Tito of Yugoslavia have been hailed (admiringly and disapprovingly) as the 'Last of the Habsburgs'. Eschewing territorial expansionism, Czechoslovakia and especially Yugoslavia tacitly admitted that they were already geographically over-extended and demographically too heterogeneous. The Czechs and Serbs, without majorities within Czechoslovakia and Yugoslavia, could not hope to govern in a manner too repressive or provocative to their powerful minorities and settled for Czech and Serb empires, reserving their hopes for more unitary, homogenous nation states for the future.

POLAND AND RUMANIA

Neither the Polish nor Rumanian state could be regarded as artificial and therefore never suffered the sense of lack of moral legitimacy which Czechoslovakia and Yugoslavia found such a handicap. But while the right of Poland and Rumania to exist was never contested, many contemporaries, most notably their national minorities, argued forcibly that they were too large. A combination of dynamic nationalist expansionism and Allied approval for making these 'bastions against Bolshevism' as formidable as possible inflated Poland and Rumania into very much more than straightforward nation states. At the same time, the demographic position of the Poles within the 'Polish Empire' and Rumanians within 'Greater Rumania' was strong enough to persuade the national governments that a more aggressive line towards their minorities would be both practical and beneficial.

The existence of a Polish state before 1795 already provided historical legitimisation for the 're-creation' of Poland in 1919 but it was perhaps the nineteenth-century Polish record that was most persuasive. Although the fighting spirit of Polish nationalism was subdued in Romanov Poland, suborned in Habsburg Poland and provoked in German Poland, the tri-partite division agreed at the Congress of Vienna showed no signs a century later of eradicating the Polish sense of national self-consciousness, indeed 'martyrdom' may well have strengthened local nationalism. The Poles were a nation deserving a state by all criteria except imperial power politics. With the collapse of all three occupying empires over the First World War, the Polish claim of national legitimacy became incontestable. Given the long-standing western sympathy for the Polish cause and the energetic patronage of France, the recreation of Poland almost automatically received the backing of the Allies, especially when reinforced by the tactical concept of Poland as a Western bastion inhibiting German *revanche* and blocking Bolshevik expansion.

Contrasting with the ease with which the principle of a new Poland was internationally recognised was the bitter controversy surrounding the territorial extent of the Polish state. Amongst the Poles themselves, opinions were (dare one say) polarised between the outlooks of the right-wing nationalist Roman Dmowski and the socialist Josef Pilsudski. Dmowski wanted a state as large as possible without endangering the numerical hegemony of the Poles and their ability to assimilate any non-Polish minorities. Pilsudski envisaged a still larger state reminiscent of the Polish Commonwealth of the past, in which a family of nationalities would be united in a federation headed by the Poles, the largest ethnic group. The Allies supported the idea of Poland being as extensive as was consistent with political, economic and military strength, in particular granting access to the Baltic by the 'grant' of German territory promptly dubbed the 'Polish Corridor' (see Map 4). In the east, Polish aggrandisement could only be at the expense of Bolshevik Russia and was therefore applauded by Western governments still actively engaged in intervention on the side of the Whites.

The frontiers of Poland were, as a result, as extended and unstable as any in eastern Europe. In the west, Polish acquisition of a Baltic 'Corridor' antagonised Germany irreconciliably, with a move to reclaim that territory awaiting only German recovery from defeat. In the south, Poland was involved in what now seem excessively acrimonious disputes with Germany over Upper Silesia and with Czechoslovakia over Teschen, which permanently soured relations between the three states. In the north, Poland provoked the new state of Lithuania by seizing and then formally incorporating the district of Vilna. Finally and most ominously, in the east a bruising Polish-Soviet War in 1920 gave notice of the eventual recovery of the military strength of Russia. In the meantime, the eastern frontier was the longest and most vulnerable of all, a geographically and ethnically arbitrary line on the landscape awaiting the inevitable pressure from a reviving Soviet Union. Although Poland was not as extensive as Pilsudski would have liked, it was too large for all its neighbours.

The national composition of Poland (see Table IXa) featured a Polish demographic dominance which was the envy of the Czechs and Serbs. Although there seems no doubt that the official censuses were less accurate statistical exercises than 'Polonisation propaganda', and the Polish percentage of the total was closer to two-thirds than appears, the strength of the Polish position could not be denied. If the racial dimension is emphasised, the Polish state was some 87.7 per cent Slav. Although there was a fair variety of non-Polish minorities within the state, four mustering over 1,000,000 people, the leading challenger was still only one-fifth the 'weight' of the Poles.

The Polish experience in the ninteenth century persuaded many gullible contemporaries that the Poles could never inflict on others what they had for so long endured themselves. An example from 1922 is the opinion of Charles Sarolea: 'A Pole cannot be a nationalist ... he has been the first to apply the federal principle in his relations with other nationalities living under the authority of the Polish state. Poland has suffered too much from the aggressive nationalism of Germany, Russia and Austria to be misled by the nationalist heresy'.[7] In reality, the Poles proved the most fanatical of heretics, with their protracted experience of 'martyrdom' under the dynastic empires serving to justify the victimisation of their own minorities after 1919.

The Ruthenes, who were incorporated into Poland through first the collapse of tsarist authority and then the failure of an independent Ukraine, remained antagonistic to Polish rule from start to finish. Although relatively backward in their nationalism, the Ruthenes had their morale raised by the close proximity of the Ruthene-Ukrainian majority just across the Soviet border. Encouraged by rumours of the considerable cultural freedom enjoyed by Ukrainians within the Soviet Union, the Ruthene minority resisted the enforced assimilation projected by the Polish authorities. A vicious circle of resistance and repression, then more violent opposition provoking stronger reprisals, reached its zenith with the infamous 'pacification' of the Ruthenes

TABLE IX National Composition of Poland and Rumania[8]

(a) *Poland (Census of 1921)*

Nationality	Population	% of total
Poles	18,814,000	69.2
Ruthenes	3,898,000	14.3
Jews	2,110,000	7.8
Belorussians	1,060,000	3.9
Germans	1,059,000	3.9
Lithuanians	69,000	0.3
Russians	56,000	0.2
Czechs	31,000	0.1
Others	78,000	0.3
Total	27,177,000	100.0

(b) *Rumania (Census of 1930)*

Nationality	Population	% of total
Rumanians	12,981,000	70.8
Magyars	1,426,000	8.6
Germans	745,000	4.2
Jews	728,000	4.1
Russians	409,000	2.3
Ruthenes/Ukrainians	382,000	2.2
Bulgars	366,000	2.1
Gypsies	263,000	1.5
Turks	177,000	0.9
Others	418,000	2.4
Total	17,895,000	100.0

by Polish cavalry in late 1930. Though a lull ensued in the 1930s it seems difficult to agree with Peter Brock that 'it looked as though, but for the war, a *modus vivendi* might ultimately have been worked out'.[9] What calm existed was the temporary product of the exhaustion of both persecuted and persecutors, not the beginnings of future consensus and co-operation.

A similar experience befell the Belorussians. With Belorussia (like the Ukraine) partitioned between Poland and the Soviet Union, the Polish government initially encouraged 'Belorussianism' to secure the loyalty of the minority population against the Soviet threat. Although Belorussian nationalists would have preferred independence of the kind they had attempted before the Treaty of Riga divided their country in March 1921, they were hopeful that they might play off the Poles against the Russians to secure preferential treatment. But the dream that partition might be a nationalist blessing in disguise, the means by which Belorussia's backward society could catch up with its larger neighbours, was soon exploded. Alarmed at the Belorussian nationalism which they had promoted – a weapon aimed at the Soviet Union which showed every sign of backfiring – the Poles switched in 1924 to a policy of forcible 'Polonisation'. As Belorussian schools, societies and newspapers were closed down, the Polish government talked blithely to the League of Nations of 'the natural process of assimilation of minority groups'. The Belorussian nationalist leader Cvikevič could not contain his disillusionment:

> Yesterday we and the Poles were two nations on the same side of the fence. Poland, 'a nation crucified', was our elder brother in the momentous struggle against tsarism, and her example gave us strength and courage. We lived in the hope that freedom would come at the same time for both our peoples – and what happened? As soon as Poland had risen from the dead, her scourge began to play over the white body of Belorussia . . . . Life has bitterly crushed our illusion.[10]

By the late 1920s Belorussian resistance was taking the form of vain protest with the other harassed minorities within the *Sejm*, the Polish Parliament , and a shift towards the political left, headed by the socialist *Hramada*. After 1928 all political nationalism in Belorussia was crushed, as was all cultural nationalism after 1936. By the mid-1930s, the choice for Belorussians under Polish rule was to acquiesce (the reluctant resort of the majority), to continue protesting (and end up in the special concentration camp reserved for Belorussian trouble-makers at Bereza Kartuska) or to emigrate (as perhaps 100,000 desperate people did over the inter-war period).

Although the German minority constituted only 3.9 per cent of the state population, it was concentrated in the compact areas of Upper Silesia and the Corridor between Germany and East Prussia, close enough to its kin state to draw continuous encouragement and sustenance for its local campaign of revisionist agitation. Polish hostility to the Germans was above all the result of the Prussianisation of Poznania over the decades before 1914. Those German settlers who had benefited from the Prussian colonisation scheme before the war were now unceremoniously dispossessed of their land, which was handed over (or 'returned') to Polish settlers. This drawn-out struggle over real estate so near the redrawn German border could not fail to fuel German hatred of Poland and enlist sympathy for Hitler's later demands for the return of the Corridor to Germany.

The Jewish minority in Poland was the largest in eastern Europe, mustering well over 2,000,000 people, or at least 7.8 per cent of the total population. The traditional policy of avoiding confrontation and sheltering from the political storm was moderately successful: despite the ready visibility of a Jewish population obstinately resistant to all attempts at integration or assimilation, the Polish government made few overt moves against the compact settlements of Jews. Azcarate, expressing the somewhat unworldly view of the League of Nations, described the official Polish attitude towards the Jews as 'very wise' and ' a model of governmental policy towards minorities'.[11] Accepting the long-established Jews as part of Poland's heritage, the Polish nationalists reserved their greatest venom for their recently acquired minorities, a perhaps surprising phenomenon in a Europe where anti-semitism was assuming epidemic proportions. It may be that the Polish government was intimidated into fatalistic inactivity by the sheer scale of its Jewish problem. Dmowski and other Polish nationalists rarely spoke of assimilation as appropriate to the Jews, only of the desirability of mass emigration, but the practical difficulties of inducing over 2,000,000 individuals, many virtually irreplacable in the commercial economy of Poland, to emigrate were too daunting. Quixotic as ever, the Poles tolerated the prime historical target of minority discrimination in order to expend most of their energies harassing their fellow Slavs.

The conspicuous advantages enjoyed by Poland, such as a universally recognised claim to statehood, strong backing from the West and a heavy Polish demographic dominance, were largely offset by the repercussions of its geographical location and territorial over-extension. Surrounded by powerful neighbours with ethnically based designs on 'Polish' territory and with a variety of minorities whose close support by their contiguous kin states was encouraged by official persecution, Poland also had the unsought distinction of being the only east European state bordering upon both Germany and Russia. This geographical predicament alone was sufficient to cancel out all the combined strengths of Poland.

Rumania was the only beneficiary of Versailles to have been in independent existence before the First World War and therefore had a practical legitimacy which was incontrovertible. Rumania had three attributes that attracted Allied favour in 1919; it had fought on the Allied side in the war (albeit belatedly and disastrously); its political complexion was pronouncedly anti-Bolshevik (a feature skilfully highlighted by the Rumanian premier Bratianu); and its geographical location was between central Europe and Bolshevik Russia. As a result, Rumania was favoured territorially by the Allies as part of their *cordon sanitaire* against the Bolshevik menace. Rumania's unfortunate wartime experience was turned to good diplomatic account as, like Serbia, its government claimed territorial compensation for sufferings incurred in the Allied cause. Over 1918, Rumania took advantage of the Russian slide into civil war to occupy the northern territory of Bessarabia, a seizure 'legitimised' a year later at Versailles. The collapse of Austria–Hungary forced the populations of Transylvania and Bukovina, with substantial Rumanian settlements but hitherto preferring membership of the Habsburg state, into the arms of Rumania. The Transylvanian Rumanians only deserted the Habsburg banner when imperial collapse was certain in late 1918, demanding the recognition of all their current privileges as an explicit condition of their union with Rumania. The Allied statesmen at Versailles recognised the greatly expanded, even territorially bloated, 'Greater Rumania' with few qualms.

A state which had grown so fast at the expense of almost all its neighbours could not expect to enjoy any border security. Only along the short frontiers with Czechoslovakia and Poland to the north were there no serious clashes. To the south, Bulgaria had every intention of reclaiming southern Dobrudja, originally lost at the end of the Second

Balkan War in 1913: to the west, Hungary was determined to recover Transylvania. As in the case of Poland, the long border with the Soviet Union to the north-east had an almost palpable impermanence (and came under increasing Russian pressure after the mid-1920s). The territorial expansion into 'Greater Rumania' effected at the end of the First World War converted what had been close to a Rumanian nation state into a Rumanian empire. Incurring the penalties of significant minorities and the wrath of all its truncated neighbours, Rumania after 1919 showed every sign of falling victim to its own success.

The national composition of Greater Rumania (see Table IXb) presented both advantages and impediments to a Rumanian demographic ascendancy. The expanded state accommodated a greater variety of national minorities than any other east European neighbour (excepting the Soviet Union): like Yugoslavia, which came second in this respect, Rumania's heritage from its geopolitical position in the conflict zone between the Romanov, Habsburg and Ottoman Empires was an egregious ethnic heterogeneity. The racial spectrum was remarkable, with some 70.8 per cent Latins, 8.6 per cent Magyars, 4.2 per cent Germans, 4.1 per cent Jews and 6.6 per cent Slavs. On the other side, the strong Rumanian position (even allowing for the usual statistical exaggeration of the dominant nationality) was reinforced by the fact that the leading challenger was less than one-eighth the size of the Rumanian majority. The overall demographic hegemony of the Rumanians persuaded them to approach Greater Rumania with policies designed to convert the new territories into integral components of a homogeneous nation state. The size of the newly acquired possessions impelled the *Regateni*, the Rumanians of the original *Regat* (or Danubian Principalities), to move in to enforce the authority of Bucharest. Even the Rumanians of Transylvania found the arrogance of the *Regateni* and their arbitrary suppression of all local autonomy repellent, and virtually formed a new national phenomenon: a minority within the majority. The fact that Transylvania, while one of the most backward areas of Austria–Hungary, was in 1919 the most advanced part of Greater Rumania encouraged the local inhabitants to resent the cruder *Regateni* and increased the determination of Bucharest to 'Romanise' its latest and most valuable acquisition. What has been termed 'integral nationalism', already discernible before 1914, dominated Rumania in the inter-war period, to the permanent detriment of its many minorities.

The Magyar minority of Transylvania was unquestionably the largest and most recalcitrant of the non-Rumanian groups. According to official Rumanian statistics, the Magyars numbered 1,426,000 or 8.6 per cent of the total population: Hungarian figures put the Magyar minority near 2,000,000 or almost 12 per cent of the total. With the simplistic social stereotype that of a Magyar intelligentsia and upper class co-resident with a Rumanian peasantry, the superior position of the Magyar minority attracted government action soon after 1919. The Magyars suddenly found themselves no longer the local bastions of Hungarian dominance but a collection of isolated and vulnerable communities within the state of the Rumanians whom they had until recently been relentlessly Magyarising. The ruling Magyars had been automatically 'disinherited' by the shift in the Hungarian-Rumanian border and now agrarian and social legislation designed to favour the local Rumanian population was threatening to 'dispossess' them too. Copious complaints were lodged with the League of Nations. Some charges were controversial: did government-sponsored erosion of the wealth and privilege of an ex-dominant minority count as 'affirmative action' to benefit the previously disadvantaged Rumanians or as persecution of a national minority requiring League intervention? Other allegations were more straightforward: the ebullient *Regateni* undoubtedly overstepped the limits of legality on a number of occasions in their headlong pursuit of the Romanisation of the minorities. Meanwhile, of course, every kind of moral, political and financial inducement was employed by the nearby kin state of Hungary to make Transylvania ungovernable and precipitate a collapse of authority which would make border revision in the Magyar favour unavoidable.

Aside from the Bulgar minority, compactly settled in the southern Dobrudja and fighting a stubborn campaign for reintegration with neighbouring Bulgaria, the other non-Rumanian groups tended to adopt a low profile, hoping that outward compliance with Romanisation would enable them in practice to retain much of their identity. The long-established German or 'Saxon' minority resident in Transylvania chose to protect its economic prosperity by avoiding provoking the Bucharest government, neither consorting with its Magyar neighbours nor fostering close links with Germany. Virtually the only substantial minority of pre-1919 Rumania, the Jews remained the principal target of Rumanian prejudice but with traditional antisemitism further 'justified' by the argument that since Bolshevism was a Jewish vehicle for world domination, the Jews in Rumania were agents of an enemy power. Local intimidation and acts of violence against the Jews were rife and, at very least, condoned by the government. The Russian and Ukrainian minorities, together comprising 4.5 per cent of the population, were concentrated in Bessarabia and Bukovina. There were few confrontations with the Rumanian authorities, largely because the Slavs were never in any doubt that their 'Rumanian captivity' was only an interlude from which the massing power of their kin state would soon secure their release.

Unlike the Czechs and Serbs, the Poles and Rumanians were not reconciled to running empires, instead aiming to convert their states into nations by whatever means seemed justified. Tantalisingly short of the ideal of the nation state, the Poles and Rumanians would not allow their minorities to stand in the way of their ambition. It was predictably the states featuring a relatively small proportion of minorities which were most tempted by 'integral nationalism'. The Poles and Rumanians, each with almost 70 per cent of their state populations, believed they had the moral right and physical strength forcibly to 'solve' their minority problems and convert their territories in the foreseeable future into nation states. Just how this was to be achieved in an age when every nationality, whether majority or minority, was acutely aware of its identity and convinced of the legitimacy of its cause could only be controversial (and very possibly bloody). The means by which majorities might 'solve' their minorities problems included the encouragement of minority emigration (perhaps even mass expulsion), assimilation into the dominant majority culture (through both encouragement and compulsion), frontier adjustments (provided of course that no territorial loss were entailed!) and, starting to emerge as a feasible option, the physical liquidation of 'unwanted' minorities. The phenomenon of integral nationalism, first identifiable among the Balkan states in the late nineteenth century and spreading to most of eastern Europe over the 1920s, was exhibited at its most forthright and unapologetic in Poland and Rumania.

HUNGARY AND BULGARIA

The states of eastern Europe created, adjusted or legitimised by the Versailles Settlement were divided all too clearly into two rival camps. The beneficiaries of Versailles, most prominent of which were

Czechoslovakia, Poland and Rumania, had all found ways of demonstrating their commitment to the Allies in the First World War and were lavishly rewarded with territory and international recognition in consequence. The victims of Versailles, comprising Hungary and Bulgaria (and of course Germany and Austria), were unfortunate enough to be on the losing side and were punished for their misjudgement by the loss of much of their territory. The outcome of the First World War was therefore institutionalised politically and territorially in the divide between the favoured 'Versailles states' and the disgraced 'revisionist states', a dichotomy which fundamentally (and probably irretrievably) undermined the structure of the new eastern Europe.

A useful indicator of the attitude of the various nationalities to the new political partition is the league table of expatriate minorities (see Table X). It is no coincidence that the favoured Czechs, Serbs, Poles and Rumanians, who were granted states at least as extensive as they ethnically deserved, appear at the foot of the list, with expatriate minorities of only 1 or 2 per cent of their total (and therefore little ethnic need or justification for territorial expansion). At the head of the list come nationalities which were for one reason or another confined to a territory which effectively excluded a significant proportion of their total, the expatriate minority, and were therefore almost automatically adherents of the revisionist camp.

The combination of substantial population size and second-highest expatriate-proportion made Hungary the leading revisionist state within eastern Europe. Just as Allied victory favoured certain rather undeserving states, so the defeat of the Central Powers somewhat unfairly penalised others. The *Ausgleich* which provided the Magyars with a blank cheque for the repression of Hungary rebounded in 1914: by the terms of the 1867 agreement, Hungary had no authoritative voice in Habsburg foreign policy and was constitutionally bound to follow Austria into war after Sarajevo. Once Austria–Hungary collapsed, the fate of Hungary itself was sealed. An eleventh-hour unilateral declaration of independence from Vienna in September 1918 and the hurried creation of a moderate Magyar government headed by Count Mihaly Károlyi shortly afterwards fooled no-one. Neither did the appointment of a well-known liberal Oszkár Jászi as Minister for Nationalities deflect the non-Magyars from their hatred of Hungary. Jászi's proposal of a Hungarian Federation of nationalities was seen in the same jaundiced light as the similar desperate offer

TABLE X Expatriate National Minorities in Eastern Europe, 1919–38[12]

Nationality	Total population (millions)	Expatriate population (millions)	Expatriate %
Albanians	1.6	0.7	44
Magyars	10.0	3.0	30
Slovenes	1.6	0.4	25
Belorussians	5.0	1.0	20
Ukrainians	30.0	5.0	17
Bulgars	6.25	1.0	16
Estonians	1.2	0.15	12.5
Latvians	1.3	0.15	11.5
Germans	70.0	8.0	11.5
Slovaks	2.7	0.2	7.5
Lithuanians	1.8	0.1	5.5
Croats	3.1	0.08	2.5
Czechs	7.4	0.13	1.8
Rumanians	13.0	0.2	1.5
Russians	90.0	0.9	1
Poles	20.0	0.2	1
Serbs	6.1	0.05	0.8
Totals	271.05	21.26	average 7.8

Notes. 1. 'Expatriate' may be defined as resident outside the state in which the majority of the membership of the nationality is located. Emigrants outside Europe are excluded.

2. Jews and Gypsies cannot be included in the table since the essence of their demographic position was the lack of any home territory. For the geographical distribution of these 'one hundred per cent expatriates', see Table XII.

of the Hungarian Parliament on the eve of disaster in July 1849. The peacetime policy of Magyarisation, together with the profoundly disquieting appearance of a 'Hungarian Bolshevik' government under Béla Kun in 1919, cost Hungary all sympathy and influence in the West. Friendless at home and abroad, Hungary was above all others the state cannibalised to provide the territorial gains of the beneficiaries of Versailles.

The punitive Treaty of Trianon left Hungary with 32.7 per cent of the territory and 41.6 per cent of the population it had previously enjoyed. All neighbouring states benefited at Hungary's expense: 36.2 per cent of Hungary's former territory was transferred to Rumania by the cession of Transylvania; 22.3 per cent in the north went to Czechoslovakia; 7.4 per cent was taken by Yugoslavia; and even the 'rump state' of Austria received 1.4 per cent. And yet the traumatic loss of over two-thirds of its former territory failed to rationalise the ethnic position of Hungary. Only 67.5 per cent of Magyars were left within the reduced state of Hungary: of the 32.5 per cent of Magyars who now found themselves outside Hungary, 16.7 per cent were in Rumania, 10.8 per cent in Czechoslovakia and 4.6 per cent in Yugoslavia. Put succinctly, two-thirds of all Magyars were confined to one-third of their former territory, while the other one-third of Magyars were forcibly incorporated into other states.[13]

'Trianon Hungary' did not even have the merit of promoting national homogeneity. According to official statistics (see Table XIa), the Magyar proportion of almost 90 per cent of the total population brought Hungary closest to the ideal of the nation state of any political entity in eastern Europe. In reality, the non-Magyar minorities mustered at least 15 per cent of the total. By the Census of 1920, based upon the criterion of mother-tongue rather than national-ity, a Hungarian government long experienced at juggling with statistics to exaggerate the Magyar hegemony completed another propaganda exercise. The German minority, certainly numbering well over the official half a million, was so entrenched within the officer corps of the army (which patriotic Magyars had been boycotting for half a century) that its position was privileged and secure. But the long-standing policy of Magyarisation, coupled with Magyar patriotic frenzy at their treatment at Trianon, constrained all lesser minorities to present the lowest possible demographic profiles in their own self-interests. The most telling instance is that of the Hungarian Jews: although statistics for religious affiliation put the Jewish population at 473,000 or some 5.9 per cent of the total, the socialist republic of Béla Kun the previous year had provoked such an outburst of anti-semitism that very few Jews cared to declare

TABLE xi National Composition of Hungary and Bulgaria[14]

(a) *Hungary (Census of 1920)*

Mother Tongue	Population	% of total
Hungarian	7,147,000	89.6
German	551,000	6.9
Slovak	141,000	1.8
Croat	37,000	0.5
Rumanian	24,000	0.3
Others (mainly Gypsy)	79,500	0.9
Total	7,979,500	100.0

(b) *Bulgaria (Census of 1934)*

Nationality	Population	% of total
Bulgars	5,275,000	86.7
Turks	618,000	9.8
Gypsies	81,000	1.3
Jews	28,000	0.4
Armenians	23,000	0.3
Rumanians	16,000	0.2
Russians	12,000	0.2
Others	25,000	0.4
Total	6,078,000	99.3

themselves officially and attract the unwelcome attentions of the 'White Terror'. Although the Magyar dominance of Hungary was guaranteed by a demographic proportion of over four-fifths of the total population, the intimidated minorities both quantitatively and qualitatively together constituted a far from negligible factor.

In terms of 'ethnic justice', Hungary suffered far more from the

Treaty of Trianon than the strictest interpretation based upon ethnic criteria could warrant. The moral principles which had been waived in order to concoct or expand the beneficiary states were also suspended for the purpose of penalising Hungary. Given the temperament of the Magyars and the political climate of the inter-war period, there was no possibility of Hungary resting content with its grotesquely reduced territory. Both in principle and practice, the ethnically iniquitous Treaty of Trianon was a disaster for Hungary and, eventually, for the whole of south-eastern Europe.

Bulgaria found itself in a similar, though less drastic, situation. Allied wrath was visited on Bulgaria for not only joining the Central Powers in the First World War but doing conspicuously well. Known as the 'Prussians of the Balkans', the Bulgars continued their late-nineteenth-century success story by capturing Serbian Macedonia, laying claim to Greek Macedonia and recovering the southern Dobrudja ceded to Rumania by the Treaty of Bucharest in 1913. But military success was dependent on the overall victory of the Central Powers and the maintenance of political and economic stability within Bulgaria. The Treaty of Neuilly of November 1919 was another punitive, almost vindictive treatment meted out by the Allies in collusion with Bulgaria's neighbours. All the territory acquired by conquest was automatically forfeit and restored to its 'rightful' owners. Extra Bulgarian territory was also made available to Yugoslavia, which gained most of Macedonia, and to Greece, which was granted enough of Thrace to deny Bulgaria once again access to the Aegean. Despite an excellent war record, Bulgaria emerged from Neuilly considerably smaller than in 1914.

The national composition of 'Neuilly Bulgaria' (see Table XIb) was most notable for featuring minorities too small or dispersed to figure prominently elsewhere. Turks constituted almost one-tenth of the population, both a heritage of the Ottoman past and an indication of the close proximity of Istanbul. Over the fifteen years before the Census of 1934, a considerable Turkish emigration occurred, suggesting a very substantial Turkish minority in Bulgaria in the early 1920s. Gypsies, who played a more significant (or at least more visible) role in Yugoslavia, Hungary and Rumania than their small numbers might suggest, comprised the third largest nationality group in Bulgaria, if admittedly at the very low figure of 1.3 per cent of the total. Stronger numerically in Bulgaria than in most other states, the Gypsies were tolerated as a traditional minority, although confined in practice to the lowest-status occupations: road-sweepers and hang-men in Bulgaria, for example, were invariably Gypsies. Jews and Armenians made up much of the remaining minority population. A notable absentee minority was the Greek: by 1934 a Greek colony numbering 50,000 in 1919 had been almost entirely 'repatriated' to Greece under the terms of population transfers under the auspices of the League of Nations. No discussion of the minorities can, however, distract attention from the fact that the Bulgars made up a formidable 86.7 per cent of the population. Given justifiable reservations about the official Hungarian statistics (which are probably not applicable to the Bulgarian), it may be that Bulgaria was the closest of the east European states, despite its more bizarre collection of minorities, to being a nation state.

By comparison with the Magyars, the Bulgars got off lightly: by the highest reputable count, expatriate Bulgars amounted to only 1,000,000, constituting an expatriate-proportion of some 16 per cent. Even so, rough treatment of their minorities outside Bulgaria fortified a rankling sense of injustice at the Neuilly Treaty to keep Bulgar pressure on every frontier insistent and provocative, most especially in Yugoslav Macedonia. Though less dramatic a victim of Versailles than Hungary, Bulgaria was a willing conspirator in manning the revisionist assault on post-1919 eastern Europe.

It is by reference to Hungary and Bulgaria in particular that the double meaning of the term 'minority' is displayed. A national minority might well be both a numerically inferior group within a particular state and a fragment of a numerically dominant group within a different state. Every majority nationality among the states of eastern Europe, from the massive Polish group to the tiny Albanian, had pockets of its people situated outside its own state borders and not subject to its jurisdiction. The attitude to these outposted expatriate minorities in an age of integral nationalism was possessive and obsessive: *all* members of a majority nationality had the right to belong to their own nation state. There were only two means by which geographically separated minorities might be united (or re-united) with their co-nationalists: population transfer and frontier expansion. Population transfer, forcibly depriving a community of the territory it legitimately owned, was universally rejected as a morally iniquitous expedient. Frontier expansion was regarded as the only answer: the single honourable recourse was to extend the borders of the kin state to include all the isolated communities of the majority nationality, despite the certainty of thereby incorporating other national minorities and antagonising *their* kin states.

The nations most obsessed with their outposted minorities were naturally the Magyars and Bulgars (to say nothing of the Germans), with their compulsive sense of grievance, contempt for Versailles and high expatriate-proportions. Hungary was preoccupied from the moment of the Treaty of Trianon with revisionism, expansionism and reunification with its minorities in other states. Many Magyars who found themselves outside Hungary after 1919 either refused to be separated from their fatherland or were effectively expelled from their new host states. The territorially much-reduced Hungary had therefore to accommodate a flood of refugees, which imposed an extra burden on the social and financial resources of Magyar society. The dispossessed Magyars recently transferred to Trianon Hungary were the most embittered of all Magyar nationalists, seeking in state expansion both an outlet for fanatical national commitment and restitution of their own lost fortunes. Dispossessed minorities formed a major social component of the Hungarian fascist movement, and revanchist secret societies like the sinisterly named Society of the Double Cross abounded. In Bulgaria, the same phenomenon occurred, with dispossessed Bulgar minorities from Macedonia and Thrace dominating the rank-and-file of the terrorist IMRO organisation.

Following the orthodox 'organic' view of the nation, Magyar nationalists insisted that, without its minorities, Hungary could not function: the Trianon state was a mutilated torso from which integral parts had been severed in an unprecedented act of international butchery. A victim of multiple amputation, Hungary was at the mercy of its enemies. Every day at school, the children of Hungary chanted the 'Magyar Creed' in unison:

> I believe in one God,
> I believe in one Fatherland,
> I believe in one divine, eternal Truth,
> I believe in the resurrection of Hungary.
> Hungary dismembered is no country,
> Hungary united is Heaven. Amen.[15]

This Magyar commitment to its minorities was shared by Bulgaria and Germany, a trio powerful enough and sufficiently widely distributed to disrupt the new eastern Europe completely. The minorities issue became a prime interface in the continuous confrontation between host and kin states throughout the 1920s and 1930s. The minorities manned the front line in a war of attrition between the two armed camps of eastern Europe, the victims and beneficiaries of the Versailles Settlement.

THE MINOR STATES

So pervasive was the ethnic heterogeneity of eastern European settlement that small size was no guarantee of a state's homogeneity, indeed the minor states of Albania, Estonia, Latvia and Lithuania featured all the nationality problems typical of the larger states. As Table VII shows, the minor states were multi-national political entities, with their proportions of national minorities varying from 11.8 per cent to 26.6 per cent. In Albania, 22.3 per cent of the population were classed as minorities, with Serbs (7.8 per cent), Rumanians (6.6 per cent) and Turks (6.0 per cent) most in evidence. In Estonia, although a substantial 88.2 per cent of the population was Estonian, there was a fair variety of minorities led by the Russians (at 8.5 per cent) and Germans (1.5 per cent). Latvia had the largest minorities problem, with 26.6 per cent of the population non-Latvian, headed once again by the Russians (12.5 per cent) and Germans (3.7 per cent) but also featuring a substantial Jewish minority (at 4.9 per cent). For Lithuania, the minorities' proportion of 16.1 per cent included Jews (7.6 per cent), Poles (3.2 per cent), Russians (2.7 per cent) and Germans (1.4 per cent).[16] Although generally featuring minority populations proportionately slightly lower than the official east European average of 20.1 per cent, the minor states were still mini-empires rather than nation states.

The minor states also followed the pattern of incorporating only a proportion of their majority nationalities within their jurisdictions. Table X demonstrates that Albania was at the very head of the league table for expatriate-proportion, with a massive 44 per cent of Albanians resident outside Albania, perhaps 500,00 in southern Yugoslavia and 200,000 in northern Greece. Some 12.5 per cent of Estonians were situated outside Estonia, mostly in the Soviet Union: it is quite possible that the largest concentration of Estonians was not in the state capital of Tallinn but Leningrad. Latvia incorporated only 88.5 per cent of Latvians, with the bulk of expatriates again within the Soviet Union.[17] Although Lithuania had a relatively low expatriate-proportion (at only 5.5 per cent), the scandalous circumstances of their 'expatriation' generated an almost hysterical nationalism: in October 1920, General Zeligowski occupied the district of Vilna, which was broadly a city with a Polish and Jewish majority within an area with a Lithuanian majority, an arbitrary action condemned by the West but 'legitimised' by the Polish government in March 1922. The result was that almost 70,000 Lithuanians were forcibly incorporated into Poland, a proportion of only 0.3 per cent of the population of the giant Polish state but constituting 70 per cent of Lithuania's expatriates. Exasperated beyond reason by this 'Polish injustice', in January 1923 the Lithuanian government seized the German port of Memel, apparently on the grounds that two wrongs must make it right. Lithuania became simultaneously too big and too small: provocatively deprived of Lithuanian territory and nationals, the state 'acquired' German territory and nationals by way of personal compensation.

The appearance of the majority nationalities of the minor states in the upper half of the table of expatriates (Table X), in the company of the Magyars and Bulgars, would suggest a marked discontent with the territory bestowed at Versailles. Although all the minor states were beneficiaries of Versailles in the sense of securing Allied blessing and support, they exhibited features which emphasised their instability. All shared the national problems of the larger east European states while being demonstrably too small to be politically, economically or militarily viable. The four minor states could barely muster 6,000,000 inhabitants between them, a demographic fact which made the glowering proximity of giants like Yugoslavia, Poland and above all the Soviet Union massively intimidating. Although none of the various minorities within the minor states was harshly treated, the identity of the minorities increased the majority's sense of foreboding. In Albania, the presence of the Serb and Greek communities always implied the possibility of territorial expansion by the Yugoslav or Greek states to incorporate all their ethnic membership, if necessary through the liquidation of Albania. In the Baltic States, the ubiquitous incidence of Russian and German communities, local representatives of the two powers which had in the past always determined the fate of the area, seemed to symbolise the external threat. Although the Baltic Germans were on the decline, steadily abandoning their traditional settlements to emigrate to Germany, the Russian minorities were increasing in demographic strength and political awareness, indicating the immediacy of the threat from the east.

That the minor states survived for some two decades was the product of fortuitous but essentially ephemeral circumstances. Albania could play off Yugoslavia, Greece and Italy against each other in self-protection for a time, but in the gloomy fear that sooner or later it would fall victim to at least one of its ambitious neighbours. The Baltic States built upon their natural advantages of relatively advanced economies and ready geographical access to the West by exploiting the collapse of Russian jurisdiction and later withdrawal of German authority during the First World War, but the Soviet Union and Germany could not realistically be expected to tolerate the independent existence of such defenceless valuable properties for very long. The political Balkanisation so feared by the Allies at Paris in 1919 perversely came closest to implementation not in the Balkans but on the Baltic, with all the impracticalities of territorial fragmentation anticipated but without compensatory ethnic rewards. With all the problems of viability associated with smallness of scale compounded by characteristic minority problems, the minor states of eastern Europe were patently the most vulnerable of all.

THE RUSSIAN BORDERLANDS

If the official attitude to national minorities on the part of the minor states always reflected the majority nationality's apprehensiveness about long-term survival, the policy towards minorities within the Soviet Union was increasingly tailored to the exigencies of future expansionism. With every cloud supposed to have a silver lining, the Soviet Union discovered that the solace of losing enormous tracts of its western borderlands to the new states of Poland, Rumania, Latvia, Lithuania and Estonia during the territorial debacle of 1917–21 was the substantial diminution of its minorities problem. While the Romanov Empire was only 44.3 per cent Russian in 1897, the Soviet Union was 58.4 per cent Russian in early 1939 (before the partition of Poland with Germany reduced that proportion again).[18] What the Soviet Union had lost in territory was at least partly compensated by a 14 per cent strengthening of Russian domination to a comfortable majority level which would have been the envy of the tsars and certainly endowed the Soviet government with a self-confidence over questions of nationality which was apparent in their treatment of all their European minorities.

This is not to say that the Soviet Union rested content with its territorial shrinkage. The doctrine of international communism and world revolution, of which the Soviet Union was the principal trustee, stipulated the overthrow of the capitalist states of eastern Europe and the induction of their populations into the idealistic campaign of the Russian people for universal emancipation. At the level of national-ism, a phenomenon increasingly viewed less as a force hostile to communism than as a useful ploy in the practical promotion of socialism, the Soviet Union advanced major claims disruptive to the new eastern Europe. Table X shows that while the Russian nation had almost 1,000,000 expatriates within the states of Poland, Rumania, Bulgaria and the Baltic, the enormous size of the Russian total resulted in an expatriate-proportion of only 1 per cent, among the lowest in eastern Europe. With their expatriate minorities offering little cause for the disruption of the present political settlement, the Russians could lay claim to east European territory only either through the supra-national appeal of communism or as patrons of their own partitioned minorities. The Belorussian and Ukrainian expatriate-proportions were respectively 20 per cent and 17 per cent (a total of 6,000,000 people), among the highest in eastern Europe, providing a nationalist justification for the Soviet Union's antagon-ism towards Poland, Rumania and Czechoslovakia. Employing nationalism as an expansionist strategem, the Soviet Union favoured its borderland minorities and, in particular, the unification under Soviet authority of the Ukrainian and Belorussian nations.

Anxious to project the most favourable image of Soviet nationality policy in the interests of 'recruitment', the revolutionary Commis-sariat of Nationalities (or *Narkomnats*) was replaced within the new Soviet Constitution in July 1923 by a separate Soviet of Nationalities. A voluntary federation of national units with varying status levels – Union Republics, Autonomous Republics and Autonomous Regions – was proclaimed, intended as a shop window for the Leninist doctrine of Self-Determination. The Soviet Socialist Republics of Belorussia and the Ukraine, both formally enjoying full sovereignty independent of Moscow, were established with maximum publicity. In reality, the shop window was more like window dressing. To quote the authoritative judgement of Richard Pipes.

From the point of view of self-rule, the Communist government was even less generous to the minorities than its tsarist predecessor had been: it destroyed independent parties, tribal self-rule, religious and cultural institutions. It was a unitary, centralised totalitarian state such as the tsarist state had never been. On the other hand, by granting the minorities extensive linguistic autonomy and by placing the national-territorial principle at the base of the state's political administration, the Communists gave constitutional recognition to the multi-national structure of the Soviet population.[19]

The formula 'National in Form, Socialist in Content' proved both an encouragment to minority self-consciousness and a denial of any subsequent ambitions for political nationalism.

Throughout the 1920s, vitually all the Soviet minorities were disposed to think kindly of their Russian masters. If the Polish Partitions of the late eighteenth century presented Russia with its Jewish problem, the early-twentieth-century recreation of Poland halved the problem for the Soviet Union. Now only 1.8 per cent of the population (as against 4.0 per cent in 1897), the Jews received infinitely less maltreatment than under the last tsars. Although still settled mainly in the ex-Pale area of Russia – 5.4 per cent of the population of the Ukrainian Soviet Socialist Republic and 8.2 per cent of the Belorussian Republic were Jewish in early 1941 – official attempts were made both to integrate the Jewish population into Soviet society and to cater for its new-found ambition for territory by establishing a Jewish Autonomous Region in Birobidzhan in the Soviet Far East.

The Germans, who now constituted 0.8 per cent of the total population as against 1.4 per cent in 1897, had borne up well under the demoralising effect of mass emigration and a local antagonism natural in time of war between Russia and Germany. Granted its own territorial units in the mid-1920s, most notably the Volga German Autonomous Republic in 1924, the German minority was permitted to develop its own cultural self-consciousness, including the promotion of a Soviet German press.

For the nationalities partitioned between the Soviet Union and the Successor States, Soviet treatment was even more indulgent. By the terms of the 1921 Treaty of Riga, Belorussia was divided into a Soviet Belorussian Republic containing some 4,000,000 people and a region of eastern Poland housing about 1,000,000. With 80 per cent of the

Belorussian population within its jurisdiction, the Soviet Union set out to undermine Poland by recommending itself to the 20 per cent expatriate minority. Both states competed to shower the Belorussians with kindnesses to guarantee border security, a tactical exercise from which Belorussian nationalists were content to benefit. A crash literacy programme was combined with official patronage of Belorussianism in the Soviet Republic in an attempt to out-bid the Polish government. For perhaps the first time, it seemed that Belorussia's location between Russia and Poland might be exploited to its own advantage, with the hope of creating a nation out of a nationality.

A similar happy experience faced the Ukrainians. The loss of significant numbers of Ukrainians to the Successor States – 4,000,000 to Poland, 500,000 to Czechoslovakia and 333,000 to Rumania – meant that some 5,000,000 lay outside the Soviet Union after 1921 and some 25,000,000 within. With jurisdiction over 83 per cent of the Ukrainian population, the Soviet Union once again planned to undermine the east European *cordon sanitaire* by ostentatiously generous treatment of the Ukraine. Over the 1920s, cultural nationalism in the Ukraine developed apace. Even the veteran Mikhail Hrushevsky, the patriarch of Ukrainian nationalism and the president of the Rada in 1918, was persuaded to return from foreign exile to lead the movement for cultural and social progress. The effect of Soviet benevolence towards its Ukrainians was to convince the expatriate minorities within Poland, Czechoslovakia and Rumania of their identities as Ukrainians rather than just Ruthenes and to engage their allegiances to a degree which could only be detrimental to their host states.

The Soviet Union's victory in the battle for the hearts and minds of the Belorussians and Ukrainians in the 1920s confirmed the governments of Poland, Rumania and (to a lesser extent) Czechoslovakia in their determination to abandon toleration for these minorities and switch over to integral nationalism. Having successfully outbid its rivals, the Soviet Union could afford to follow suit, cancelling its earlier concessions in the course of the 1930s. Like the Poles, the Russians became alarmed that the cultural nationalism that they promoted as a weapon against others might well be turned against themselves. The Kremlin feared that the Leninist policy might be turned on its head as ambitious minorities achieved a situation which was 'Socialist in Form, National in Content'. Far from converting minorities to communism, generous treatment showed clear signs of backfiring on the Soviet Union.

Even minorities which presented no demographic or strategic threat came under increasing attack. The Jews experienced a steady re-assertion of traditional anti-semitic discrimination, especially in the light of the failure of the Soviet Jewish homeland of Birobidzhan to attract more than a tiny proportion of the Jewish population. The Germans of central European Russia, industrious peasant farmers almost to a man, resisted the agrarian collectivisation implemented after 1928. As a result, perhaps 50,000 were exiled to Siberia, a disproportionately high figure for a small, and now very chastened, minority of only some 1,250,000 people.

Predictably, the volte-face in Soviet minorities policy was most marked with regard to the Belorussians and Ukrainians. In Soviet Belorussia, the whole national leadership was purged and later executed as either 'bourgeois nationalists' or (most commonly) 'Polish spies'. To quote the opinion of Vakar, 'the wholesale purge which began in 1929 and continued far into 1933 was immeasurably more ruthless than anything the Belorussian nationalists had ever experienced in Poland'[20] Belorussian culture was officially ridiculed and proscribed, censorship was universally imposed. Coinciding with the wider collectivisation campaign, the suppression of Belorussian cultural and political nationalism in the 1930s left the local population materially impoverished and emotionally demoralised. In 1938, Belorussian was officially redefined as neither a political nor cultural identity, nor even a separate language but only 'a dialect of Russian'.

In the Soviet Ukraine, an official campaign against 'national deviationism' gathered momentum over the same period. Purges of the nationalist intelligentsia culminated in the expulsion of Hrushevsky and the imprisonment of all collaborators on the prestigious academic journal *Ukraïna*. Once again, it was no coincidence that the nationality purges were contemporaneous with the collectivisation purges. Over the 1920s, the Ukraine had grown prosperous, developing far more than its share of the *kulak* class which benefited so dramatically from the New Economic Policy in operation from 1921 to 1928. With more to lose from collectivisation than elsewhere, the Ukraine became the principal arena of confrontation between central authority and local private enterprise. As a direct result, in the judgement of John Armstrong, Ukrainians formed a 'disproportionate, if not predominant part of the hopeless millions deported as "kulaks" to Siberia'.[21] As with Belorussian, Ukrainian was denied first a political, then a cultural and finally even a linguistic separate identity. By the late 1930s, Ukrainians had been deprived of all their early privileges and were firmly reduced to the position of subordinate minority within the Soviet Union.

The territorial shrinkage of the Romanov Empire, 44.3 per cent Russian and 73 per cent Slav, into the Soviet Union, 58.4 per cent Russian and 78 per cent Slav, strengthened the demographic dominance of the Russian establishment. In the 1920s, a combination of residual respect for socialist principle and an appreciation of the tactical advantages of concession persuaded the Soviet government to permit, often to foster, the cultural nationalism of its minorities. Disillusionment for these minorities came with the 1930s, when a blend of administrative centralisation (not to say dictatorship), fear of national disintegration and a burgeoning Russian integral nationalism induced the Stalinist establishment to withdraw all the benefits distributed so lavishly a decade before. The Soviet Union was not as imperviously sealed behind its border as has often been suggested and was susceptible to the trend towards integral nationalism sweeping all the east European states and aware of the expansionist opportunities presented by the expatriate minority populations immediately beyond its ephemeral European frontier. Never having set its signature to the Versailles Settlement, the Soviet Union had no allegiance to the new eastern Europe. Having lost considerable territory as the result of a settlement imposed at a time of uncharacteristic weakness, the Soviet Union could be included in the revisionist camp together with Hungary, Bulgaria and Germany. As the Soviet Union, like Germany, recovered much of its former vigour by the 1930s, the imperial and expansionist traditions reasserted themselves. Throughout eastern Europe, whether in the Soviet Union or the Successor States, the position of the national minorities came under mounting threat.

HOPES INTO FEARS

All too soon the hopes of the 1920s were replaced by the fears of the 1930s. Although the Versailles Settlement created the new phenomenon of the 'national majority' in eastern Europe, any hope that majorities might foster stability and toleration quickly evaporated. The hybrid nature of the new states – neither empires with experienced dominant-minority leadership nor nation states without external or internal minorities – only exacerbated the national problem. Promoted beyond their immediate abilities by the cataclysmic First World War, the new majority nationalities were chronically insecure, over-ambitious and unconscionably competitive. A feature shared by all the east European states was an obsessive territorial acquisitiveness, a pastime compulsive not only for the rewards of extra land it might earn, a symbol of national virility, but for the intensity of majority nationalism generated. The very novelty of territorial repartition, the natural hypersensitivity of new states about their sovereignty and the imperfect implementation of the principle of national self-determination all served to put the beneficiaries of Versailles on the defensive and the 'victims of Versailles' on the offensive over their minorities. Although the scale of the minority problem in eastern Europe was halved by Versailles, the investment of nationalist emotion on the part of the new majorities and the raised (but frustrated) expectations of the one-quarter of the population which were still minorities made the issue more explosive than ever.

Within most of the new states, the style of government which was to become typical was established within five years of Versailles; only in the Soviet Union was a hardening of official attitudes towards minorities delayed until the 1930s. By the mid-1920s, most minorities could recognise the future pattern of treatment by the host state wished upon them at Versailles. 'Penetration', the degree to which government impinges on society, was strongly promoted by the First World War, leaving all post-war establishments with greater ambitions for the integration or liquidation of minorities than the dynastic empires had entertained. The desire of majority nationalities to convert their present heterogeneous multi-national states into future monolithic nation states was universal, with only the exigencies of individual circumstances moderating the application of integral nationalism. The pre-war dynastic empires had been content with passive acquiescence from their minorities; the post-war states demanded positive commitment. The general trend towards integral nationalism not only exploded the hopes of the remaining minorities for more understanding from the new 'majority states' but subjected them to worse treatment than they had suffered under the dynastic empires.

The political trend of the 1920s was confirmed and accentuated by economic disaster. The Wall Street Crash of late 1929 and the long

Depression that followed hit eastern Europe very hard. The substantial economic progress achieved during the 1920s was everywhere halted and in some cases almost wiped out. To the minorities, who had been excluded from their proper share of the past benefits of prosperity, the Depression was less of a shock, even though the economies of minority areas generally suffered most. To the majority nationalities, becoming almost complacent after a decade of growing prosperity and rising prospects, the deflation of their excessively inflated hopes prompted a major crisis of morale. As with all scenarios featuring the dashing of raised expectations, the unexpected gap between what were regarded as legitimate aspirations and the hard reality favoured political extremism of both the left and right. With the economy floundering, unemployment in an already overpopulated environment rose to unprecedented levels, undermining the stability of society and furnishing a volatile, potentially explosive element which threatened to burst the bonds of conventional social control.

As the unemployed masses increased and the prospects for employment decreased, the majority nationality typically demanded priority over minorities in the job market. At its simplistic worst, the majority nationality secured full employment through a jobs monopoly, condeming the minorities to languish in universal unemployment. The social consequence was for the minorities, already politically harassed, to become increasingly desperate and frustrated, often attracted to extremist solutions which they had scorned in earlier periods of relative prosperity. On the other side, the more-employed and better-employed majority nationalities condemned the minorities as parasites and took to enquiring rhetorically of one another just how long they were expected to maintain these idlers by their own honest toil. The Depression worsened relations between majorities and minorities, reinforced pejorative national stereotypes and fostered violence and extremism as solutions where consensus and negotiation had demonstrably failed. The gross effect was to weaken all eastern Europe in relation to the Great Powers, putting its economic viability at risk and making poor majority-minority relations even worse.

Traditional options offered ever-dwindling relief to the oppressed minorities. The 'fight option' continued its decline. After 1919 all the new armies of eastern Europe played the same, essentially conventional role: to employ compulsory universal conscription to impose the new state identity, encourage a sense of solidarity, blur internal divisions and assimilate minorities. The indispensability of the peacetime army as an instrument of social control and manipulation was generally recognised as a technique of the past empires which was even more appropriate in new states whose political legitimacy was far from universally accepted. Although mass conscription offered some genuine opportunities to backward national minorities for advancement, the new armies were overwhelmingly the military, social and even political bastions of the majority nationality of the state. The prospects for 'fight' by national minorities were even less realistic under integral nationalism than under empire.

'Flight' was, as ever, a useful crude indicator of mass attitudes towards the status quo in eastern Europe. In the first years after Versailles, the traditional pattern of substantial emigration from eastern Europe in both westerly and easterly directions was actually reversed. On the eastern border, a vast population movement of refugees fleeing the economic breakdown of Russia (which claimed 5,000,000 deaths by starvation in 1921–3 alone) and the Bolshevik 'Red Terror' flooded into the other Slav states of Poland, Czechoslovakia and Yugoslavia in particular. From the west came an influx of emigrants returning from America. Migrants in America often combined an extravagant nostalgia for their homelands with a hard-nosed Yankee drive which made them welcome additions to the Successor States. The new states needed teachers, administrators, architects, lawyers, generals, bankers, industrialists, entrepreneurs and politicians for their new personnel establishment. The American-trained individual of east European birth or extraction was presented with a unique opportunity to combine nationalism and personal advancement. Emigrants of new majority nationalities, notably the Poles and Czechs, were most susceptible to the appeal of the east European states after 1919. Immigration into eastern Europe from east and west was an expression of preference, an indication of hope and confidence in a new society.[22]

Emigration never stopped, although it altered in volume, nature and direction. The most significant single event in east European migration occured half a world away: from 1921, the United States introduced a progressively more restrictive quota system for immigration. Although the system was based upon the current migrant population of the United States and therefore favoured immigrants from nationalities which had loomed large in the past (like many in eastern Europe), the quotas were not high enough to satisfy the demand. Contrary to conventional wisdom, the First World War did not ease the overpopulation of eastern Europe: since the war caused proportionately more damage to the material resources of the area than to its inhabitants, overpopulation actually increased despite the widespread human casualties. Population pressure was therefore mounting when America effectively brought an end to mass immigration. All east European emigration had now to operate at a reduced volume and divert from America, whose 'Open Door' was now barely ajar, to more hospitable destinations.

The new most popular destination, partly because of traditional links, mostly because its own traumatic experience of the First World War had created a manpower shortage more acute than anywhere else in Europe, was France. Migration to France was much less permanent than it had been to America. The geographical proximity of France to eastern Europe encouraged the Poles in particular to seek work in the West but to return home whenever finances permitted. The French government too played its part, employing foreign labour whenever necessary but showing no compunction about either giving its own nationals preferential treatment or expelling immigrants if they became redundant or troublesome. The overall migration pattern soon reverted to its traditional pre-war pattern: the excess population of Soviet Europe was channelled once more into Siberia, some willingly, others (like the victims of the collectivisation purges) involuntarily; the excess in independent eastern Europe attempted to flow west. Emigration to America dwindled for reasons of deliberate exclusion rather than a decline in either 'push' or 'pull' factors, and was only partly compensated by a more local ebb-and-flow between eastern and western Europe.[23]

Emigration did represent a practical, voting-with-the-feet plebiscite on the new order in eastern Europe. The majority nationalities' short-term but heavy traffic demonstrated both general commitment to 'their' states and resignation to those states' economic limitations. Like the dominant nationalities of the Balkan states before 1914, the new majority nationalities after 1919 viewed emigration not as a permanent escape but as a technique for the survival and enrichment of their nation states.

As in the nineteenth century, the minorities continued to be highest in the proportionate emigration statistics and more likely to be permanent emigrants. For example, while the loss through emigration from Poland in the inter-war period was almost 500,000 Poles (about 2.5 per cent of the Polish population), it was almost 100,000 Belorussians (or some 10 per cent of the Belorussian population). Similarly, although Croats made up only 25 per cent of the population of inter-war Yugoslavia, Croat emigrants constituted some 60 per cent of the Yugoslav total. Again, the Jewish minority in Poland had an emigration rate five times the national average, although the effect of the American quota legislation was to reduce the pre-war flood to a trickle and divert it into Zionism: the Zionist prayer 'Next Year in Jerusalem' became a chorus only because of the unavailability of 'Next Year in New York'. The traditionally high participation of minorities in available emigrant activity was confirmed from the early 1920s, demonstrating that their allegiances had not been engaged by new states in which they were all too often the victims of the integral nationalism of the majorities. The majority nationalities may have emigrated out of hope; the minorities, as ever, emigrated out of despair and fear.[24]

A final conclusion on 'flight' must be that the reduced and diverted emigration of the 1920s and 1930s was even less an answer to the problems of east European society than before 1914. The emigrant safety-valve had barely functioned in the nineteenth century and with rural overpopulation (actually heightened by the First World War) outstripping the ability of the expanding east European economies to absorb it, the demographic situation went from bad to worse. The fatalistic lesson seemed to be that neither war nor emigration provided effective safety-valves, let alone solutions, to over-population. At the same time, the increasing unavailability of emigrant outlets, by rendering the safety-valve concept anachronistic, lent a certain inevitability in the popular imagination to the prospect of another war.

Exaggerated hopes for the 'New Europe' were cruelly dashed after 1919: the national majorities were encouraged in the 1920s only to be disillusioned by the 1930s; the minorities were frustrated in the 1920s and embittered by the 1930s. The deteriorating relations between national majorities and minorities were symptomatic of, and con-tributory to, a deeper malaise in east European society which could only be resolved by another war more terrible than the last.

7. War and the Minorities

THE conventional wisdom is that no-one benefits from wars, and especially not minorities. The Jewish Holocaust is always cited as unanswerable proof for the most sceptical, should evidence be needed, that it is the ordinary, the weak and above all the innocent who suffer most in war. In reality, the historical record of the impact of war upon national minorities has been extraordinarily mixed, sometimes proving unexpectedly advantageous, occasionally inflicting damage literally unthinkable in peacetime. The Jewish experience of attempted genocide should not automatically be assumed as typical of the wartime treatment of minorities, even by the Nazis in the Second World War. A more objective coverage of the many national minorities in eastern Europe over the century after 1848 shows war as complex, ambivalent and downright contradictory a phenomenon of human society as peace, with a similar paradoxical crop of national survivors and fatalities, winners and losers.

VICTIMS OF WAR

The very geographical location of the minorities has condemned them to regular and occasionally catastrophic damage in wartime. The natural centrifugal expansion of state development outwards from the heartland of the dominant nationality means that national minorities tend to be situated on the peripheries of multi-national states. As a direct result, the outbreak of hostilities between states is bound to affect the minorities first and (very probably) most. The moment when the victorious state incorporates all its enemy's minorities and threatens the enemy heartland is very often the time for surrender or negotiation in order to spare the dominant nationality heavy casualties. In this geopolitical sense, national minorities are often 'natural victims' in wars between larger nations and states.

Eastern Europe has always, moreover, constituted a power vacuum attracting invasion from east and west. In two world wars, the dominant continental powers of Germany and Russia have argued, fought and even struck deals over the bodies of the inhabitants of interposing eastern Europe. The Romanov Empire, arriving historically relatively late upon the scene after its 'Mongol Captivity', was eager to acquire eastern Europe's economically valuable resources and the strategic access to the open sea which its occupation guaranteed. Deprived of a warm-water port with unrestricted access to the wider world, Russia exhibited a claustrophobic geopolitical urge to possess eastern Europe both for what it was and for where it led. Germany's interest went much further back in time. As early as the tenth century, Saxon bishops were urging their flocks to 'go East':

> The Slavs are abominable people but their land is very rich in flesh, honey, grain, birds and abounding in all produce of fertility of the earth when cultivated, so that none can compare with it . . . . Wherefore, O Franks, Saxons, Lotharingians, men of Flanders most famous, here you can both save your souls and, if it please you, acquire the best land to live in.[1]

This early expression of the *Drang nach Osten*, the colonising German drive to the east, almost uncannily contains the component of racial contempt for the Slavs which was to infuse the *Lebensraum* (living-space) doctrine of the twentieth century. Motivated by a concept which retained its appeal almost unchanged for a millennium, the Germans penetrated eastern Europe to establish colonies for century upon century. In both world wars, Germany established east European empires, one lasting only a few months in 1918, the other surviving a few years in the early 1940s, which realised ambitions so deep-rooted as to be almost instinctive. When two states which by the late nineteenth century dominated continental Europe both claimed the same territory as their rightful estate, the prospects for the population of the property could only be gloomy.

As an inevitable battle zone between ambitious Powers and also a territorial prize on which Germany and Russia had set their sights, eastern Europe could only be the loser. In the First World War, the front line between the Central Powers and Russia shifted steadily across Poland and Rumania over 1915 and 1916, passed the Baltic provinces in 1917 and traversed the whole of the Ukraine by 1918. The physical damage, economic dislocation and loss of life to the indigenous population of mainly minority nationalities was enormous. The some 3,250,000 direct casualties of the First World War in eastern Europe were subsequently eclipsed by the 22,000,000 casualties of the Second World War. A speedier German and Soviet takeover of eastern Europe spared the local populations high war casualties over 1939–40 but not the ferocious Nazi and Soviet occupation regimes nor the casualties of the German retreat through eastern Europe before the Red Army over 1944–5. The collapse in public services precipitated by the world wars often claimed more lives than the hostilities themselves: over the decade 1914–23 'only' 2,000,000 Russians died in the First World War but an astonishing 14,000,000 may have died in the Civil War and its attendant disease and famine. With one-half of the population before 1914 and one-quarter after 1919 counting as national minorities, eastern Europe was in a real sense the 'innocent victim' of the two world wars.[2]

It can also be argued that the very numerical inferiority of minorities increases their 'natural wartime vulnerability. With the growing modern weaponry potential for mass destruction, minorities are proportionately at greater risk of major demographic damage than majorities. At its most apocalyptic, a single atomic bomb could inflict damage on a small national minority amounting to complete genocide, an action which a larger group would survive through greater numbers and wider territorial settlement. In April 1941, for example, German bombing of Yugoslavia destroyed Zemun, the Gypsy quarter of Belgrade, destroying in one day a substantial proportion of the Yugoslav Gypsy population. Although the German 'Operation Punishment' was aimed at the Serbs not the Gypsies, the incidental – even accidental – effect of an unlucky coincidence of wartime bombing on a compact minority settlement was disproportionately destructive to the Gypsy community.

In wartime, certain human phenomena surfaced which regularly affected minorities only, reinforcing their claim to be considered as particular victims of war. One was the suspicion of a minority being actively or passively treacherous to the host state. The kind of patriotic fever which induced phlegmatic Englishmen in 1915 to kick dachshunds for being German easily led to a nationalist hysteria which seems almost incomprehensible in retrospect but was commonly the reaction of a populace frustrated at its inability to serve the war effort. It was at the very beginning of wars (when patriotism acted as an intoxicant) and at the times when wars were going badly (and society needed an anti-depressant) that majority hysteria was likely to vent itself on a minority. At its most elemental, the public mood made no attempt even to concoct a charge against a minority, still less to prove the accusation: a scapegoat was required, or a whipping-boy on whom to expend rage and frustration.

The Jews involuntarily filled this role (as so frequently) in Russia during the First World War. Anti-semitic organisations like the Black Hundreds had been intensifying their campaign for a 'solution' to the Jewish problem well before 1914 and the war itself, especially when Russia suffered alarming and ignominious reverses in 1915, reinforced the peacetime prejudice. To add point to the traditional charges, accusations of treason were now levelled: stories of Jews signalling to German troops and acting as Habsburg spies were legion. What added poignancy to the *canards* was that, of all Romanov minorities, the Jews lost most from Russia's retreat. As the Central powers advanced through the 'Vistula Provinces', the evacuating Russian military authorities expelled the Jews from the war zone on suspicion of espionage. The Pale of Settlement leaked like a colander as tens of thousands of Jewish refugees flocked eastward to seek even temporary refuge from the Germans at their backs and the Russians all around. The Romanov Jews simultaneously were the greatest victims of the enemy advance and held responsible for Russian defeat. with such uncharitable inconsistency of logic on the part of the dominant nationality, nothing the Jews did – or omitted to do – made any difference to their treatment. In the emotional circumstances of wartime rout in Russia, the Jewish minority was cast in its traditional role of scapegoat.

That victimisation of a harmless minority is a predictable (if lamentable) majority reaction under stress may be observed in the Second World War too. In a sense, the Jewish minority was resorted to as the Russian whipping-boy in the First World War because of the limited availability of the most obvious target. Within a Russia at war with Germany, it was natural that resident Germans were most suspect. A law of 1916 against 'German influence' projected a mass expulsion of Germans from the Volga region in April 1917, an action only forestalled by the fall of tsarism. In the Second World War, with the success of 'Operation Barbarossa', the German invasion of the Soviet Union launched in June 1941, Stalin ordered the physical transportation to Siberia of all Soviet citizens with German connections. It would seem that the entire German population of European Russia, numbering some 1,400,000 people, was transported in a massive transfer over August 1941. Although almost all the Germans in the Soviet Union had been resident for many generations, their allegiance was considered sufficiently suspect to justify mass deportation as 'a precautionary security measure'. Later in 1943–4, six minor nationalities from southern Russia and the Caucasus were also deported, allegedly for actual collaboration with the occupying German forces.

The Russian 'victimisation' of suspect minorities shows a definite progression between the First and Second World Wars. Much of the harassment of the Jews after 1915 was fundamentally unorchestrated, more the social consequences of military events over which the tsarist government had little control than deliberate tsarist strategy. However the tsarist ambition to build upon its experience of sponsorship of mass emigration to Siberia to move on to forcible transfer of a national minority was plain from its policy towards the Volga Germans, even if unrealised. What the tsars planned but were unable to achieve was effected by Stalin. Twenty-five years after revolution saved the Volga Germans, the power of state intervention had developed to the point when mass deportation could be undertaken at a time when the *Wehrmacht* was battering at the gates of Moscow and Leningrad. The transfers of 1941–4 were enormous logistical exercises conducted in the midst of the most catastrophic war ever to involve Russia by a government whose nerve was shaken but whose resolve and resources were unscathed. A new dimension was opening up for the 'solution' of the minorities issue in eastern Europe.

A more positive use to which national minorities were put by the state in wartime was as cannon-fodder. By employing minority nationality troops at the front and keeping majority or dominant minority troops in reserve, the state was certain to benefit. At best, military victory was won with little blood shed by the dominant nationality, while the commensurately greater casualties suffered by minority troops reduced the scale of the minorities problem within the state. At worst, if victory was not achieved and majority troops were fruitlessly invested, the lack of military success was still compensated to some degree by the improvement in the demographic dominance of the leading nationality. The early, frequent and preferably exclusive employment of minority troops rapidly became a standard wartime tactic: victory should always carry a double significance; defeat need never be total.

The Habsburgs employed the Croats, long organised on military lines to combat threats to imperial security, most consistently against both domestic rebels (like the Italians in 1848 and 1859, and the Magyars in 1848–9) and external enemies (notably the Serbs, Rumanians and Italians over 1914–18). But it was the Soviet Union during the 'Great Patriotic War' of 1941–5 that furnished the clearest examples of the Machiavellian technique of deliberate over-investment of minority troops. The unfortunate Far Eastern and Central Asian regiments were most frequently employed against the German advance: aside from politico-demographic considerations, their alien culture and language made fraternisation or surrender to the Germans almost literally impossible. At a time when Stalin was deeply concerned at the incidence of mass desertion to the enemy by Red Army personnel, the Asian troops were the least susceptible and therefore ideal front-line regiments.

More sophisticated and nationally aware groups were occasionally provoked into protest or even mutiny by such callous treatment. When in late 1941 an army was raised from Polish detainees on Soviet territory, Stalin attempted to employ this hastily gathered 'Polish Legion' immediately at the front, where the Red Army was hard pressed. Repeating essentially the same argument that Napoleon had used almost 150 years before, Stalin asserted that Polish freedom had to be earned by valour on the battlefield. In 1942 however, the attempted manipulation of the Polish Legion proved unsuccessful: the Polish commander General Anders refused to allow his new army to be cajoled into military suicide. After a long stalemate, Anders's obstinacy paid off: the Polish Legion was transferred over 1943 via Persia to the West, where its fighting performance was soon put to the test but appreciated without being unduly exploited.

It would be unhistorical to suggest that in wartime national minorities were exclusively the victims of cynical Great Powers: rival nationalities were often quite as deadly. The unfortunate Serbs, who suffered so heavily in the First World War, fared no better in the

Second, though at different hands. The antagonism between Serbs and Croats, far from calmed by the *Sporazum* of 1939, reached its bloody climax in the early 1940s when the fascist *Ustasha* movement declared a 'holy war' of 'purification' on all non-Croats. The fortunes of war reversed the peacetime Serb domination over a Croat minority in Yugoslavia to establish Croat dominance over a Serb minority within the Italian client state of Croatia. The result was a bloodbath of 'revenge' wreaked by one member of the South Slav family on another. Of the 2,300,000 military and civilian casualties of the Second World War suffered in the Mediterranean area, probably 1,800,000 were lost in Yugoslavia, the majority in the internecine civil war between Croats and Serbs. The ferocity of the *Ustashi* of Ante Pavelić in systematically liquidating Serbs and Gypsies in their jurisdiction invites comparison with the bloodiest acts of the Second World War.[3]

Even so, despite notorious instances of minorities taking advantage of the disruptions of wartime to settle old scores, the Great Powers were still the most likely to victimise the smaller nationalities. The principal combatants were always prepared to accept (and often to cause) high casualties among minority nationalities on the expedient argument that the cause of the majority 'outvoted' lesser considerations. The Soviet attitude to the Poles in the Second World War comes under this heading. In September 1939, the Germans and Russians partitioned Poland, spending the next eighteen months destroying the Polish nationalist leadership on their respective sides of the territorial divide. After the German invasion of the Soviet Union, Stalin suddenly needed the Poles he had so recently repressed. The acutest embarrassment was caused in spring 1943 when the Germans discovered in the Katyn Forest near Smolensk the grisly evidence of a Soviet massacre of over 4000 Polish officers and other leaders of society three years before. All the inmates of the Kozielsk camp for Polish detainees had been consigned to a mass grave at Katyn. Another 10,000 inmates of the Ostashkov and Starobielsk camps were likewise never heard of again and must be assumed to have met their 'Katyn' elsewhere in Russia. All the available evidence points to the cold-blooded Soviet liquidation of some 14,000 prominent Poles, considered an actual or potential threat to Soviet domination of Poland, an action described by Louis Fitzgibbon as 'the worst crime against prisoners-of-war ever committed and perhaps the worst single unpunished crime in history'.[4]

However in the eastern Europe of the Nazi 'New Order', practical considerations – even the merciless power politics which dictated the Katyn Massacre – were increasingly subordinated to the fanatical ideology of racial destiny, a preoccupation which accounted for more deliberate and widespread outrages against national minorities than ever before. In the course of the 1930s, Hitler and his ideological specialist Alfred Rosenberg developed racial prejudice into a complex and mystical strategy for the future of Europe based upon the premise that race created a natural hierarchy which predetermined the career of every nationality. The behaviour of nationalities was of secondary importance: biological predestination not political self-determination decided the fate of a nation. Nazi ideology insisted that nationality automatically marked out the individual for pre-determined treatment: responsibility and privilege for the Germans at one extreme, mass extermination for the Gypsies and Jews at the other.

The position of the Gypsies was deteriorating alarmingly long before the Nazis conquered eastern Europe. The diffused nature of their distribution, too stubbornly peripatetic to be called 'settlement', prevented the Gypsies ever having the demographic weight to influence a host state. The concomitants of Gypsy nomadic culture and strict endogamous tradition were commonly educational backwardness and material deprivation. There is a plausible link between the struggle for the Balkan heartland of Macedonia, the last territory to be partitioned between the new nation states, and the growing vulnerability of the Gypsies, who were now deprived of what had traditionally served as their refuge from persecution elsewhere (and therefore came closest to a Gypsy homeland).[5] Composed not of a single homogeneous nationality but a spectrum of distinctive *vitsi* or tribes, the Gypsies found that internal disunity further weakened their chances of avoiding ethnocide or even genocide. (Before the 1930s, the commonest cause of Gypsy deaths was not *gadjo* enmity but inter-tribal vendettas.) By the 1920s however, the attitudes of the sedentarised east European nationalities to the Gypsies were hardening: in 1927, for example, a group of Gypsies was brought to trial in Slovakia on a charge of cannibalism, a traditional slur last formally entertained in the time of Josef II in 1782.

Nazi inclinations were for quite literally liquidating the problem from the start: as early as 1933 an SS study recommended drowning the Gypsies at sea! From 1936 a Racial Hygiene and Population Biology Research Unit was considering the options for a 'final solution' of the Gypsy issue. In 1937, new legislation condemned 'asocials', defined as 'those who by anti-social behaviour, *even if they have committed no crime*, have shown that they do not wish to fit into society'. This general warrant for persecution was made specific in 1938 when a Decree on the Fight against the Gypsy Menace was passed. Dachau and then Buchenwald became the leading concentration camps for Gypsies. At this stage, deportation to such destinations as Abyssinia and Polynesia was still considered the only practical policy and, in the meantime, Poland was designated as a general dumping-ground for Gypsies and all other racial undesirables. A policy of mass sterilisation, the tacit toleration of the present generation in return for the forcible prevention of another, marked a new phase in the escalation of Nazi terror. Once the 'Euthanasia Programme' proved viable, particularly with the first gas-chambers proving their efficiency in autumn 1941, the switch to an official policy of mass extermination was agreed in mid-1942. In December 1942 came the order from Heinrich Himmler claiming jurisdiction over all Gypsies in German-dominated Europe and consigning most to the gas-chambers of Auschwitz.

Just why the Gypsies were singled out for victimisation still defies rational explanation. The Nazi concept of racial hierarchy was far from unequivocal about the Gypsies: as an Indo-European ethnic group, the Gypsies featured a measure of 'Aryan respectability' which persuaded even the purity-obsessed Himmler to make a distinction between the 'superior' Sinti and Lalleri Gypsy tribes (whom he was prepared to tolerate) and the 'inferior' half-breed Rom and Kale tribes (whom he readily consigned to destruction). More practical considerations seem to have been paramount. The landless, nomadic life-style of the Gypsies offended the Teutonic sense of order, stability and hierarchy. The generally low levels of Gypsy literacy and hygiene fostered the reputation of a sub-human race of 'untouchables' who were incorrigibly resistant to integration, sedentarisation and civilisation. Gypsies were regarded as at best an unnecessary burden on the social services of the state, at worst a disruptive, criminal, social nuisance implacably antagonistic to legitimate authority. There was also, predictably, a demographic fear: a statistic often cited was that in Austria over the period 1890–1933, the German population had risen by 20 per cent and the Gypsy by 400 per cent, partly by immigration but principally through an exceptionally high birth-rate. Nazi propaganda always stressed the shameless promiscuity of

Gypsy women and the loathsome priapism of Gypsy men. As with most instances of violent prejudice against a racial minority, a legend of sexual menace played a significant part. The commonest scenario was the sanctimonious insistence of the majority nationality on preserving the virtue of its defenceless womankind from the ubiquitous sexual threat of the animalistic males of the minority nationality. The cumulative result was a policy of extermination based less upon logic (or even ideology) than upon emotional insecurity and blind prejudice.

However arcane the motivation for Nazi persecution of the Gypsies, the tragic repercussions of their campaign are all to obvious (see Table XIIa). Wherever Germany assumed control during the Second World War, Gypsies were rounded up, confined in concentration camps and exterminated. Local considerations did, however, ensure that the pattern of Gypsy liquidation was far from uniform. Where the Germans had most direct local authority, as in the Baltic states, Poland and Bohemia, the Gypsy death rate was highest. The *Ustashi* opted to out-herod Herod by launching massacres which virtually eliminated the entire Gypsy minority within Croatia. Other states, especially those with a relatively large, long-established Gypsy population, paid only lip-service to Nazi Gypsy-phobia: Rumania and Bulgaria, with proportionately the largest Gypsy minorities at respectively 1.5 per cent and 1.3 per cent of their total populations, harassed their Gypsies as little as possible without incurring the active displeasure of their German masters, consistently preferring deportation to extermination. Slovakia assumed the traditional role of Macedonia as the Gypsy refuge of eastern Europe. The overall 22 per cent death rate suffered by Gypsies in eastern Europe was less the result of independent action by local nationalities than that of the policy of extermination either imposed upon reluctant dominated states by Nazi authority or directly implemented by German SS units operating as *Einsatzgruppen*.[6]

If the Gypsies were conspicuous victims of Nazi persecution, it was of course the Jews who had the greatest martyrdom of all thrust upon them. As with the Gypsies, the hopes of the 1920s for better treatment for the Jews had faded long before the advent of the Second World War. Although Jewish communities existed in every east European state, their distribution was too sparse to enable them to acquire any political clout: the highest Jewish proportion of a state population was 7.8 per cent in Poland, followed by 5.9 per cent in Hungary and 4.1

TABLE XII Gypsy and Jewish Deaths in Eastern Europe, 1939–45[7]

(a) *Gypsy*

State	Population in 1939	Deaths by 1945	% casualty
Croatia	28,500	28,000	98
Poland	50,000	35,000	70
Baltic States	7,000	4,500	64
Bohemia	13,000	6,500	50
Hungary	100,000	28,000	28
Serbia	60,000	12,000	20
Soviet Union	200,000	30,000	15
Rumania	300,000	36,000	12
Bulgaria	80,000	5,000	6
Slovakia	80,000	1,000	1
Total	918,000	206,000	22 *average*

(b) *Jewish*

State	Population in 1939	Deaths by 1945	% casualty
Poland	3,300,000	3,000,000	91
Baltic States	253,000	228,000	90
Bohemia	90,000	80,000	89
Slovakia	90,000	75,000	83
Hungary	650,000	450,000	69
Yugoslavia	43,000	26,000	60
Rumania	600,000	300,000	50
Soviet Union	2,850,000	1,252,000	44
Bulgaria	64,000	14,000	22
Total	7,940,000	5,425,000	68 *average*

per cent in Rumania. Although the Jews collectively comprised some 5 per cent of the total east European population, or one-fifth of the minority population after 1919, their numerical weakness within each individual state combined with their ubiquity increased both their social visibility and vulnerability. The outward emigrant flow of Jews was diverted by American quota legislation into a demographic fillip for Zionism but without any prospect of effecting a solution to the enormous resident Jewish problem in eastern Europe. Within the Soviet Union, the Jewish Autonomous Region of Birobidzhan quickly proved a failure. Inhospitably located on the Soviet-Chinese border, what had been hailed as a Soviet Jewish homeland first became an extended ghetto, a geographical transplantation of the tsarist Pale, and then lost its Jewish character almost entirely. By 1936 Birobidzhan had failed to engage Soviet Jewish sympathies to the point that Jews constituted a national minority of only 30 per cent within a territory specifically designated for their settlement. Integration, assimilation, emigration and territorial concentration had all failed to answer the Jewish Question.

The impact of the Nazi 'Operation Reinhardt' on the Jewish population of eastern Europe is too well-known to require extensive description. However, certain salient features of the Jewish experience should be emphasised. As shown by the Jewish casualty rate in the Second World War (see Table XIIb), the highest figures occurred in areas of direct Nazi intervention. Even in traditionally anti-semitic states like Rumania, the death rate was significantly lower than elsewhere and often the product of overt German pressure rather than local prejudice. Areas where Jews had secured more tolerant treatment in the inter-war years, like Hungary, Czechoslovakia and Poland, sooner or later featured the most comprehensive anti-semitic operations through the exercise of direct Nazi control. Elsewhere, the *Einsatzgruppen*, the specialist extermination squads of the SS, followed the advance of the German army across eastern Europe into the Soviet Union, executing isolated Jewish communities and concentrating larger numbers in ghettoes and prison compounds to await the summons to the death camps once the technology of mass murder had been perfected.

A comparison of Jewish and Gypsy persecution shows that while the geographical pattern was similar – both Jews and Gypsies were most likely to survive in Rumania and Bulgaria, least likely to survive in Poland and the Baltic States – the intensity of victimisation was markedly different. The Jews lost not only over 5,000,000 more dead than the Gypsies but suffered a casualty rate over three times higher. For the Gypsies, a lower level of Nazi commitment to their extermination allowed a substantially higher proportion, some 78 per cent, to survive the Second World War. For the Jews, the Nazi obsession with their total liquidation was only slightly modified in impact by states outside direct German rule, resulting in a survival rate of only some 32 per cent. Slovakia furnished a refuge for the Gypsies, but not for the Jews. For the Jews, there was no hiding place from their Nazi pursuers and poor prospects for escape or survival.

Almost incredibly, there was something for the Jewish people to salvage from the Holocaust. The horrific experience of the German Jews, the most assimilated of all European Jewish minorities, discredited the concept of assimilation and channelled the increased current of Jewish endeavour definitively into Zionism. Jewish organisations proved effective at lobbying the Great Powers, orchestrating demands on guilty consciences and appealing to the humanitarianism of a world shocked to discover the extent of Nazi atrocities. The new state of Israel testified both to reinforced Jewish commitment to a physical homeland and Great Power recognition of the moral debt owed to the survivors of the Holocaust. The almost obscene lesson was that the Holocaust was necessary to effect a decisive victory for the Jewish cause. The near-genocide of the Jewish minority at the hands of the Nazis enormously strengthened its position, first morally and then politically and territorially, to withstand any future anti-semitic onslaught.

The Gypsies were unluckier. Whilst recognising that the possession of a territorial homeland was the best guarantee of ethnic survival, Gypsy organisations were few and unable effectively to press their demands for the establishment of a 'Romanestan'. The nearest the Gypsies came to a recognised homeland was during the last years of the Second World War: *Ustasha* persecution of the Gypsies drove the survivors into such fanatical commitment to the partisan cause that in 1945 Tito seriously considered granting a Gypsy autonomous area in Macedonia. But although the Gypsies both 'deserved' recompense (like the Jews after 1945) and had 'earned' a homeland through their contribution to the war effort (like the Serbs after 1918), the reward of territory and a measure of future security eluded them. Less successful at engaging world attention than the Jews, the Gypsies were soon forgotten and their minority nationalism was relegated once again to the insulting level of a 'social problem' for host states. Without undervaluing the Jewish experience, Gypsy spokesmen have been known to argue that it was the Gypsies who were ultimately the greatest victims of war in eastern Europe: the Jews lost a great deal in the Second World War but gained some practical recompense; the Gypsies lost less but gained nothing.

And yet the Jewish casualty rate in the Second World War sets them apart from all other national minorities as historical victims. Fanatical in their pursuit of Jewish minorities and merciless in their consignment of astronomically high numbers of Jews to death by gassing, the Nazis failed to achieve complete genocide only because German defeat in the wider war came too soon. The almost indescribable sufferings of the Jews under the Nazi New Order meant that even those fortunate enough to survive the experience commonly sustained physical, emotional and psychological damage too extensive to permit full recovery. The deliberate murder of almost 5,500,000 people, comprising over two-thirds of the Jewish population of eastern Europe, must make the Holocaust the ultimate citation of a national minority as the supreme victim of war.

BENEFICIARIES OF WAR

Even almost 40 years after the event, there is a danger of the Jewish Holocaust distorting overall perspective on the question of national minorities. It may be true that the problem is less that the Jewish ordeal has been *over*-emphasised than that the experiences of many other minority nationalities have been grossly *under*-emphasised, even shamefully ignored. The Holocaust may have been not only unprecedented in scale but also entirely untypical of the wartime careers of the bulk of the minorities of eastern Europe.

One argument propounded suggests that the numerical inferiority of minorities is in practice an advantage for survival in wartime. Too small to be a threat to the principal combatants, minorities are typically incidental not deliberate casualties of war, sustaining damage through being caught in crossfire rather than being the targets of campaigns or *Blitzkrieg*. Although the lottery of war might inflict a direct hit on a compact minority, the small size of the target meant that the odds were against it. Many minorities, moreover, were widely spread rather than compact in settlement; the actuarial risk of substantial 'accidental' war damage on diaspora groups like the Jews and Gypsies was therefore slight. By this argument, military action alone results in minorities either being badly hit (if unlucky) or sustaining below-average damage in wartime.

Minorities heavily hit by 'incidental' war operations or 'deliberate' wartime persecution have understandably been the most publicised. The Jews undoubtedly suffered most in the Second World War and possibly in the First World War too. The Gypsies appear high on the casualty lists of both world wars. The Serbs incurred massive human losses in both world wars, probably in the order of 20 per cent of their population on each occasion. The Poles lost up to 15 per cent of their population in 1914–20 and again in 1939–45. The Ukrainians and Belorussians too suffered disproportionately high demographic damage through their location in the war zone for so much of the First and Second World Wars.

However, dominant nationalities too generally sustained human losses of a very high order in wartime, quite enough to justify calling Russians and Germans victims of war, although not necessarily as innocent as Jews and Gypsies. In the First World War, the Russians lost about 1,700,000 men from a total imperial population of perhaps 135,000,000, a casualty rate of 1.25 per cent; in the Second World War, they lost up to 20,000,000 from a population of almost 200,000,000 a death rate of around 10 per cent. The German casualty rates were proportionately higher than the Russian, reaching 2.6 per cent in the First World War and 11.1 per cent in the Second. The wartime casualty rates of the major nations were quite steep enough to bear comparison with those of many minorities and were appreciably higher than some.[8]

In practice, minorities appear on wartime casualty tables at all levels of damage. A significant number managed by various combinations of good luck and good management to attract low casualty rates. Appearing consistently at the foot of the proportional casualty table for both world wars were the Czechs. The destruction of the village of Lidice as a reprisal for the assassination of Heydrich in May 1942 has lent the Czechs the undeserved reputation of heroic resisters of Nazi rule. Heydrich's death was actually ordered (by London) to halt his successful policy of attracting Czech collaboration and to provoke Nazi reprisals which would permanently wreck Czech-German relations. The Czechs had 'no heart for open rebellion and little for secret resistance' so their tactic of 'playing possum' ensured that they emerged from both world wars, like the Good Soldier Schweik, hardly covered in glory but relatively unscathed, at a peacetime advantage over more heroic and war-damaged neighbours.[9]

The overall spread of minorities in wartime casualty statistics would suggest that the well-known appearance of certain minorities at the top has falsely moulded popular perceptions into thinking of minority nationalities as 'natural victims'. It may be true that *certain* minorities appear so regularly at the head of the list as to appear 'natural victims' but they are not necessarily typical. There is little historical or statistical evidence to suggest that in eastern Europe the national minorities *per se* were marked down as natural, typical or inevitable victims of war.

War was often employed by minorities to attempt to improve their subordinate peacetime situations. In time of emergency, the state need for unity could be exploited by a minority in a way impossible in peacetime. The prospect of 'double victory' was opened up for the politically aware: the military victory of the host state, in which the minority would share; and the political victory which the minority would earn as the price of its loyalty. Minorities entered into negotiations with majorities to create an arrangement of 'conditional loyalty', a deal in which the minority was promised tangible reward for rallying to the establishment, usually in the form of political concessions like the grant of extensive autonomy. The greatest difficulty for a minority was in exacting payment for its negotiated loyalty. Russian Jews in the First World War wryly claimed that the Tsar had promised full civil rights to all Jewish soldiers killed in action. The very denial of automatic, unreserved loyalty antagonised the dominant nationality, which was then disposed to welsh on the deal whenever possible. If the state lost the war, the majority-minority deal was rendered void by the failure of their alliance. If the state won the war, the army was at such a peak of performance and ebullience that a minority hesitated to present its account for payment. Dominant nationalities had a self-interested tendency to forget compacts which failed and ignore alliances once they had achieved their objective. The consequence was increased bitterness on the part of minorities whose legitimate claims were being shrugged off, and increased aggressiveness on the part of majorities congratulating themselves on manipulating their minorities into obedience without payment.

A more extreme course was for a minority to exploit war as its only chance to escape the jurisdiction of a state too powerful to defy in peacetime. War inevitably made higher demands on the state than peace, and if the supply of resources could not keep pace with war demand, the state was stretched and weakened. The disciplinary powers of the state would be reduced and probably diverted to the war effort: the army reinforcement to the civil police which guaranteed the establishment security in peacetime could be despatched to the front, leaving a much-undermined law enforcement machinery behind. The authority of the dominant nationality was never weaker than in wartime. War was therefore exploited by ambitious minorities on the principle that 'the state's difficulty is our opportunity'.

Previous to the First World War, the most successful minority to employ this tactic was the Magyar, the least successful the Polish. The Magyars seized the opportunity of Habsburg defeat by Prussia in 1866 to intimidate the demoralised imperial establishment into the *Ausgleich*. A similar crisis arrived for the Romanovs during the Crimean War of 1854–6. Nicholas I found himself in a cruel dilemma: if he transferred his best regiments quartered in Poland to the Crimea, his chances of victory against Britain and France were greatly enhanced but he risked a Polish rebellion; if he maintained his troops in Poland, the Empire was territorially secure but he must resign himself to ignominious defeat in war. Nicholas chose not to risk losing Poland but to lose the war instead. It was perhaps typical of the Poles that on the only occasions when rebellion had a sporting chance – in 1848 and during the Russian wars of 1854–6 and 1877 – they neglected the opportunity, reserving their defiance of Romanov authority for 1830–1 and 1863, peacetime occasions when all the odds favoured the tsars.

A very rewarding pursuit for minorities in wartime was what may be termed 'periphery politics'. Given that their geographical location often made minorities contiguous to an enemy state, official policy towards minorities tended to be either to repress the periphery so that its population was incapable of desertion to the enemy or to attempt to buy the allegiance of the minorities through concessions. In wartime, the position of minorities became simultaneously more dangerous physically (for they could not avoid damage in the conflict of the two states) and more advantageous politically (for they could now play off one state against the other and offer their final allegiance to the highest bidder). Patronage of the enemy's national minorities became a standard wartime stratagem. Western Great Powers composed of a single nationality were the most enthusiastic proponents of the 'nationalities game', discerning a political weapon damaging to the multi-national empires of eastern Europe which was incapable of backfiring or being employed in retaliation.

Identity (or at least similarity) of interests encouraged some ostensibly bizarre political relationships. Three of the most unlikely bedfellows were the Finns, the Poles and the Japanese. The Russo-Japanese War of 1904–5 found the Russians unable to employ the nationalities game against the united Japanese nation; but the Japanese had learned enough from the West to consider exploiting the multi-national composition of the Romanov Empire. Finns, Poles and Japanese discerned a community of interest: Nicholas II was having to keep Russian armies in Finland and Poland to forestall nationalist rebellion at a time when the troops were urgently needed both to fight the Japanese in Manchuria and to suppress the developing 'Revolution of 1905'. The tri-partite relationship never amounted to much. The Japanese realised that their military superiority was sufficient to defeat Russia without recourse to political stratagems. The Romanov minorities appreciated that their interests were tactically the opposite of Japan's: while the Finns and especially the Poles (led by Pilsudski) urged the Japanese to step up the war to increase the pressure on the Tsar to transfer troops from Finland and Poland to Manchuria, the Japanese wanted the Finns and Poles to rebel against the Tsar to pin down more troops in Europe so that their own victory in the east could be cheaper and easier. Self-interest may have identified a common enemy in the Romanov Empire but it also differentiated the Finns, Poles and Japanese and made a coherent anti-Russian strategy elusive. Finally, as with his namesake half a century before, Nicholas II reconciled himself to defeat in war rather than risk either his empire to the nationalists or his throne to the Russian revolutionaries. Although the nationalities game became a standard wartime exercise by the early twentieth century, the clash of interest between national minority and foreign patron severely limited the effectiveness of the stratagem.

It was in the First World War that the overlap of military and political warfare first dramatically and substantially benefited national minorities in eastern Europe. The approximate balance of resources between the Allied and Central camps forced all the Powers to invest increasingly in unconventional warfare to break the military deadlock. As the Russian, German and Austro-Hungarian armies faced each other across the 'Vistula Provinces', for instance, the Poles found themselves in the happy position of being ardently wooed by their Great Power neighbours on a spectacularly rising scale of political bribery. Setting one camp against the other, the Poles were almost too successful in exploiting periphery politics: although Polish opinion was split over whether to support the Allied or Central Powers, the fact remained that by early 1917 an independent Poland had been promised by both alliances. In the literal sense, from 1917 it no longer mattered to the Poles who won the First World War.

But while encouraging wider employment of both the nationalities game and periphery politics, than ever before, the greatest contribution of the First World War favouring the minorities was undoubtedly its precipitation of the collapse of traditional imperial authority. None of the empires of eastern Europe was defeated in the war in the sense of suffering catastrophic military reverses; rather the empires collapsed under the strain of conducting over an extended period a high-intensity, more 'total' war than ever previously experienced. The effect of the collapse of imperial authority was to revolutionise the prospects for the minority nationalities of eastern Europe.

Within the Russian sphere of influence, the abject failure of the Provisional Government of 1917 to fill the power vacuum left by the demise of tsarism invited all national minorities to take advantage of a situation which might never be repeated. Before March 1917, only leading Romanov minorities like the Poles and Finns participated in periphery politics and then only to improve their bargaining position *vis-à-vis* tsarism. After March 1917, the collapse of imperial authority precipitated a nationalist free-for-all in which all minorities made bids for independence. The Finns made dramatic progress, first agitating against the Provisional Government's reluctance to concede more than Grand Duchy status, then using the pretext of the Bolshevik seizure of power in Russia to declare their independence in December 1917. The Ukrainians moved rapidly from cultural to 'emancipatory nationalism' over 1917, winning reluctant autonomy from the Provisional Government for their *Rada* in July, a concession which only whetted nationalist appetites and led to a declaration of independence from Russia in January 1918. The Belorussians too developed a political movement for the first time, eventually having the effrontery to announce an independent Belorussian republic in March 1918. The Estonians, Latvians and Lithuanians all followed the same line, elaborating political demands in the course of 1917, then exploiting the Russian civil war provoked by the Bolshevik coup of November 1917 to assert their complete independence.

Unfortunately, the Russian collapse which permitted all the minorities a chance of national sovereignty also promoted a German takeover of much of European Russia. A mass break-out from the tsarist 'Prison of Nations' was promptly succeeded by the arrival of new jailors. All the emerging nationalities had to come to terms with Germany as the Central armies swept into their territories. The final German settlement of eastern Europe was established by the Treaty of Brest-Litovsk in March 1918, by which an enormous German empire incorporating a variety of national client states was created (see Map 5). Hoping for greater autonomy under the Germans than they had experienced under the Russians, the national minorities accepted the exigencies of the military situation and reconciled themselves to 'independence' under licence from Germany.

The Estonians, Latvians and Lithuanians settled uneasily into their subordinate new states, particularly unhappy that the resident Baltic German minorities were now acting as the local agents of the Central Powers. The Belorussian Republic was treated with amused contempt by Germany: as Nicholas Vakar remarks, 'it has been said that nationhood came to the Belorussians as an almost unsolicited gift of the Russian Revolution; it was, in fact, received from the hands of the Austro-German Occupation Army authorities and depended on their goodwill'.[10] The Poles meanwhile discovered that German takeover of the whole of Poland nullified their earlier triumphs with periphery politics: with the value of Poland in the nationalities game now greatly reduced, Germany was exasperated by demands for immediate independence, finally snubbing the Poles publicly by handing over the eastern territory claimed by Poland to the Ukrainians at Brest-Litovsk. Much encouraged by this sign of favour, the Ukrainians initially hoped to treat with the Germans on equal terms but shortly after the Brest-Litovsk Treaty (which confirmed their territorial separation from Bolshevik Russia), the occupying forces overthrew the *Rada* and established their own puppet Ukrainian government under Pavlo Skoropadski. Even the Finns, although spared German occupation, were compelled to accept German military intervention under General von der Goltz in early 1918 to ensure their new state's survival against the Bolshevik threat.

Although dissolved with the defeat of the Central Powers in November 1918 after only some eight months in existence, the

MAP 5 Eastern Europe under the Treaty of Brest-Litovsk,
March to November 1918

Source: J. M. Roberts, *Europe 1880–1945* (London: Longman, 1970)
p. 281.

German east European empire proved profoundly significant. All the ex-Romanov nationalities found German hegemony at least as odious as the Russian but they received an immense stimulus to their nationalisms. The more mature nations closer to the west, adroit enough to hedge their political bets by maintaining contacts with both Allied and Central Powers – the Poles, Finns and, to a lesser extent, the Estonians, Latvians and Lithuanians – survived the Allied victory despite extensive past collaboration with Germany and were soon bastions of the new Europe. Immature nationalities relying upon Germany alone – like the Ukrainians and Belorussians – were ruined by the Allied victory and soon after the German withdrawal suffered reabsorption by a transformed but still expansionist Russian state through the brutal agency of the Red Army. All the minorities had to some degree been beneficiaries of the war: many had achieved independence for the first time; the others, although defeated, had experienced 'telescoped nationalist development', making enormous political advances and gaining a fleeting, tantalising taste of independence which could never be forgotten.

Within Austria–Hungary, the impact of the First World War was similarly revolutionary. Although the Habsburg state weathered the storm well, eventually the war had the same disintegrative effect as upon the Romanov Empire some eighteen months previously. By comparison with their Romanov counterparts, the Habsburg minorities were much less successful at exploiting periphery politics and the nationalities game, partly because of allied reluctance to resort to tactics which could rebound against Russia, partly because the Central Powers were apparently so strong and self-assured until the last months of the war. Only after the Allies turned against the retention of Austria–Hungary in early 1918 were *emigré* nationalist groups like the Czech able to secure any firm assurances about future independence from the Allies. On the other hand, the downfall of Habsburg authority was total and irreversible in a way that the Romanov collapse was not: while the Bolsheviks gradually assumed the tsarist imperial mantle, reclaiming national territories as soon as their resources permitted, Austrian imperial authority had been destroyed forever. From October 1918, all the constituent minorities indulged in feverish and frequently vicious competition for territorial expansion – what Palmer has described as 'the greatest claim-jumping exercise in history' – a nationalist debacle into which the Allies attempted to introduce some order by the Versailles

Settlement.[11] In a different way, the ex-Habsburg minorities owed as much to the First World War as the ex-Romanov minorities.

It may be argued that the east European minorities had abiding cause to be grateful to the First World War throughout the inter-war period. The traditional predators of eastern Europe, positioned on its periphery but constantly tempted to stray into its interior, were all struck down by the war. For the Habsburg and Ottoman Empires, ruin was permanent and irreversible. For the Romanov and German Empires, military disaster and territorial shrinkage were eventually overcome as traditional expansionism reappeared in new guises within the Soviet Union and Nazi Germany. But for two decades, the smaller nationalities of eastern Europe had an opportunity granted by the First World War to pursue their own goals without direct interference from imperial authority. The war saw the Germans and Russians decimate each other, to the demographic enhancement and political advantage of most national minorities. In a very real sense, the independent eastern Europe of the 1920s and 1930s was the political gift of the First World War to the formerly repressed nationalities.

The Second World War was more ambivalent in its impact upon the minority nationalities. For some eighteen months after their symbolic repartition of Poland in September 1939, Nazi Germany and the Soviet Union shared the territory of eastern Europe: having already occupied most of Czechoslovakia, Germany continued its economic, political and military penetration of Hungary, Bulgaria, Rumania and finally Yugoslavia; the Soviet Union reabsorbed Estonia, Latvia and Lithuania and wrested the territories of Bessarabia from Rumania and western Karelia from Finland. The tacit division of the territorial spoils of eastern Europe ended in June 1941, when Operation Barbarossa was launched against the Soviet Union. From autumn 1941 until 1944, all of eastern Europe and much of European Russia were occupied by Germany, a deliberate revival of the 'Brest-Litovsk Empire' of 1918 (see Map 6).

In the Soviet 'zone' of eastern Europe which lasted from late 1939 until mid-1941, the treatment of the newly incorporated nationalities was uniformly grim. After half-hearted attempts to ingratiate themself with the Poles, Estonians, Latvians, Lithuanians, Bessarabians, west Karelians, west Ukrainians and west Belorussians during the first months of their forcible reclamation, the Russians abandoned the soft line in favour of overt Sovietisation. National leaders and

MAP 6 The German Mastery of Europe 1942

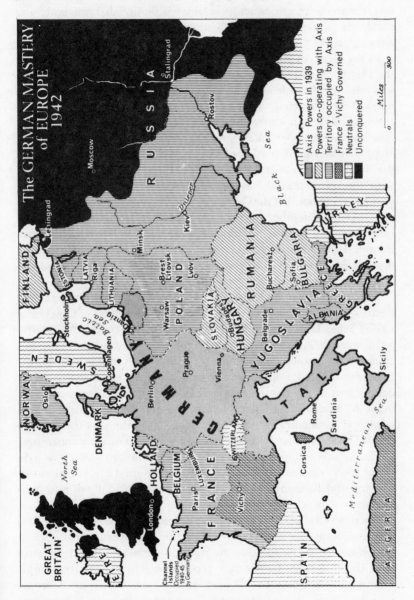

Source: Gilbert, *Recent History Atlas*, *p.72*.

sometimes most of the educated classes were transported to Siberia, where many were subsequently liquidated. Nationalist resistance was ruthlessly eradicated by specially transferred Asian troops of the Red Army to effect complete Soviet domination.

In the German zone, during both the early 'partition period' and the first years of the later 'imperial period', treatment of minorities was relatively flexible and discriminating. One set of nationalities was marked down as victims of German expansionism. The Czechs were repressed and humiliated under the German 'Protectorate of Bohemia and Moravia' from the instant of military takeover in March 1939. The German invasion of Yugoslavia in April 1941 precipitated the disintegration of the state and the direct annexation of Serbia, with the result that the Serbs suffered most of all the South Slav groups at the hands of the Germans. The Poles suffered perhaps worst of all. After September 1939, the Polish Corridor was reincorporated into Germany (as the *Wartheland*) and the remainder of German Poland organised into a 'General Government' which was promptly designated as a vast Nazi concentration camp for all the 'undesirables' of eastern Europe.

The common denominator of the Czechs, Serbs and Poles was their position as prime beneficiaries of Versailles. The states of Czechoslovakia, Yugoslavia and Poland, all underwritten by the Allies after 1919, were deliberately and methodically smashed by Germany in a spirit of unbridled revisionism. The German minorities of the Sudetenland and Polish Corridor provided an extra incentive for destruction of Czechoslovakia and Poland, but the identical treatment of Yugoslavia, with its tiny and relatively docile German minority, demonstrates that the primary Nazi aim was the dismantling of the Versailles Settlement. Even when not directly concerned, Germany was willing to condone Soviet depredations over 1939–40 in the other Versailles beneficiary states of Estonia, Latvia, Lithuania, Finland and Rumania. Whether benefiting territorially or not, Nazi Germany was set on the annihilation of 'Versailles Europe'.

There was a constructive as well as a destructive side to Nazi policy. The enormous German empire created by the invasion of the Soviet Union could not be ruled by military power alone, even by a force with the *Wehrmacht*'s invincible reputation. Having secured ample *Lebensraum*, the empire of 1941–4 then swallowed up German resources (and especially personnel) at an alarming rate, prompting a chronic manpower shortage. If eastern Europe could not be held by military force alone, local collaborators had to be found. Building on the precedents of the Napoleonic and First World Wars, Hitler promoted those nationalities subordinated in peacetime to create a new national hierarchy. At its most grandiose, Nazi strategy envisaged a reversal of fortunes for east European nationalities: the beneficiaries of Versailles were to become the principal victims of the German empire; the victims of Versailles were to become the beneficiaries of the Nazi New Order. Those minority nationalities disappointed by Versailles or Soviet reclamation over the period 1919–21 now had the opportunity to rectify the injustices of peacetime by collaborating with the triumphant Nazi establishment. Versailles majorities were forcibly converted into minorities; peacetime minorities might secure promotion to majority status under German patronage.

Hungary reclaimed about one-half of the territory lost at the Treaty of Trianon through a succession of 'awards' from Germany: by the Vienna Award of November 1938 Hungary acquired southern Slovakia with its substantial Magyar minority; in March 1939 Hungary exploited the German partition of what remained of Czechoslovakia to occupy Ruthenia; in August 1940 northern Transylvania, with the largest Magyar minority, was transferred from Rumania by the Second Vienna Award; and finally in April 1941, the German partition of Yugoslavia included the transfer of the Bačka district, with another Magyar minority, to Hungary. Bulgaria too, seeking the cancellation of the Treaty of Neuilly and the restoration of 'Big Bulgaria', was prepared to make painful political concessions to Germany to gain territory: the southern Dobrudja was transferred from Rumania in September 1940; and in mid-1941 Bulgaria received most of Yugoslav Macedonia. Neither Magyars nor Bulgars were satisfied with their gains – Hungary wanted southern Transylvania and Bulgaria Greek Macedonia – but Hitler was astute enough to keep his beneficiary nationalities subordinate by providing just enough territory to ensure self-interested loyalty but insufficient to warrant an independent stance.

Almost whimsically favoured by Hitler rather than seeking a political bargain with Germany, the Slovaks were in March 1939 converted from a Czechoslovak minority into a nation state. Just how much popular support 'independent' Slovakia under Monsignor Tiso enjoyed is debatable. To Hugh Seton-Watson in 1945, perhaps articulating Western wishful thinking, Slovakia was a 'Quisling state' whose leaders, headed by 'the ridiculous Tiso' were 'the laughing-stock of their people and of Europe'. To partisan Stanislav Kirsch-baum, it is plain that 'the Tiso-state did not have to fear a plebiscite, that it was accepted by the majority of the Slovak nation, and that the liquidation of the Czechoslovak Republic was not considered in Slovakia as a national disaster but rather it was greeted as the liberation from twenty years of Czech domination'.[12] Regardless of which judgement came closer to reality, the experience of even spurious independence was unforgettable, boosting Slovak national-ism into a force impossible to suppress long after the demise of the Slovak Republic.

Croatia was promoted as a nominally independent fascist state upon the ruins of Yugoslavia. However the atrocities perpetrated by the *Ustashi* upon all those Serb, Gypsy and Jewish minorities unfortunate enough to be within reach alienated much of the local Croat population. The aggressiveness of the *Ustashi* towards defence-less minorities was matched by their cravenness towards their masters: by the Roman Treaties of May 1941, Pavelić both surren-dered ethnically Croat territory to Italy and invited a member of the Italian Savoy dynasty to become King of Croatia. The combination of external obsequiousness and internal repression reduced the support for the *Ustasha* regime to a very narrow band of society and disgraced Croat nationalism before an international audience. Even so, as in the case of Slovakia, even pseudo-independence and a shameful record lent an aura of viability to the notion of a Croat state long after the overthrow of the *Ustasha* in 1945.

After June 1941, the leading national minorities of the Soviet Union became eligible for German patronage. The initiative for pragmatic treatment of the various nationalities came from Rosenberg, formally appointed in July 1941 to run the *Ostministerium*, the German ministry for occupied Soviet territory. While Hitler viewed all Slavs indiscrimi-nately as *Untermenschen*, Rosenberg envisaged a hierarchy of national discrimination which would allow the *Reich* to foster minority nationalism against the Russians. Following the Promethean strategy, political blocs based upon anti-Soviet and anti-Russian consciousness would be constructed (including the Ukraine, Belorus-sia, *Baltikum*, the Caucasus and Greater Finland) to build into a German *cordon sanitaire* against 'Muscovy', what remained of the Soviet Union after the German-encouraged rampage of its peripheral nationalities. Selective discrimination between the Slav minorities in particular would induce the crucial Ukrainians and Belorussians to switch allegiance and accept German hegemony to escape the worse fate of remaining under Soviet Russian jurisdiction. The Ukrainians and Belorussians had not forgotten their brief taste of independence in 1918, were irretrievably alienated by the Soviet collectivisation of the early 1930s and accordingly welcomed the *Wehrmacht* soldiers as emancipators over summer 1941 with an enthusiasm which surprised even Rosenberg. The prospects for a Nazi-engineered 'living dam' against the Bolshevik Russian flood were considered most promising.

For the first years of the Second World War, national minorities were patently divided by crude self-interest in their attitudes to the Nazi New Order. The Czechs, Poles and Serbs had been demoted from peacetime majority status to wartime minority status through the exercise of German power and resented their downfall bitterly. The Jews and Gypsies who bore the brunt of Nazi persecution naturally added their voices to the chorus of opposition. Favoured nationalities were understandably more mixed in their attitudes. The Magyars and Bulgars saw German patronage as a necessary evil, the only available means of regaining territory unjustly confiscated at Versailles. The Belorussians, Croats, Slovaks and Ukrainians were peacetime no-chancers who saw Germany as the only external force powerful enough to offset the domination of an overweening neighbour, without whom there was no possibility of national self-expression.

Most nationalities favoured by Germany, feeling they had at least as much to gain from the Nazi New Order as the Germans themselves (and perhaps even more to lose), became the staunchest supporters of the *Reich*. Not only were favoured national minorities prepared to fight openly at the side of the *Wehrmacht*, forming *Ostlegionen* like the Ukrainian 'Nightingale' and 'Roland' battalions (and later even joining the renegade Russian 'Vlasov Army'), they were anxious to stake their claims to statehood under German licence. In May 1943, the SS admitted Ukrainians for the first time, and by the end of the war, of the total 1,000,000 personnel of the SS, only one-quarter were German, another quarter *Volksdeutsche* and the bulk of the remainder – up to 400,000 men – were from eastern Europe. For every SS soldier staffing the death camps of Treblinka, Belzec and Sobibor, there were seven Ukrainian auxiliaries. It was no accident that willing 'Quisling' organisations like the Croat *Ustashi* and Ukrainian *Benderovtsy* frequently outdid the Nazis themselves in their ruthlessness.

Over 1944–5, the defeat of the *Wehrmacht* brought the Red Army storming into eastern Europe, serving as an abrupt political guillotine on a Nazi New Order always patently dependent on military success. Hitler's promise of a 1000-year *Reich* from which previously penalised nationalities could benefit was bankrupted by military defeat within five years; but long before military collapse, even the favoured nationalities had been alienated by their wartime experience. The demographic demands of the New Order became too high. At the front line, the Rumanian army and Slovak contingent lost a full half of their men at Stalingrad in January 1943, a casualty figure matched by the Hungarian army at the battle of Voronezh in July 1943. On the home front, the manpower shortage of the Nazi Empire acted like a huge pump, sucking in non-German labour from eastern Europe to serve in Reich industry and agriculture and thereby release Germans for slaughter on the Russian front.[13] All the 'favoured' nationalities were disproportionately penalised by the *Ostarbeiter* scheme, which demanded ever greater and more frequent sacrifices which could only arouse the resentment and eventual opposition of groups like the Magyars, Bulgars, Slovaks and Croats.

The ex-Soviet nationalities were treated worst of all and were consequently alienated most of all. Despite the obvious community of self-interest between Germans and national minorities, relations became worse than in 1918. Local nationalism was strong enough to resent German domination but insufficiently vigorous to negotiate more advantageous terms (especially in Belorussia). More than any other minorities, the Ukrainians and Belorussians were shamelessly press-ganged to serve as the helot class of German industry: by 1944, two-thirds of the *Ostarbeiter* in Germany were Ukrainian. The more pragmatic policies of the *Ostministerium* were increasingly circumvented by, or subordinated to, the fanatical race-obsessed line of more traditional Nazi institutions, notably the SS, whose *Einsatzgruppen* spread terror, outrage and finally rebellion amongst the national minorities.

As in 1918, it was probably the racially based German contempt for the eastern *Untermenschen* that irremediably antagonised all the 'beneficiary nationalities'. The Ukraine, by its population size and economic resources the greatest potential ally of Germany in eastern Europe, was gratuitously alienated by Nazi treatment. Hatred of the Russians was such that even tolerable treatment after 1941 would have paid rich dividends, and concessions like an independent

Ukrainian Church and especially the de-collectivisation of agriculture might well have committed the Ukrainian population to the New Order. Instead, the Nazi 'Brown Tsar of the Ukraine', Erich Koch, dissipated the early goodwill of the populace quite wantonly, turning opinion irrevocably against the German occupation forces. Describing the Ukrainians publicly as 'a colonial people' who should be treated 'with a whip, like negroes', Koch set out to liquidate not only all the resident Jews but the entire nationalist intelligentsia (most horrifically by the massacres at Babi Yar outside Kiev). In May 1943, a despairing Rosenberg demanded that the *Führer* decide between Koch and himself; when Hitler chose Koch, the already compromised nationalities strategy of Rosenberg collapsed completely. To quote Alexander Dallin, 'a unique opportunity had presented itself . . . Germany bungled it, and aroused against itself those it claimed to free . . . . Like other occupied areas, the Ukraine, lost on the field of battle, had even earlier been lost by Germany in the minds and hearts of men'.[14] The crass errors of the Germans in their east European empires both in 1918 and 1939–44 thrust any national minorities unable to stand alone into the repressive jurisdiction of the victorious Soviet Union.

As the frequency, scope and intensity of war grew over the century following 1848, the impact of hostilities on the careers of national minorities in eastern Europe increased commensurately, both for good and ill. The relatively rare and small-scale wars of the late nineteenth century offered few opportunities and often only modest rewards to ambitious minorities but also prevented their incurring extensive damage. By contrast, twentieth-century war had an increasingly dramatic effect upon the fortunes of minorities. As the political stakes were raised to unprecedented heights, so were the risks consciously or involuntarily run by the minorities. In the First World War and the Versailles Settlement which followed, many more national minorities proved beneficiaries than victims. In the Second World War, however, all minorities sooner or later suffered from the experience of German eastern Europe. Although in the early years of the Second World War east European nationalities were conspicuously divided between victims and beneficiaries of the New Order, well before 1945 all the favoured nationalities had joined the victimised nations in condemning Nazi Europe. Although some national minorities lost more than others, none were ultimately beneficiaries. By 1945 all national minorities in eastern Europe had become victims of war.

8. A Century in Perspective

NATIONAL majorities did not exist in eastern Europe in 1815; yet by 1945 national majorities constituted probably some 90 per cent of the total population. Such a dramatic shift from a minority-populated society partitioned into empires to a majority-dominated community organised into nation states would appear to be evidence of remarkable political achievement, but the paradoxes of eastern Europe render a definitive judgement on the apparent near-resolution of the minorities problem elusive and controversial.

Until the Versailles Settlement, national majorities existed only in the new states emerging from the territorial shrinkage of Ottoman Europe: in Habsburg and Romanov Europe, there were only national minorities. The Turks, Austrians and Russians were all demographic minorities within dynastic empires embarrassed by a nationalism which undermined their essentially supra-national rationale. Since all nationalities within the Habsburg and Romanov Empires were minorities numerically, minority status as such was almost meaningless, forcing attention to devolve upon the political question of whether a minority was 'dominant' or 'subordinate'.

As 1848 proclaimed the advent of the Age of Nationalism in the supreme confidence that 'there is nothing so irresistible as an idea whose time has come', the 'dominant' or 'imperial' minorities responded very differently to the challenge from their increasingly *in*subordinate minorities. The Ottoman Empire retreated complaisantly before the threat of Balkan nationalism until all its former European domain was converted into smaller political entities claiming to be nation states. The Habsburg Empire, well-versed in traditional imperial stratagems like 'ethnic divide and rule' and 'territorial re-divide and rule', survived by inventing new political and social techniques to contain the nationalist challenge: alerted to the danger by 1848 and Italian Unification, the Habsburg establishment recognised the necessity of a compact between the traditionally dominant Austrian minority and the challenging Magyar minority to create a near-majority partnership which resisted the combined threat from the remaining minorities for half a century. The Romanov Empire, headed by the numerically strongest but qualitatively weakest dominant minority in eastern Europe, relied upon the 'stick' of its army and the 'carrot' of economic prosperity to resist its most advanced minorities, and upon a pre-emptive campaign of Russification to retard the nationalist development of its less mature minorities.

Over the course of the late nineteenth and early twentieth centuries, external intervention through territorial partition, the classic instrument of multi-national Great Power consensus, transformed the political map of eastern Europe. The Peace of Paris in 1856, the Congress of Berlin in 1878 and especially the Paris Peace Conference of 1919 concocted (or condoned) territorial settlements which far from satisfied all the interested parties but were still constructive attempts to stabilise dangerously volatile local situations. The outlook for the national minorities as the collapse of the dynastic empires spawned a host of 'successor states' seemed promising. The trend towards smaller political entities automatically allowed minorities to 'float' upwards in social visibility and nationalist aspiration: the Slovaks, for example, constituted 3.8 per cent of the population of the Habsburg Empire before 1867, 9.4 per cent of Hungary after 1867 and some 16 per cent of Czechoslovakia after 1919.[1] The Versailles Settlement alone halved the numerical scale of the minorities problem, contriving by territorial repartition to reduce the subordinate minorities' proportion from one-half to one-quarter of the total population of eastern Europe, a striking achievement.

After Versailles, the whole of eastern Europe for the first time featured a political phenomenon hitherto confined to the Balkans: not the nation state but the national majority. In every state, including the Soviet Union, a particular nationality comprised the demographic majority (or near-majority in the instances of Czechoslovakia and Yugoslavia), encouraging it to consider the state as exclusively its own domain. The national minorities, averaging 25 per cent of the populations of the new states, expected better treatment from avowedly democratic governments but typically experienced a 'majority tyranny' in which they suffered more than under the dynastic empires. With their minorities a relatively small proportion of the total population, the majority nations were tempted to convert their inheritances, essentially mini-empires, into nation states. The majority emphasis switched abruptly from ethnic 'self-determination', the moral justification for their own emancipation, to 'national determinism', the rationalisation for their suppression of the nationalism of others. The idealistic nineteenth-century slogan 'Every nation a state' was now accompanied by the sinister corollary 'Every state a nation'. In the words of Josef Pilsudski, 'it is the state that makes the nation, not the nation that makes the state', as succinct an expression of Polish 'integral nationalism' as may be found. By this loaded definition, the new east European political entities were less 'nation states' than 'state nations'.

The natural, organic and often spontaneous growth of 'nationalism' which had proved so beguiling in the nineteenth century was replaced in the twentieth century by a contrived, government-engineered and mechanistic campaign of 'nation-building' or 'nationism'. National minorities already disappointed at failing to gain political recognition at Versailles and therefore disposed to challenge the legitimacy of their host states were subjected to sustained campaigns of attempted assimilation which provoked them, often actively encouraged by their kin states, into overt opposition and made the minorities issue a major threat to the stability of inter-war Europe. The overall effect of Paris, Berlin and Versailles on eastern Europe was therefore to 'enfranchise' the leading subordinate minorities of moribund or defunct empires, converting them into national majorities which promptly set out to suppress those smaller minorities which had failed to secure promotion. Multi-national entities pursuing the ideal of the nation state, the new states of eastern Europe were essentially too big for their political philosophies.

The confrontation between majorities and minorities could not be relieved by any traditional factors. The 'fight option' steadily declined over the century after 1848. Even in the Balkans, the notion of 'fighting for independence' against Ottoman authority was largely spurious, a device for attracting Great Power intervention. Government's increasing penetration of society provided multiple opportunities for identifying and defusing nationalist crises before they became explosive. The armies which had always been bastions of the imperial establishment and were intelligently conscripted by the Habsburgs and Romanovs for peacetime counter-offensives against nationalism became cruder instruments of oppression by national majorities after 1919. Against determined modern governments with large peacetime armies, the fight option would have been suicidal had it not become impossible.

'Flight' never provided a solution to the minorities problem. Even when mass emigration was at its height in the late nineteenth century, the volume of traffic never constituted more than an open safety-valve on chronic overpopulation. Emigration could not solve overpopulation, indeed could not prevent overpopulation from getting worse. All emigration could do was to prevent human congestion from getting as bad as it would otherwise have become. Though not inflicting substantial damage on the national minorities, emigration provided little advantage; the net result was that mass emigration made little difference to eastern Europe. After the American quota legislation of the 1920s, the era of mass emigration from eastern Europe came to an end except for renewed Russian colonisation of Siberia, seasonal migration in search of work and specific national causes like Zionism. The limitations of a migrant safety-valve on the demographic pressures of nineteenth-century society were apparent enough: in the twentieth century, the situation became worse as the safety-valve was effectively turned off.

International intervention proved disappointing in arbitrating between national majorities and minorities. Efforts at trans-national partnership between minorities in the interests of self-preservation foundered over national rivalries. Extra-national patronage was always a disruptive element and, as nationalism gathered momentum, the temptation for a Great Power to sponsor its own minorities within other states became irresistible, adding fuel to the flames of minority grievance. The shortcomings of successive exercises in multi-national partition only encouraged minorities to challenge the morality of settlements imposed from outside, too novel to command immediate respect and often flouting the 'ultimate legitimacy' of national self-determination. Finally, the deficiencies of international protection were cruelly spotlighted in the inter-war period as the League of Nations, never intended as an organ of government, only of arbitration based on moral pressure, inevitably failed to live up to the exaggerated hopes invested by the remaining national minorities.

As 'fight' was rendered impossible, 'flight' increasingly marginal and intervention either ineffectual or mischievous, the confrontation between national minorities and state authority became more stark. The demographic trend served constantly to undermine the majorities and dominant minorities, and favour the subordinate minorities. More advanced 'Historic' nations featured a lower birth rate than the more backward 'Un-Historic' nationalities, a decline in biological fertility linked to both the population shift from the countryside to the towns and a universal human response to improved social stability and material prosperity. The fertility-differential was the means by which the backward nationalities tended to overhaul the early lead established by the advanced nations, increasing the demographic pressure for better treatment. Once the leading minorities secured majority status, their fertility dipped and they lost the 'demographic initiative' to their own minorities. Throughout the early twentieth century, the minorities seized the initiative from the majorities in the 'breeding wars' which always underlay the politics of majority-minority relations. In Czechoslovakia, for example, the fertility rate increased dramatically from west to east as the social maturity of each national minority declined: in Bohemia, the rate of increase between 1921 and 1930 was 6.1 per cent: in Moravia 9.6 per cent: in Slovakia 15.1 per cent: and in Ruthenia 22.5 per cent.[2] The differential fertility rate, consistently favouring subordinate minorities over dominant minorities in the nineteenth century and minorities over majorities in the early twentieth century, put demographic pressure on political establishments from the moment of their creation. Invariably favouring the 'Opposition' against the 'Establishment', the demographic trend in eastern Europe after 1848 provided a classic 'conflict model' of society.

Regular and preferably continuous conflict was a necessary component of a 'movement' as dynamic as nationalism. Activated by nationalist psychological impulses, majorities and minorities both craved conflict to create and then reinforce their senses of identity and solidarity. In the inter-war period, the majorities demanded, and if necessary fabricated, constant stimulation for their nationalism. Sometimes nationalist fervour was directed outwards, seeking excitement through frontier incidents with, and territorial claims against, neighbouring states. Often nationalist hysteria sought a more accessible target, with minorities type-cast in the roles of Trojan Horses and Fifth Columns. Nationalism was 'a love affair too hot *not* to cool down' and with the likelihood of nationalist ardour rapidly abating after the consummation of independence, the fires of chauvinism had to be stoked regularly, if only to distract attention from the indifferent performances of inexpert majority-nationality governments desperate to furnish alibis for their shortcomings. The minorities too needed the stimulation of a majority nationality. Commonly at an earlier stage of national self-consciousness, minorities needed an external threat to develop their sense of a unique identity and to reinforce their nationalist solidarity. Whilst rarely courting persecution, a minority typically needed at very least the close proximity of another nationality to accelerate its national self-awareness. It was a fundamentally symbiotic, mutually sustaining relationship: national majorities and minorities needed each other to a degree which neither could ever publicly admit.[3]

Even so, the peacetime political and social status quo was always preserved, to the consistent advantage of the dominant minorities before 1914 and the national majorities after 1919. The instances of minorities securing substantially improved treatment from the establishment, for example raising their subordinate status to any significant degree, were very rare in peacetime. Even more than the victims of war, minorities were typically the casualties of peace.

War was the only external factor powerful enough to break the hold of a dominant minority or majority, to the temporary or permanent advantage of subordinate minorities. Even limited wars provided opportunities quite impossible in peacetime: 'conditional loyalty', 'periphery politics' and the 'nationalities game' could all be exploited by minorities in the hope of improving their positions. Of course, not all wars benefited all minorities; but not a war passed in eastern Europe over the century after 1848 without at least one minority making substantial direct or indirect gains. The Crimean War of 1854–6 paved the way for the foundation of Rumania. The Austro-Prussian War of 1866 was an indispensable factor in the negotiation of the Austro-Magyar *Ausgleich*. The Russo-Turkish War of 1877 precipitated the state of Bulgaria. Even the Russo-Japanese War of 1904–5 earned the Poles and Finns a temporary respite from tsarist Russification.

The world wars brought commensurately greater gains for minorities as they precipitated the overthrow or collapse of the peacetime establishment. The First World War permitted minorities like the Czechs, Poles, Finns, Estonians, Latvians and Lithuanians to secure majority status in independent states, enhanced the positions of existing majority nations like the Serbs, Albanians, Greeks and Rumanians and prompted a first nationalist experience for the Ukrainians and Belorussians. Even nations penalised at Versailles, like the Magyars, Bulgars, Austrians and Germans, lost only territory, not sovereignty and independence. The lesson of the period 1914–19 seemed to be that national minorities had little to lose and a great deal to gain from world war.

The Second World War brought temporary advantage to established majorities like the Magyars, Bulgars and Finns, offered second chances to disadvantaged nationalities like the Ukrainians and Belorussians, and provided first experiences of independence to aggrieved minorities like the Slovaks and Croats. Compared to the First World War however, the Second was a great disappointment to minorities and majorities alike. The First World War so weakened Germany and Russia that traditional authority collapsed, promoting a power vacuum which permitted the political enfranchisement of the leading nationalities and two decades of independence. The Second World War, far from again ruining German and Russian authority and offering eastern Europe another (largely undeserved) chance of independence, cancelled many of the gains of the First World War and laid the foundation for the incorporation of almost all eastern Europe into a vast Soviet empire. Even so, war ensured that over the century after 1848 all the principal national minorities of eastern Europe were exposed to the experience of political statehood and independence (albeit often only briefly), an opportunity never afforded in peacetime.

War tended to simplify the minorities issue demographically. Protracted war had a disentangling or segregating effect on areas of mixed settlement: under the threat of majority persecution or enemy attack, minorities sought their own ethnic company in self-protection. Diaspora minorities like the Jews and Gypsies proved most vulnerable in wartime, suffering both 'accidental' and 'deliberate' extensive numerical damage. The overall effect of the world wars was thus to reduce the size of the diaspora minorities and encourage mixed minority settlement to become more compact, thereby making frontier revision on ethnic lines increasingly realistic, or at least less unrealistic. With war decimating and 'compacting' minorities, successive peace conferences were faced by a progressively diminishing minorities problem which rendered the traditional recourse of territorial repartition steadily more satisfactory.

War hardened majority attitudes towards minorities. The temptation for minorities to play periphery politics, entertain overtures from enemy Powers or at very least negotiate conditional loyalty naturally antagonised the dominant minority or majority. Conversely, the likelihood of majorities overemploying minorities to minimise their own casualties or using minorities as innocent scapegoats for disaster angered the subordinate minorities. Actions against minorities inconceivable in peacetime became acceptable in wartime as justified by national emergency. At the most apocalyptic level, genocide was only attempted as a majority option in wartime, with the Turkish onslaught on the Armenians and Greeks in the First World War and the German destruction of the Jews and Gypsies in the Second World War.

To a considerable extent, war brutalised majority nationalities in their minority policies after the coming of peace. Majority options considered inadmissible before 1914 became so widespread during the First World War that they became almost standard practice after 1918. Subsequently, majority tactics considered reprehensible in the 1920s and 1930s were so commonly applied in the Second World War that they were included in the post-1945 settlement. War became the pretext for an escalation in the severity of majority practices towards minorities, employing techniques which had already become possible through technical advances but requiring a wartime atmosphere to render them politically acceptable. Population transfer, for example, was confined to emigration on private initiative before about 1900, appeared as an experimental tsarist option in demographic engineering just before 1914, occurred spontaneously on a massive scale over 1914–18 and was tried out as an international solution to the minorities question in the 1920s. Although discredited by the Greek-Turkish 'exchanges' validated by the League of Nations, population transfer was revived and employed on an unprecedented scale by the governments of Nazi Germany and the Soviet Union during the Second World War. After 1945, physical liquidation of a national minority (as attempted during the war by both Hitler and Stalin) was abhorred by the victors as a Nazi crime against humanity but population transfer was tacitly recognised as an acceptable peacetime option – if only for use against the scattered German minorities still bedevilling eastern Europe.

The Allies can be forgiven for running out of patience with the minorities issue. The *reductio ad absurdum* of nationalism was that there was no logical limit to the fissiparous reproduction of minorities. As E. H. Carr remarks, 'national self-determination became a standing invitation to secession . . . . Given the promise of nationalism, the process was natural and legitimate and no end could be set to it'.[4] Precisely the point at which subdivision should be arrested could not be determined by objective criteria. For every majority, the existing state was a viable organic unity and the minority secessionist challenge a mischievous and bogus provincial masquerade. For every emerging national minority, the host state was an illegitimate empire, a state prison from which escape was politically and morally imperative. The state itself represented the power equilibrium when the strongest nationality could secure independence from its former superiors yet simultaneously deny sovereignty to its own juniors. With naked self-interest the cardinal factor, any decision imposed by external intervention was bound to be arbitrary and contentious. With the ongoing wrangle between states and their minorities becoming so dangerous, national majorities and Great Powers alike were increasingly drawn to apply more drastic remedies.

Almost obsessively aware of the prominent role played by east European minorities in triggering both world wars, the victorious Allies determined upon major demographic surgery after 1945 to forestall another minorities-provoked war. The combined effects of wartime deaths, minority territorial compaction, frontier revision on a massive scale and wholesale population transfer halved the pre-war minorities' proportion of the population, bringing the post-1945 level down to near 10 per cent of the total. The Versailles practice of attempting to draw frontiers around nations was superseded by the more drastic expedient of fitting nations into pre-determined boundaries. Politics had been unable to tailor a stable system to the existing demographic pattern: so the only recourse was to alter the demography to make political sense. The nation state was brought a stage closer: just as the First World War effected a transition from dynastic empires to mini-empires, so the Second World War promoted another shift in the direction of the ethnically homogeneous, minorities-refined nation state. Minorities were required to transport themselves to their kin states or accept the consequences. Minorities without kin states were implicitly expected either to create one miraculously (like the Jews with Israel) or submit to assimilation by the majority nationality of their host states with good grace, preferably without making embarrassing demands on the consciences of the Powers. Although the human cost was high, the exercise was regarded as acceptable in the interests of permanent peace, especially as the price had to be paid only by the minorities and defeated majorities.

If (as Gandhi is reputed to have said) 'civilisation is to be judged by the treatment shown to minorities', then the century after 1848 saw eastern Europe becoming increasingly uncivilised in the interests of its national majorities. The internecine nationalist competition of eastern Europe reflected the social Darwinist nightmare of a 'law of the jungle' geared to the 'survival of the fittest'. 1848 promised that all minorities might be winners under idealistic nationalism: 1919 warned that while stronger minorities could secure promotion to majority status and political independence, others would not: and 1945 demonstrated that not even national majorities were necessarily winners and minorities could only be losers. With politics becoming 'the art of creating majorities', the national minority became an inevitable victim of the development of modern east European society.

Notes and References

The place of publication is London unless otherwise stated.

1. THE DEMOGRAPHIC INHERITANCE

1. For the most graphic account of the Asiatic colonisation of Europe, see Geoffrey Barraclough (ed.), *The Times Atlas of World History* (Times Books, 1978) pp. 84, 98–9, 111, 128 and 140.
2. Jaroslav Krejci and Vitezlav Velimsky, *Ethnic and Political Nations in Europe* (Croom Helm, 1981) pp. 26–9 and 247–50.

2. MINORITY NATIONALISM

1. Robert Ardrey, *The Territorial Imperative: A Personal Enquiry into the Animal Origins of Property and Nations* (Collins, 1967; pbk edn, Fontana, 1972) pp.10, 13, 132 and 359–60.
2. Constantin C. Giurescu, *Transylvania in the History of Rumania: An Historical Outline* (Garnstone Press, 1970) pp.16–35; John R. V. Prescott, *The Geography of Frontiers and Boundaries* (Hutchinson, 1965) pp. 102 ff.
3. Frederick Hertz, *Nationality in History and Politics* (Kegan Paul, 1944) pp. 147–8 ; J. V. Stalin, 'Marxism and the National Question', in J. V. Stalin, *Works* vol. II, 1907–13 (Lawrence and Wishart, 1953) p. 307.
4. Ardrey, *Territorial Imperative*, pp. 330 –1.
5. Anthony D. Smith (ed.), *Nationalist Movements* (Macmillan, 1976) p.12.
6. Krejci and Velimsky, *Nations in Europe*, p.11; Prescott, *Frontiers and Boundaries*, p. 102; Ardrey, *Territorial Imperative*, p.189.
7. W. J. Argyle, 'Size and Scale as Factors in the Development of Nationalist Movements', in Smith (ed.), *Nationalist Movements*, pp.35–7.
8. Elie Kedourie, *Nationalism*, 3rd ed. (Hutchinson, 1966) pp. 61–8; Krejci and Velimsky, *Nations in Europe*, p. 155.
9. Statistics abstracted from Colin McEvedy and Richard Jones, *Atlas of World Population History* (Penguin, 1978) pp.53, 76, 79, 81, 85, 93, 97 and 113.
10. Ibid., p. 84.
11. Francois Fëjto, 'Conclusion', in Fëjto (ed.), *The Opening of an Era 1848: An Historical Symposium* (New York: Fertig, 1966) pp.420–1.

12. V. Kiernan, 'Nationalist Movements and Social Classes', in Smith (ed.) *Nationalist Movements*, p. 111.

13. Carlo M. Cipolla, *Literacy and Development in the West* (Penguin, 1969) pp. 118 and 127–9.

14. Alan W. Palmer, *The Lands Between : A History of East-Central Europe since the Congress of Vienna* (Weidenfeld and Nicolson, 1970) p. 18; Renan, quoted in Boyd C. Shafer, *Faces of Nationalism: New Realities and Old Myths* (New York: Harcourt Brace Jovanovitch, 1972) p. 336.

15. Kedourie, *Nationalism*, pp. 97–101; also Anthony D. Smith, *Theories of Nationalism* (Macmillan, 1971) p. 33.

16. Kedourie, *Nationalism*, pp.27–30.

17. Renan, quoted in Hertz, *Nationality*, p.12.

18. Smith, *Theories of Nationalism*, pp. 53, 107 and 248–50 ; also Krejci and Velimsky, *Nations in Europe*, pp. 38 and 61.

3. THE IMPERIAL PERSPECTIVE

1. Statistics from Robert Kann, *The Multinational Empire: Nationalism and National Reform in the Habsburg Monarchy 1848–1918*, 2 vols (New York: Columbia University Press, 1950) vol. II, pp. 305–6.

2. C. A. Macartney, *Hungary: A Short History* (Edinburgh: Edinburgh University Press, 1968) p. 138.

3. Quoted by Arnost Klima, 'Bohemia', in Fëjto (ed.), *Opening of an Era*, pp. 281–97.

4. William V. Wallace, *Czechoslovakia* (Benn, 1977) p. 24.

5. Krejci and Velimsky, *Nations in Europe*, pp. 68–9.

6. Kann, *Multinational Empire*, vol II PP 3034

7 UGH ETON-ATSON *Eastern Europe between the Wars 1918–1941* (Cambridge University Press, 1945 ; 3rd ed. pbk, New York: Harper and Row, 1967) p. 43; C. A. Macartney, *National States and National Minorities* (RIIA, 1934; New York: Russell and Russell, 1968) pp. 118–22.

8. Kann, *Multinational Empire*, vol. II, p. 302.

9. A. J. P. Taylor, 'The Opening of an Era, 1848', in Fëjto (ed.), *Opening of an Era*, p.xvi; Donald W. Treadgold, *The Great Siberian Migration* (Princeton, NJ: Princeton University Press, 1957) pp. 31–5.

10. Benjamin Goriely, 'The Russia of Nicholas I in 1848', in Fëjto (ed.), *Opening of an Era*, p. 412.

11. Richard Pipes, *The Formation of the Soviet Union: Communism and Nationalism 1917–23* (Cambridge, Mass.: Harvard University Press, 1964) pp. 300–1.

12. *Entsiklopedicheskii Slovar'*, 40 vols (St Petersburg: Brockhaus-Efron, 1890–1904) vol. xxxv, p. 918 ('Finlandia').

13. Cipolla, *Literacy and Development*, pp. 17 and 82.

14. *Gosudarstvennaya Duma: stenograficheskie otchyety, sozyv II, sessia 2, chast'* 1 (St Petersburg: Gosudarstvennaya Tipografia, 1907) p. 142.

15. Quoted in Leo Errera, *The Russian Jews: Extermination or Emancipation?* (New York: Macmillan, 1894; reprinted New York: Greenwood Press, 1975) p. 37.

16. Ibid., p. 187.

17. Pipes, *Soviet Union*, p. 2; Krejci and Velimsky, *Nations in Europe*, p. 24.

18. T. Y. Burmistrova and V. S. Gusakova, *Natsional'nii Vopros v Programmakh i Taktike Politicheskikh Partii v Rossii 1905–1917* (Moscow: Mysl', 1976) pp. 45–53.

19. Nicholas P. Vakar, *Belorussia: The Making of a Nation* (Cambridge, Mass.: Harvard University Press, 1956) p. 92.

4. FIGHT OR FLIGHT?

1. Palmer, *The Lands Between*, p. 67; also Michael Roller, 'The Rumanians in 1848', in Fëjto (ed.), *Opening of an Era*, pp. 299–311.

2. Marin V. Pundeff, in Peter F. Sugar and Ivo J. Lederer (eds), *Nationalism in Eastern Europe* (New York: University of Washington Press, 1969) pp. 110–26.

3. Fëjto, *Opening of an Era*, p. 9.

4. Ibid., p. 420.

5. For a comprehensive essay on the problems facing the historian of emigration, see Frank Thistlethwaite, 'Migration from Europe Overseas in the Nineteenth and Twentieth Centuries', in Herbert Moller (ed.) *Population Movements in Modern European History* (Macmillan, 1964) pp. 73–92.

6. Most prominent among the authorities employed in compiling this league table were Carl Wittke, *We Who Built America: The Saga of the Immigrant* (New York: Case Western Reserve University Press, 1939; revised ed. 1967) and Samuel Joseph, *Jewish Immigration to the United States from 1881 to 1910* (New York: Columbia University Press, 1914; reprinted New York: Arno, 1969).

7. Wittke, *We Who Built America*, pp. 453–7; Joseph, *Jewish Immigration*, pp. 34–6, 69-77, 105–8.

8. Most of the statistical detail as to relative emigrant volume, literacy, occupation and return-rate is drawn from Joseph, *Jewish Immigration*, pp. 87–123 and 165–94.

9. Treadgold, *Siberian Migration*, pp. 31–5, 227–8 and 241–2.

10. Wittke, *We Who Built America*, pp. 431–3.

11. George J. Prpic, 'Croat Emigration', in Francis H. Eterovich (ed.), *Croatia: Land, People, Culture*, 2 vols (Toronto: Toronto University Press, 1964 and 1970) vol. II, pp. 397–9.

12. Ibid., p. 399.

13. Quoted in Sugar and Lederer (eds), *Nationalism in Eastern Europe*, pp. 37–8.

14. Quoted by Leonard Schapiro, 'Introduction', in Lionel Kochan (ed.), *The Jews in Soviet Russia since 1917* (London: Oxford University Press, 1970) p. 3.

15. Joseph, *Jewish Immigration*, pp. 46–7 and 67; Errera, *Russian Jews*, pp. 23 and 87–9.

16. Charles Sarolea, *Letters on Polish Affairs* (Edinburgh: Edinburgh University Press, 1922) pp. 16 and 21.

5. EXTERNAL INTERVENTION

1. Macartney, *National States*, pp. 183, 191 and 394–5.

2. Pablo de Azcarate, *League of Nations and National Minorities: An Experiment* (New York: Macmillan, 1945; repub. New York: Kraus, 1972) p. 131.

3. Inis L. Claude Jr, *National Minorities: An International Problem* (Cambridge, Mass.: Harvard University Press, 1955; repub. New York: Greenwood Press, 1969) pp. 7–8.

4. Claude, *National Minorities*, p. 13; Macartney, *National States*, p. 211.

5. Claude, *National Minorities*, p. 8; Azcarate, *League of Nations*, p. 170.

6. J. E. S. Fawcett, *The Law of Nations* (Penguin, 1968) pp. 28–30, 123–5, 134-41 and 160–77.

7. Stephen P. Ladas, *The Exchange of Minorities: Bulgaria, Greece and Turkey* (New York: Macmillan, 1932) pp. 27–327 (Greece–Bulgaria) and 335–588 (Greece–Turkey).

8. Ibid., pp. 592–7 (Bulgars), 618–704 (Greeks), 705–15 (Turks) and 720–6 (Conclusions); also Azcarate, *League of Nations*, p. 16.

9. Azcarate, *League of Nations*, pp. 43, 67, 82 and 185; Claude, *National Minorities*, pp. 15–17, 24–6, 29–30 and 31–50.

6. A NEW EUROPE?

1. Based upon Oscar I. Janowsky, *Nationalities and National Minorities* (New York: Macmillan, 1945) p. 111, but with additions and estimates from a variety of contemporary sources (cited below under individual states).

2. Cited in Antony Polonsky, *The Little Dictators: The History of Eastern Europe since 1918* (Routledge and Kegan Paul, 1975) pp. 160 and 162.

3.   For a different estimate, see Macartney, *National States*, p. 525.

4.   Seton-Watson, *Eastern Europe*, pp. 180–1.

5.   Quoted in Macartney, *National States*, p. 242.

6.   Some authorities put the Serb total as low as five million, for example Macartney, *National States*, p. 534.

7.   Sarolea, *Polish Affairs*, p. 3.

8.   Polonsky, *The Little Dictators*, pp. 158 and 163.

9.   Peter Brock, 'Polish Nationalism', in Sugar and Lederer (eds), *Nationalism in Eastern Europe*, p. 363.

10.   Quoted in Vakar, *Belorussia*, p. 125.

11.   Azcarate, *League of Nations*, p. 34.

12.   Table based on a variety of authorities, led by Macartney, *National States*, pp. 518–40 (Appendix III) and Seton-Watson, *Eastern Europe*, pp. 413–7.

13.   Statistics from Count Albert Apponyi *et al.*, *Justice for Hungary* (Longman Green, 1928) annotated ethnographic map.

14.   Polonsky, *The Little Dictators*, p. 159; Seton-Watson, *Eastern Europe*, p. 416.

15.   Quoted in George Barany, 'Hungary: From Aristocratic to Proletarian Nationalism', in Sugar and Lederer (eds), *Nationalism in Eastern Europe*, p. 288.

16.   Statistics from Royal Institute of International Affairs, *The Baltic States* (Oxford University Press, 1938) pp. 30–38.

17.   Jaan Pennar, 'Nationalism in the Soviet Baltic States', in Erich Goldhagen (ed.) *Ethnic Minorities in the Soviet Union* (New York: Praeger, 1968) pp. 200–4.

18.   Janowsky, *Nationalities and National Minorities*, p. 75.

19.   Pipes, *Soviet Union*, pp. 296–7.

20.   Vakar, *Belorussia*, p. 146.

21.   John A. Armstrong, *Ukrainian Nationalism 1939–1945* (New York: Columbia University Press, 1955; revised ed. 1963) p. 17.

22.   Eugene Kulischer, *Europe on the Move: War and Population Changes 1914–47* (New York: Columbia University Press, 1948) pp. 53–71 and 246–7.

23.   Ibid., pp. 120–45 and 240–6.

24.   Ibid., pp. 135–44; Vakar, *Belorussia*, p. 133; Oscar Janowsky, *A People at Bay: The Jewish Problem in East-Central Europe* (New York: Praeger, 1938) p. 149.

7.   WAR AND THE MINORITIES

1.   H. A. L. Fisher, *A History of Europe*, 2 vols (Eyre and Spottiswoode, 1935; Fontana pbk, 1961) vol. 1, p. 217.

2.   McEvedy and Jones, *World Population History*, pp. 34–5; Kulischer, *Europe on the Move*, p. 71.

3.   L. A. Kosinski, 'Yugoslavia and International Migration', *Canadian Slavonic Papers*, xx, 3 (September 1978) 319.

4.   Louis Fitzgibbon, *Katyn: A Crime without Parallel* (Tom Stacey, 1971) p. 6.

5.   Konrad Bercovici, *The Story of the Gypsies* (Cape, 1939) p. 46.

6.   Donald Kenrick and Grattan Puxon, *The Destiny of Europe's Gypsies* (Heinemann–Sussex University Press, 1972) pp. 59 ff.

7.   Gypsy statistics from Kenrick and Puxon, *Europe's Gypsies*, pp. 183–4; Jewish statistics adapted from Lucy Dawidowicz, *The War Against the Jews 1939–45* (Weidenfeld and Nicolson, 1975; Penguin pbk, 1977) p. 480.

8.   John Major, *The Contemporary World: a historical introduction* (Methuen, 1970) p. 233.

9.   Wallace, *Czechoslovakia*, p. 223; Joseph F. Zanak, 'Nationalism in Czechoslovakia', in Sugar and Lederer (eds), *Nationalism in Eastern Europe*, pp. 197–200.

10.   Vakar, *Belorussia*, p. 105.

11.   Palmer, *The Lands Between*, p. 143.

12. Seton-Watson, *Eastern Europe*, p. 410; S. Kirschbaum, 'Slovak Nationalism in Socialist Czechoslovakia', *Canadian Slavonic Papers*, XXII 2 (1980) 223.

13. Kulischer, *Europe on the Move*, p. 264.

14. Alexander Dallin, *German Rule in Russia 1941–5: A Study of Occupation Policies* (Macmillan, 1957) pp. 166–7.

8. A CENTURY IN PERSPECTIVE

1. Kann, *Multinational Empire*, pp. 304–5; Seton-Watson, *Eastern Europe*, p. 414.

2. Kulischer, *Europe on the Move*, pp. 148 and 201.

3. Henri Tajfel, *The Social Psychology of Minorities* (Minority Rights Group, Report 38) pp. 9–18.

4. E. H. Carr, *Nationalism and After* (Macmillan, 1945) p. 24.

Bibliography

BY CHAPTER

1. THE DEMOGRAPHIC INHERITANCE

Geoffrey Barraclough (ed.), *The Times Atlas of World History* (Times Books, 1978).
Jaroslav Krejci and Vitezlav Velimsky, *Ethnic and Political Nations in Europe* (Croom Helm, 1981).

2. MINORITY NATIONALISM

Robert Ardrey, *The Territorial Imperative: A Personal Enquiry into the Animal Origins of Property and Nations* (Collins, 1967; Fontana pbk, 1972).
Carlo M. Cipolla, *Literacy and Development in the West* (Penguin, 1969).
Alfred Cobban, *The Nation State and National Self-Determination* (Collins and Fontana, 1969).
Frederick Hertz, *Nationality in History and Politics* (Kegan Paul, 1944).
Elie Kedourie, *Nationalism*, 3rd edn (Hutchinson, 1966).
Hans Kohn *The Idea of Nationalism: A Study in its Origins and Background* (New York: Macmillan, 1946; repub. 1961).
Colin McEvedy and Richard Jones, *Atlas of World Population History* (Penguin, 1978).
Kenneth R. Minogue, *Nationalism* (Oxford University Press, 1969).
J. R. V. Prescott, *The Geography of Frontiers and Boundaries* (Hutchinson, 1965).
Royal Institute for International Affairs, *Nationalism* (Oxford University Press, 1939; repub. New York: Cass, 1963).
Anthony David Smith (ed.), *Nationalist Movements* (Macmillan, 1976).
        Theories of Nationalism (Duckworth, 1971).
Peter F. Sugar (ed.), *Ethnic Diversity and Conflict in Eastern Europe* (Oxford: Clio Press, 1980).
Peter F. Sugar and Ivo J. Lederer (eds), *Nationalism in Eastern Europe* (New York: University of Washington Press, 1969).

3. THE IMPERIAL PERSPECTIVE

Francois Fëjto (ed.), *The Opening of an Era 1848* (New York: Fertig, 1966).
Robert Kann, *The Multinational Empire: Nationalism and National Reform in the Habsburg Monarchy 1848–1918*, 2 vols (New York: Columbia University Press, 1950).

C. A. Macartney, *The Habsburg Monarchy 1790–1918* (Weidenfeld and Nicolson, 1968).
Arthur J. May, *The Habsburg Monarchy 1867–1914* (Cambridge, Mass.: Harvard University Press, 1965).
Hugh Seton-Watson, *Nations and States* (Methuen, 1977).
    The Russian Empire 1801–1917 (Oxford University Press, 1967).
Peter N. Stearns, *The Revolutions of 1848* (Weidenfeld and Nicolson, 1974).
A. J. P. Taylor, *The Habsburg Monarchy 1809–1918* (Hamish Hamilton, 1948; Peregrine pbk, 1964).
Edward C. Thaden (ed.), *Russification in the Baltic Provinces and Finland 1855–1914* (Princeton, NJ: Princeton University Press, 1981).

4. FIGHT OR FLIGHT?

Herbert Moller (ed.), *Population Movements in Modern European History* (Macmillan, 1964).
Joseph O'Grady (ed.), *The Immigrants' Influence on Wilson's Peace Policy* (Louisville, USA: Kentucky University Press, 1967).
Donald W. Treadgold, *The Great Siberian Migration* (Princeton, NJ: Princeton University Press, 1957).
Carl Wittke, *We Who Built America: The Saga of the Immigrant* (Case Western Reserve University Press, 1939; rev. edn, 1967).

5. EXTERNAL INTERVENTION

Pablo de Azcarate, *League of Nations and National Minorities: An Experiment* (New York: Macmillan, 1945; repub. Kraus, 1972).
Inis L. Claude Jr, *National Minorities: An International Problem* (Cambridge, Mass.: Harvard University Press, 1955; rep. 1969).
James E.S. Fawcett, *The International Protection of Minorities* (Minority Rights Group, Report 41, 1979).
Stephen P. Ladas, *The Exchange of Minorities: Bulgaria, Greece and Turkey* (New York: Macmillan, 1932).
Hans Kohn, *Pan-Slavism: Its History and Ideology* (Bloomington, Indiana: University of Notre Dame Press, 1960).
C. A. Macartney, *National States and National Minorities* (RIIA, 1934; repub. New York: Russell and Russell, 1968).
L. P. Mair, *The Protection of Minorities* (Christophers, 1928).
L. D. Orton, *The Prague Slav Congress of 1848* (New York: Columbia University Press, 1980).
Claire Palley, *Constitutional Law and Minorities* (Minority Rights Group, Report 36, 1978).
Jacob Robinson (ed.), *Were the Minorities Treaties a Failure?* (New York: Institute of Jewish Affairs, 1943).
Julius Stone, *International Guarantees of Minority Rights* (Oxford University Press, 1932).

6. A NEW EUROPE ?

Oscar I. Janowsky, *Nationalities and National Minorities* (New York: Macmillan, 1945).
Otto Junghann, *National Minorities in Europe* (New York: Covici, Friede Inc., 1932).
Eugene M. Kulischer, *Europe on the Move: War and Population Changes 1914–1947* (New York: Columbia University Press, 1948).
C. A. Macartney and A. W. Palmer, *Independent Eastern Europe: A History* (Macmillan, 1962).
Alan Palmer, *The Lands Between: A History of East-Central Europe since the Congress of Vienna*

(Weidenfeld and Nicolson, 1970).

Antony Polonsky, *The Little Dictators: The History of Eastern Europe since 1918* (Routledge and Kegan Paul, 1975).

Hugh Seton-Watson, *Eastern Europe between the Wars 1918–1941* (Cambridge University Press, 1945; repub. New York: Harper and Row pbk, 1967).

Hugh and Christopher Seton-Watson, *The Making of a New Europe* (Methuen, 1981).

R. W. Seton-Watson, *Europe in the Melting-Pot* (Macmillan, 1919).

J. S. Stephens, *Danger Zones of Europe: A Study of National Minorities* (Hogarth, 1929).

7. WAR AND THE MINORITIES

Robert Conquest, *The Nation Killers* (Macmillan, 1970).

Alexander Dallin, *German Rule in Russia 1941–5: A Study in Occupation Policies* (Macmillan, 1957).

Jon Evans, *The Nazi New Order in Poland* (Left Book Club, 1941).

Louis Fitzgibbon, *Katyn; A Crime without Parallel* (Tom Stacey, 1971).

Ihor Kamenetsky, *Secret Nazi Plan for Eastern Europe: A Study of Lebensraum Policies* (New York: Bookman, 1961).

Vojtech Mastny, *The Czechs under Nazi Rule: The Failure of National Resistance 1939–42* (New York: Columbia University Press, 1971).

George L. Mosse, *Towards the Final Solution; A History of European Racism* (Dent, 1978).

Richard Pipes, *The Formation of the Soviet Union: Communism and Nationalism 1917–23* (Cambridge, Mass.: Harvard University Press, 1964).

Gerald Reitlinger, *The House Built on Sand: The Conflicts of German Policy in Russia 1939–45* (Weidenfeld and Nicolson, 1960).

Joseph B. Schechtman, *European Population Transfers 1939–45* (Cornell University Press, 1946; repub. New York: Russell and Russell, 1971).

8. A CENTURY IN PERSPECTIVE

Antony E. Alcock (ed.), *The Future of Cultural Minorities* (Macmillan, 1979).

E. H. Carr, *Nationalism and After* (Macmillan, 1945).

A. C. Hepburn (ed.), *Minorities in History* (Arnold, 1978).

Henri Tajfel, *The Social Psychology of Minorities* (Minority Rights Group, Report 38, 1979).

BY NATIONAL MINORITY

ALBANIAN

Stefanaq Pollo and Arben Puto, *The History of Albania; from its origins to the present day* (Routledge and Kegan Paul, 1981).

Stavro Skendi, *The Political Evolution of Albania 1912–1944* (Princeton, NJ: Princeton University Press, 1954).

The Albanian National Awakening 1878–1912 (Princeton, NJ: Princeton University Press, 1967).

BELORUSSIAN

Nicholas P. Vakar, *Belorussia: The Making of a Nation* (Cambridge, Mass.: Harvard University Press, 1956).

BULGAR

G. C. Logio, *Bulgaria Past and Present* (Manchester: Manchester University Press, 1936).
Mercia Macdermott, *A History of Bulgaria* (New York: Praeger, 1962)
J. Swire, *Bulgarian Conspiracy* (London: Grant Richards 1930).

CROAT

Francis H. Eterovich (ed.), *Croatia: Land, People, Culture*, 2 vols (Toronto: Toronto University Press, 1964 and 1970).
E. Paris, *Genocide in Satellite Croatia* (Chicago: American Institute for Balkan Studies, 1962).
Francis Preveden, *A History of the Croatian People*, 2 vols (New York: Philosophical Library, 1955 and 1962).
R. W. Seton-Watson, *Absolutism in Croatia* (Constable, 1912).

CZECH

Jaroslav Hašek, *The Good Soldier Schweik* (Penguin, 1976).
J. Korbel, *Twentieth-Century Czechoslovakia* (New York: Columbia University Press, 1977).
Stanley Z. Pech, *The Czech Revolution of 1848* (Chapel Hill: North Carolina University Press, 1969).
R. W. Seton-Watson, *A History of the Czechs and Slovaks* (Hutchinson, 1943).
William V. Wallace, *Czechoslovakia* (Benn, 1977).
Elizabeth Wiskemann, *Czechs and Germans*, 2nd edn (Macmillan, 1967).

ESTONIAN (also under Latvian and Lithuanian)

John Hampden Jackson, *Estonia* (Benn, 1941; repub. 1948).

FINNISH

David G. Kirby (ed.), *Finland and Russia 1808–1920: From Autonomy to Independence* (Macmillan, 1975).
C. Jay Smith Jr, *Finland and the Russian Revolution 1917–21* (Atlanta: University of Georgia Press, 1958).
John H. Wuorinen, *A History of Finland* (New York: Columbia University Press, 1965).

GREEK

Richard Clogg, *A Short History of Modern Greece* (Cambridge University Press, 1979).
Douglas Dakin, *The Greek Struggle for Independence 1821–1833* (Batsford, 1973).

GYPSY

Konrad Bercovici, *The Story of the Gypsies* (Cape, 1930).
Jean-Paul Clebert, *The Gypsies* (Vista, 1963; Penguin, 1969).
Donald Kenrick and Grattan Puxon, *The Destiny of Europe's Gypsies* (Heinemann-Sussex University Press, 1972).

JEWISH

Lucy Dawidowicz, *The War against the Jews 1933–45* (Weidenfeld and Nicolson, 1975; Penguin pbk, 1977).
Leo Errera, *The Russian Jews: Extermination or Emancipation?* (New York: Macmillan, 1894; repub. Greenwood Press, 1975).
Martin Gilbert, *Final Journey: The Fate of the Jews in Nazi Europe* (Allen and Unwin, 1979).
Louis Greenberg, *The Jews in Russia: The Struggle for Emancipation* (Newhaven, Conn.: Yale University Press, 1951).
Celia S. Heller, *On the Edge of Destruction: The Jews of Poland Between the World Wars* (New York: Columbia University Press, 1977).
Oscar I. Janowsky, *The Jews and Minority Rights 1898–1919* (New York: Jewish Institute, 1933).
Samuel Joseph, *Jewish Immigration to the United States 1881–1910* (New York: Columbia University Press, 1914; repub. Arno, 1969).
Lionel Kochan (ed.), *The Jews in Soviet Russia since 1917* (Oxford University Press, 1970).

LATVIAN

A. Balmanis, *A History of Latvia* (Princeton, NJ: Princeton University Press, 1951).
Georg von Rauch, *The Baltic States: The Years of Independence 1917–40* (Hurst, 1970).

LITHUANIAN

Royal Institute of International Affairs, *The Baltic States* (Oxford University Press, 1938).
Alfred Erich Senn, *The Emergence of Modern Lithuania* (New York: Columbia University Press, 1959).

MACEDONIAN

E. Barker, *Macedonia: Its Place in Balkan Power Politics* (Royal Institute of International Affairs, 1950).

MAGYAR

Count Albert Apponyi *et al.*, *Justice for Hungary* (Longman Green, 1928).
George Barany, *Stephen Széchenyi and the Awakening of Hungarian Nationalism 1791–1841* (Princeton, NJ: Princeton University Press, 1968).
Istvan Deák, *The Lawful Revolution: Louis Kossuth and the Hungarians 1848–9* (New York: Columbia University Press, 1980).
Sir Robert Gower, *The Hungarian Minorities in the Succession States* (Grant Richards, 1937).
C. A. Macartney, *Hungary and her Successors* (Oxford University Press, 1937).

Hungary: a Short History (Edinburgh: Edinburgh University Press, 1962).
R. W. Seton-Watson, *Racial Problems in Hungary* (Constable, 1908).

POLISH

Jan T. Gross *Polish Society under German Occupation: the Generalgouvernement 1939-1944* (Princeton, NJ: Princeton University Press, 1981).
Stephen Korak, *Poland and her National Minorities 1919-1939* (New York: Vantage, 1961).
Robert F. Leslie, *Polish Politics and the Revolution of 1830* (London University Athlone Press, 1956).
  Reform and Insurrection in Russian Poland 1856-65 (London University Athlone Press, 1963).
  (ed.), The History of Poland since 1863 (Cambridge University Press, 1980).
Antony Polonsky, *Politics in Independent Poland 1921-39* (Oxford University Press, 1972).
Charles Sarolea, *Letters on Polish Affairs* (Edinburgh: Oliver and Boyd, 1922).

RUMANIAN

Gerald S. Bobango, *The Emergence of the Romanian Nation State* (New York: Columbia University Press, 1980).
Stephen Fischer-Galati, *Twentieth-Century Rumania* (New York: Columbia University Press, 1970).
Constantin C. Giurescu, *Transylvania in the History of Romania :An Historical Outline* (Garnstone Press, 1970).
T. W. Riker, *The Making of Roumania* (Oxford University Press, 1931).
R. W. Seton-Watson, *A History of the Roumanians* (Cambridge University Press, 1934; repub. New York: Archon, 1963).

RUTHENE

P. R. Magosci, *The Shaping of a National Identity: Sub-Carpathian Rus' 1848-1948* (Cambridge, Mass.; Harvard University Press, 1978).
Michael Winch, *Republic for a Day* (Longman Green, 1939).

SERB

H. C. Darby *et al.*, *A Short History of Yugoslavia* (Cambridge University Press, 1966).
Vladimir Dedijer, *The Road to Sarajevo* (MacGibbon and Kee, 1967).
Ivo J. Lederer, *Yugoslavia at the Paris Peace Conference: A Study in Frontiermaking* (Newhaven, Conn.: Yale University Press, 1963).
Harold V. Temperley, *History of Serbia* (Bell, 1917).

SLOVAK (also under CZECH)

Peter Brock, *The Slovak National Awakening* (Toronto: Toronto University Press, 1976).
Dorothea H. El Mallakh, *The Slovak Autonomy Movement 1935-9* (New York: Columbia University Press, 1979).
Y. Jelinek, *The Parish Republic: Hlinka's Slovak People's Party 1939-45* (New York: Columbia University Press, 1976).

Joseph M. Kirschbaum (ed.), *Slovakia in the Nineteenth and Twentieth Centuries* (Toronto: Canadian Slovak League, 1978).
R. W. Seton-Watson, *The New Slovakia* (Allen and Unwin, 1929).

SLOVENE

Dragotin Loncar, *The Slovenes* (Cleveland, Ohio: American Slovene League, 1939).
Carole Regel, *The Slovenes and Yugoslavia 1890–1914* (New York: Columbia University Press, 1977).

UKRAINIAN

John A. Armstrong, *Ukrainian Nationalism 1939–1945* (New York: Columbia University Press, 1955: 2nd edn 1963).
Michael Hrushevsky, *A History of the Ukraine* (Newhaven, Conn.: Yale University Press, 1941).
Anatoli Kusnetsov, *Babi Yar* (McGibbon and Kee, 1967).
Alexander J. Motyl, *The Turn to the Right: The Ideological Origins and Development of Ukrainian Nationalism 1919–29* (New York: Columbia University Press, 1980).
John S. Reshetar, *The Ukrainian Revolution 1917–20: A Study in Nationalism* (Princeton, NJ: Princeton University Press, 1952).
Robert S. Sullivant, *Soviet Politics and the Ukraine 1917–57* (New York: Columbia University Press, 1962).

Index